D1601509

The Writing of Orpheus

The Writing of Orpheus

Greek Myth in Cultural Contact

Marcel Detienne

Translated by Janet Lloyd

The Johns Hopkins University Press
Baltimore and London

This translation was brought to publication with the generous assistance of the French Ministry of Culture.

An earlier version of this work was published as *L'Écriture d'Orphée*,

Published 2002
Printed in the United States of America on acid-free paper
9 8 7 6 5 4 3 2 1

The Johns Hopkins University Press
2715 North Charles Street
Baltimore, Maryland 21218-4363
www.press.jhu.edu

Library of Congress Cataloging-in-Publication Data
Detienne, Marcel.
[Écriture d'Orphée. English]
The writing of Orpheus : Greek myth in cultural context / by Marcel Detienne ; translated by Janet Lloyd.
p. cm.
Includes bibliographical references and index.
ISBN 0-8018-6954-4 (hardcover : alk. paper)
1. Mythology, Greek. I. Title.
BL783 .D4813 2003
292.1'3—dc21
2003006673

A catalog record for this book is available from the British Library.

Contents

Author's Note

This is a new version of a book that appeared in French in 1989, in the Infini series edited by Philippe Sollers, the Archangel of the "musicians of life," to whom I am greatly indebted. I should like to thank Gregory Nagy for having encouraged me to select additional texts and in some cases to choose new words to communicate to those living in the gardens of America a few brief essays in homage to the writing of Orpheus. I should also like to thank my friend Janet Lloyd for once again making communication possible through the art of translation.

Translator's Note

I have used the following translations of ancient texts:

Penguin Classics, Harmondsworth, Middlesex, England
—Herodotus, *Histories*, translated by Aubrey de Sélincourt, 1971
—Homer, *Iliad*, translated by Martin Hammond, 1987
—Homer, *Odyssey*, translated by E. V. Rieu, 1991

The Complete Greek Tragedies, University of Chicago Press, Chicago and London
—Aeschylus, *The Libation Bearers*, translated by Richmond Lattimore, 1953
—Aeschylus, *The Eumenides*, translated by Richmond Lattimore, 1953
—Sophocles, *Oedipus at Colonus*, translated by Robert Fitzgerald, 1954

The Loeb Classical Library, Harvard University Press, Cambridge, Mass.
—Aristotle, *The Constitution of Athens*, translated by H. Rackham, 1935
—Ovid, *Fasti*, translated by James G. Frazer, 1931
—Pausanias, *Description of Greece*, translated by W. H. S. Jones, 1965
—Plato, *Critias*, translated by R. G. Bury, 1929
—Plato, *Euthydemus*, translated by W. R. M. Lamb, 1924
—Plato, *Laws*, translated by R. G. Bury, 1967
—Plato, *Phaedrus*, translated by W. R. M. Lamb, 1952
—Plato, *Politicus*, translated by W. R. M. Lamb, 1952
—Plato, *Timaeus*, translated by R. G. Bury, 1929
—Pliny the Elder, *Natural History*, translated by H. Rackham, 1971
—Plutarch, *Table Talk*, translated by W. C. Hembold, 1971
—Virgil. *Aeneid*, translated by H. Rushton Fairclough, 1974

Preface to the English-Language Edition

I chose the title of this series of essays on Greek mythology, *The Writing of Orpheus: Greek Myth in Cultural Context*, deliberately in order to combine a mythical figure who possesses a more or less universal resonance with the work of writing, which has invaded mythology ever since it became a subject for reflection and analysis. The Greek Orpheus surrounded by his texts is not altogether separate from Eurydice's lover who triumphed over the deities of the underworld through the power of his voice and music.

The singing of Orpheus provides an introduction to the orality of myths that were commonly told, and the writing that he invented reveals the many relations between mythology and mythography. Furthermore, that same Orpheus, rewriting the city gods, invites us to recognize that mythology as a framework of thought must be understood in its connection to polytheism and the system of relations that obtains among the various divine forces.[1]

The telling of stories is our first basic element. Indeed, it prompted one of the Greek language's most ancient formulations of the idea of "mythologizing." In the *Odyssey*, the blind bard Demodocus has just fallen silent after singing of the wooden horse brought within the city walls and of Troy in flames; everything is about to start, for now Odysseus begins to recount his adventures, the impossible return journey and, following the disaster of the cattle of the sun, his pleasures with Calypso. His stories follow one upon another, in a chain, but when they come to an end—as they must—he declares that, as a good bard, one must never "retell a story already told": in Greek one must never "mythologize" *(mythologeuein)*.[2] Repetitiveness is thus set in opposition to the "performance" of a storyteller, which I am used to describing as the "impromptu interaction between the oral and the aural." It is at this point that memory, along with transmission, makes its appearance.

If it is true that mythology is an invention in which both the ancient Greeks and ourselves are implicated, why not compare, on the one hand, the stories of the *Odyssey*, told in the course of an impromptu oral/aural performance by Odysseus, such a clever storyteller and inventor of tales, and, on the other, the interchange, this time in the eighteenth century, between Greeks and Americans—that is to say, the tales of the ancients and the myths of the savages? The intellectual activity at work in stories that seemed to produce echoes resounding all the way from the New World to the ancient world, and from Oceania and Africa to Hesiod's native village and the mountains of Arcadia gave rise to the first attempt at comparative ethnology. As for the interpretation of myths, this made its appearance, also in Greece, as soon as other stories came to be evoked on the periphery of those already told: for example, the stories on the fringes of the adventures of Achilles and of Nestor, to which the *Iliad* referred, thereby setting both sets of stories in perspective.

As for myself, captivated by those Greeks who move from exegesis into interpretation within a space of time that always seems so short, I am struck by the fact that mythology is something that gets written down.[3] Mythography seems to pounce upon mythology, although not as death pounces upon the living, or vice versa. For in mythography, the writing down of myths, there is as much life, invention, and showmanship as there is in the art of weaving together stories to the strains of a lyre. We now appreciate that so-called mythical thought is not radically opposed to what is called rational thought, except as a different form of intelligibility—an idea bequeathed by the sociological discourse that, at the beginning of the twentieth century, sought to find an all-encompassing structure from which all other subsequent forms of thought could be deduced.[4]

If we remain on the intensively exploited Greek terrain, the history of what happened between the eighth and the sixth centuries B.C. is, however, probably more complex. For example, when did people begin to feel free to readjust and reshape the stories that we like to call "fiction" or even "literature"? And how decisive a role was played by the practice of antagonistic debate within circles in which certain equal rights were claimed, such as those in which the Homeric warriors take part? Would it not be more to the point, today, to do as Geoffrey Lloyd suggests?[5] Namely, to make a differential analysis of types of proof and ways of elaborating distinctions between discourse that is true and discourse that is not? (That would be to replace the assumption of a radical and definite distance separating two kinds of logic, one said to be ambiguous, the other based on the principle of the excluded middle.)

Most of the analyses collected in this volume were conducted while I was pondering upon the status of myth and the invention of myth as an object, and questioning the veracity of metalinguistic models. I think it only fair to indicate what seems to me to constitute the common parameter of these studies written between 1974 and 1996, and to explain the procedures adopted in the interpretations suggested here. Some of my studies have been in circulation for several years already. They have included the stories of Thebes, Calydon's boar hunt, the battle between the Centaurs and the Lapiths, the grief of Niobe, the fall of Troy, the adventures and misadventures of Hephaestus the divine blacksmith, the wanderings of Dionysus, the childhoods of the gods, and many other subjects. Such stories constitute the expanding material of mythology seen as a tradition—a tradition that was certainly treated in a variety of ways but that continued to be transmitted, without interruption, right down to the end of antiquity. It forms a mythological framework within which, in the first place, the stories constantly interrelate. It is a kind of system of thought, based upon a cultural knowledge shared over as many as a dozen or so centuries. This mythological framework is intertwined with what we call the polytheism or the polytheisms that relate to the native view of the world and that consist of a flexible yet close network of relations among the divine powers—always a plurality of deities or a *polytheos*, as the Greeks would say. Mythology and polytheism are the constitutive elements of the culture of Greek societies, as they are for societies on other continents, such as India or Japan. But within this framework it may be helpful to distinguish a mythological lore. This may begin with unobtrusive comments on the tradition, such as Odysseus' remarks about repetitiveness as being so "unpleasant." It may then continue with various ways of writing down mythical stories: local "archaeologies," historical memoirs, genealogies—all practices in which stories and more or less scholarly interpretations are intermingled. The probable existence of "doctors of memory," or specialists who took in hand whole collections of stories, in no way justifies our doubting the overall unity of the mythological tradition as a framework of thought. Some scholars argue that there would be no mythology were it not for the application of "rules" to the poetic genres.[6] Others maintain that tragedy, for example, unfolds in an autonomous space in which the plots elude the "domain" of mythology.[7] But neither Euripides' *Bacchae* nor Sophocles' *Oedipus the King* is cut off from Theban mythology, which is haunted by the bloody foundation of Thebes and the defilements introduced by Cadmus. There is no reason to imagine any deep cleavage between, on the one hand, "real" myths that are bound to rituals deeply anchored in beliefs, and, on the other, stories that have become literary and seem no longer to have anything to do with the mythological tradition.

The type of analysis adopted in these essays on mythology may be described as a series of informed guesses.[8] First comes the hypothesis that terms considered in isolation never carry any intrinsic meaning, for meaning is always a matter of relations and stems from the way that terms stand in opposition to one another. My second proposition is that analyzing a myth involves taking account of the transformations that occur between one version and another of that myth and also between that myth and others akin to it, so that neither one single version nor a synthesis of several versions constitutes an adequate object for analysis. The third, and certainly the most important, principle is that this type of analysis always demands a knowledge of the ethnographic context. To repeat: the mythological framework is part of the cultural system, and it is indissociable from the polytheistic network and the whole collection of so-called religious representations and institutional practices.

What should we understand by "ethnographic context"? It must certainly be independent of the mythical material itself, and it can be discovered and apprehended through an understanding of the manifold of objects, values, and institutions that make up the culture of the society in which the chosen myths are told. Plants, animals, social practices, geographical data, ecological systems, astronomical phenomena, technological know-how: the interpreter-decipherer of myths needs to possess knowledge of all these, just as does an encyclopedist of his own times. For beneath a mass of curious or seemingly insignificant details, the analyst must identify the multiplicity of levels of meaning that bestow upon the mythical account its full richness. All possible registers of culture must be mobilized in the inquiry: vegetables, hunting and fishing techniques, types of foods, and calendars—and in as many societies as seem relevant to a comparison between neighboring or opposed myths. This type of analysis aims to associate knowledge of concrete things with experimentation with intellectual structures in combinations that are sometimes local, but sometimes of a more general nature. One thus needs to work on several levels of meaning, for at each level latent properties may be extracted from a particular field of experience. It is up to the analyst to put them to the test by confronting them with the data provided by other areas of human experience.

It would thus be fair to say that these analyses pursued between Hera's lettuce and Lycaon's table aim to be at once combinatory and experimental. Of course, it would be possible to select terms other than those I have chosen. And likewise, the ethnographic context is no doubt richer than I have taken it to be and may also be organized differently. It seems to me to go without saying that the interpretations that I have suggested under the sign of Orpheus need to be checked out, reconsidered, and challenged from different perspectives. Such an analysis may be combinatory according to the terms initially chosen, but that is not to say that it need necessarily be interminable. Like any interpretation that accepts constraints, the analysis must set limits for itself. For example, instead of amassing ever increasing numbers of more or less "homologous" figures from all over the world, the type of analysis practiced here chooses to select certain abstract schemata, with the help of which it sets out to reconstruct an organized semantic field and to see how elements that appear to belong to the same configuration interact there. It is certainly a matter of constructing, reconstructing, and bringing together the widest possible range of data from many particular areas of knowledge, but of doing so within the confines of a specific culture—not in order to close this upon itself, all twelve centuries of it, but in order, at best, to acquire the means to confirm the relevance of the features noted and the relations established. Three areas are thus staked out in these mythological forays. The first has to do with gender, and here the inquiry moves from the Danaids, half-female, half-male, to Hestia who, positioned at the heart of politics, is both a virgin and misogynous. It is a way of wondering, as others have, about the sex of mythology. In the second area, we investigate the table manners of men and those of the gods, the treatment meted out to a murderer afflicted by madness, and the affinities between ephebes and olive trees. The third is devoted to writing, to the intellectual horizon that went with the invention of writing, to the rewriting of the gods in the Orphic tradition, and to certain games involving the writing of mythology, as reflected upon by a philosopher: the Plato of the *Timaeus* and the *Critias*, who never stopped problematizing the status of mythology, particularly true mythology, caught between the city and the effects of fiction.

Part I / From Myth to Mythology

CHAPTER ONE

The Genealogy of a Body of Thought

Today, thinking about myth involves, first, recognizing and to some extent succumbing to the fascination that mythology and its imaginary representations continue, as always, to exert upon us and upon the history of our most intimate thinking. This fascination stems from an uninterrupted reading, enriched by every analogy presented by the course of history ever since the earliest Greek beginnings. The word *myth*, in itself, is in no way deceptive. But when its semantic shifts are carefully studied, its transparency becomes somewhat clouded. For this reason, the best approach to adopt seems to be a reflexive one that does not deflect the analysis of myths from its object but firmly encourages it to take account of the complexity of the material.

Readers seeking more information on the topics covered in chapters 1–4 should consult Marcel Detienne, *The Creation of Mythology*, trans. Margaret Cook (Chicago: University of Chicago Press, 1986); and Marcel Detienne, ed., *Transcrire les mythologies. Tradition, écriture, historicité* (Paris: Albin Michel, 1994).

On the Fables of the Americans and Those of the Greeks

In the early eighteenth century mythology and the nature of mythology fueled a debate that involved the Americans and the Greeks—or, to be more precise, the first inhabitants of the New World and the people of early antiquity. The debate, prompted as early as the seventeenth century by contact with Native Americans, intensified in 1724, the year that saw the publication of works by both Fontenelle and Lafitau. Fontenelle's was a pamphlet "On the Origin of Fables," while Lafitau's work concerned "The Mores of the Savages of America Compared to the Mores of the Earliest Times." This, the first work of comparative ethnology, was devoted to the intellectual activity of the ancient Greeks and that of the "savages" of America, as expressed through their respective, remarkably similar, fables and mythology. The resemblance between the form and content of the stories of the Iroquois and those of Hesiod's Greeks provided the basis for a kind of comparative mythology. Everywhere and always, it seemed, people invent fables, but to what kind of thought do these belong? The originality of Lafitau lay in showing the strange "conformity" between the mores and customs of the Native Americans and those of the ancient Greeks—a conformity detectable in their practices of abstinence, their modes of initiation, their sacrificial rites, and even the shape of their huts, all of which indicated a "collection of duties" and a "civil religion" in which cult practices were organized as a public service, useful to society. Right from the earliest days, the great body of customs that extends from the ancient to the New World bears the imprints of religion: hieroglyphics, symbols, and emblems, mysterious figures designed to teach the secrets of initiations and mysteries. Long antedating Christianity and the Bible, Lafitau discovered a kind of religion, that of early paganism, upon which the "conformity" between the Greeks and the Native Americans was founded. But what was to be made of the fables and mythology of the Native Americans and those of the ancient Greeks? In contrast to religion, mythology proliferates with ignorance, is fueled by passions, makes its appearance when a cult begins to fall apart. Fables emerged out of the decadence of that early paganism, full of carnal notions as gross and ridiculous among the Greeks as in the Iroquois societies: notions that constituted a gangrene in the fine "collection of duties" that the representatives of that original world were recognized to possess.

While Lafitau, a Jesuit, conceded to primitive humanity the virtues of a religion antedating Christianity, Fontenelle, a man of the Enlightenment who was also curious about this strange product of the human spirit, could see in its fables and mythology nothing but a common ignorance that was shared by both the ancient world and the New World in their earliest days. In those uncouth centuries that did not yet speak the language of Reason, human beings, wanting to explain phenomena and the world, invented fables. In their ignorance, they could make out nothing but prodigies and were thus led to tell stories about chimeras and strange, dreamlike figures. Perhaps those barbaric and infantile societies—whether Greek, Iroquois, Kaffir, or Lapp—were engaged in a primitive kind of philosophic activity. But Fontenelle could distinguish in it nothing but stammerings—foolishness that, as he saw it, made the grave mistake of "turning into religion," among most of those peoples, at least.

Where Lafitau thought that religion came first and was then degraded into fables, the author of *The Origin of Fables* chose to regard all those absurd and senseless stories as the first forms of what would later become religion, for the ancients and the barbarians of both yesterday and today. To the credit of the Greeks and Romans, Fontenelle declared that, for them, fables also became a source of pleasure, initially for the ear and later—thanks to the images conceived and produced by painters and sculptors—also for the eye. For him, that was enough to justify the effort that he and his contemporaries had made to trace the mythological subjects of so many pictures and also the stories invented by the ancients, stories that constituted the sources of so many literary works.

Myth, Language, and Comparison

In early eighteenth-century France, mythology thus found neither a place nor an image that made it distinctive. Although they were in agreement as to the erroneous and vain nature of fables, neither Fontenelle nor Lafitau was in a position to generate any real comparative mythology. Even then, in their view, myth and mythology surely had to be apprehended in relation to the subject that, between the eighteenth and the nineteenth centuries, commanded universal attention—that is to say religion, whether this was regarded as a massive, general Christian institution or, by the sixteenth century, a subject that raised overt problems, as shown by the religious wars and the earliest conflicting interpretations of Christianity. It was only thanks to new ways of thinking about language that, in the nineteenth century, an approach to mythology as such was initiated. In the early years of the nineteenth century a whole series of discoveries and advances modified the status of language: these included the publication of the *Vedas* and the appearance of Sanskrit philology; the first studies, in French and English, of the *Gâthâs* and the *Avesta;* and in 1816, in Germany, the publication of the first elements of a comparative grammar by Franz Bopp. In the wake of the natural sciences and with the introduction of linguistics, comparison became a paradigm, a theoretical model that the new science of language would extend to other areas, including those of myth and mythology.

The connection between myth and language was made through phonetics and the study of sounds. Sounds, syllables, and roots, liberated from the letters that happen to transcribe them, are so many formal elements, whose modifications are governed by the laws of phonetics. Meanwhile, there emerged the idea of language as the speech of the people, the sonorous shifts of which testify to the constant activity that seems inseparable from movement and history. A speech of the people and the nation was thus discovered. At a deeper level, at the origins of the human race revealed by the Sanskrit of the *Vedas*, primitive language seemed to consist of both speech and song. It could cope with neither abstraction nor deceit. That primitive language, which antedated civilized languages, possessed the energy and grandeur of original, faithful expression. Within this new space of sounds the myths of the ancients became the object of scholarship that mobilized comparison between these stories of ancient civilizations and those of the primitive societies in which, a little later, the founders of anthropology took an interest.

Friedrich-Max Müller (1823–1900) was to found a veritable school of comparative mythology. In his book *The Science of Language*, he set out a stratigraphy of human speech, in which he distinguished three phases: thematic, dialectal, and mythopoetic. In the first phase, terms were forged to express the most necessary ideas. In the second, the grammatical system acquired its specific characteristics once and for all. The mythopoetic phase saw the appearance of mythical discourse that was not at all a conscious product of language. As Müller saw it, just as grammatical structures silently took shape in the abysses of language, so too the first myths appeared like bubbles bursting at the surface of the words and phrases that rose to the lips of the earliest human beings. At the dawn of history, a human being possessed the faculty to pronounce words that gave direct expression to the essence of the objects perceived by the senses. Things awakened within the individual sounds that materialized as roots and engendered phonetic types on the basis of which a body of language was progressively formed. However, the human mind did not long retain the privilege of "giving articulated expression to concepts produced by reason." Once human beings ceased to "resonate" before the world, a sickness invaded language. Soon the human race would become a victim of the illusions produced by words.

The earliest language possessed a kind of mythopoetic energy that allowed the earliest human beings to apprehend the original meaning of words such as *night* and *day* or *morning* and *evening* and, at the same time, to conceive of them as powerful beings marked by a particular sexual nature. However, as soon as the primitive essence of the words *night* and *day* or the names Night and Day changed and became clouded, mythical figures swarmed into the field of representation. The human beings of the third phase found themselves assailed by the illusions of a language invaded by the strange and disconcerting discourse of myths. For Müller, mythology—in the first place that of the ancients—was a sickness in language. Linguists, now acting as clinicians, detected in the fables and stories of mythology a pathlogical form, not so much of thought, but of language and the excess of meaning from which it suffered at one point in its development. At a stroke, the paths of interpretation were marked out: all that was necessary was to diagnose behind the major narratives of mythology the forms taken by the spectacle of nature that impressed the human race of the earliest times. Thus, whether in India or in Greece, myths reflect a tragedy of nature in which a sense of storms and tempests alternates with impressions produced by the spectacle of sunshine and light.

Mythical Thought: The Foundation of Anthropology

The "science of language" that turned into comparative mythology took mythical narratives apart and disintegrated them, only too happy to burst the bubbles that had once risen to the surface of the words and sentences of human beings now long forgotten. Comparative mythology was partly motivated by the same sense of scandal that seems to have been felt by the new observers of humankind who, in the 1880s, turned into anthropologists. They were scandalized by the obscene and odious discourse purveyed by the mythology of the Greeks, which told of the emasculation of Ouranos and the death of Dionysus, cut into pieces and barbecued on a spit. All those who devoted themselves to the "science of myths" or "comparative mythology"—Edward Burnett Tylor (1832–1917), Adalbert Kuhn (1812–1882), Andrew Lang (1844–1912), Paul Decharme (1839–1905)—concurred as to the urgency of the task of explaining, not the wonderful stories produced by those early human beings, but the "savage and meaningless" tales about the appearance of death or of the sun, and the "monstrous and ridiculous" adventures, involving incest, murder, and cannibalism, which befell the gods. Between 1850 and 1890, from Oxford to Berlin and from London to Paris, the "science of myths" was established on the basis of the common opinion that bodies of myth were full of notions of a "revoltingly immoral" nature. That was certainly true right across the world, but also and above all in so many ancient societies that appeared to have attained a high degree of civilization. Beneath the surface, the ancient Greek and the Vedic priest were obsessively linked to the "savage" and the Iroquois.

But the strategy adopted by Tylor was quite unlike that of Müller. The earliest concept of anthropology is reflected in the proposed aim, taken over from Lafitau and Fontenelle, of revealing the "astonishing conformity between the fables of the Americans and those of the Greeks." Now the comparisons that were prompted by the scandalous nature of myth were extended to include the whole body of stories told among Australian Aborigines, Native Americans, Boschimen, and also the representatives of ancient societies. Stories that an anthropologist could now bring back from his missions in distant places could not be explained away as resulting from a misunderstanding of a few particular expressions. Studies of the peoples of the forests and savannas prompted anthropologists to follow a different line of investigation—but one that still involved language and the sovereign power it wielded in the earliest days of the human race. This was the power of naming, of creating sounds and giving them meaning. For Tylor, too, the primordial state of humanity to which native peoples alive in his own day continued to testify made it possible to understand why, in the beginning, all languages are governed by the same "intellectual art." The coincidence of language and myth is a sign of those earliest times for human beings, when a real life was attributed to nature as a whole and when language exerted a full and total tyranny over the human mind. In conditions such as these, mythology is everywhere, impregnating grammar, invading syntax, proliferating in metaphors. But mythology only possesses that force for a while, at the very beginning of the development of the human mind. It is a time of childhood that will pass away as the human mind evolves and reaches maturity: next comes the time of reason and philosophy. Mythology reveals the human mind in its primordial state. It falls to anthropologists to observe it on the African continent, in the Americas, wherever they can encounter "savage" peoples—that is to say, representatives of the human race who are still "at the stage of creating myths."

The basic assumption is that in the beginning the human mind "mythologizes" spontaneously. Myth and language evolve contemporaneously, testifying to a first stage of thought that has an autonomy of its own and that needs to be observed and analyzed. Tylor postulated the existence of thought of a mythical kind, with characteristics sufficiently specific to enable historians and anthropologists alike to recognize it immediately wherever it appears, either directly or indirectly. Myth is *a natural and regular product of the human mind reacting to particular circumstances*, and in such circumstances, Tylor declares, the human mind is bound to mythologize. That proposition comes quite close to what Claude Lévi-Strauss was to say in the 1960s. But there is one major difference. For Tylor, myth, that spontaneous cultural product of the human mind, is a sign of childishness and weakness. For him, the intellectual art that mythology represents is a "philosophy of the nursery." For Lévi-Strauss, in contrast, the savage thought that is manifested freely in a body of myth is complex and involves a wealth of intellectual operations. It is true that, in Greece, for example, it was to "desist" and give way to philosophy, the philosophical thought that emerged there "as the necessary forerunner to scientific reflection." But from Tylor onward, right down to the present day, mythology became an essential element in the functioning of the human mind.

Mythical Thought among Philosophers and Sociologists

Anthropologists are not prone to read philosophers, and vice versa. Nevertheless, it was a German philosopher, Schelling, who in 1856 published the fundamental work on mythology. In his *Introduction to the Philosophy of Mythology*, Schelling's idealism showed that a basic inclination of the human mind is manifested in mythology. It involves a kind of process that is necessary to consciousness and has nothing to do with inventiveness. Schelling sets out to reconcile the monotheism of reason and the polytheism of the imagination within a rational mythology. He constructs a theogony of the Absolute, thereby alerting Ernst Cassirer and Marcel Mauss to the fact that the only way to interpret myth correctly is to adopt a "tautegorical" method. In other words, the meaning of myth lies in what it recounts, not elsewhere. In Germany, in the wake of Cassirer's neo-Kantian scholarship, Walter F. Otto cultivated the values of epiphany and of the revelation of the sacred, which emerged as specific features of myth and are still considered to be so today. Greece, par excellence, produced a body of myth that testifies to what Otto, among others, calls "original experience *made manifest*"—experience that, as he sees it, is also what makes rational thought possible. Alongside the philosophical and spiritual path opened up by Schelling, we should be aware of a parallel track, which was to be particularly favored by philology and historicism. Before becoming a rut, this was the route that the poet-historian Karl-Ottfried Müller (1797–1840) had opened up in the early nineteenth century. In his view mythology is a form of thought marked by the naivete and simplicity of the earliest times, but it takes shape slowly, reflecting the impact of events and circumstances. Understanding this essential product of the human mind involves rediscovering an original landscape and fathoming the realities that led human intelligence to articulate relations in the form of actions that, more often than not, revolve around a proper name, in an original story. For this traveler, both a Romantic and a historian, the land of myths was a forgotten world, which could be recalled by discovering the landscape that alone could authenticate the story produced long ago by that particular locality. K.-O. Müller thus introduced a way of analyzing mythology that was to continue to fascinate historians and philologists dealing with antiquity. It consisted in stripping away from myths the concretions that, in the course of time, had rendered them unrecognizable, and then—courtesy of Pausanias or some other ancient traveler who, for his part, had truly seen and heard—getting through to some home-grown stories and replacing these in their historical and geographical context.

On the subject of mythical consciousness and mythical thought, Durkheim's sociology was to rival the philosophy of Cassirer, while at the same time bestowing upon it the strength of its own convictions. In the first place Durkheim, as early as 1899, in the first issue of *L'Année sociologique*, set out one of the major theses of *Les Formes élémentaires de la pensée religieuse:* mythology—or religion, for Durkheim made no distinction between them—"contains within it, right from the start but in a confused state, all the elements which, as they separated out and became defined, interacting in a thousand ways, engendered the divers manifestations of the collective life." Then, eleven years later, in 1910, Durkheim repeated his definition of the nature of religion and mythology: this is the most important of all kinds of thought and encompasses everything. It is both itself and more than itself. Mythical thought is no longer seen as a stage in thought, or as a particular phase in the consciousness of the mind. It possesses an astonishing power to engender the fundamental concepts of knowledge and the principal forms of culture. Durkheim's treatment of this subject was somewhat summary compared to the philosophical approach of Cassirer, who devoted to mythical thought one whole volume of his trilogy, *The Philosophy of Symbolic Forms.* In his analysis *Mythical Thought*, published in 1924, the

German philosopher postulated that mythical consciousness defines an autonomous order of knowing and represents a particular mode of human intellectual development. Mythical thought is neither infantile nor feeble. It is an original form adopted by the mind. It is a thought of "concrescence," the temporal and spatial intuitions of which are concrete and qualitative. Mythical thought, ruled by intuition, is fascinated by the universe that is immediately present and can be apprehended through the senses. Captivated by the contents of intuition, it knows nothing of representation and remains alien to conceptual action. The self engaged in mythical thought, assailed by the desire or fear prompted by every fleeting impression, speaks only haltingly of differences. It distinguishes and separates things, but without ever really pulling free from original, undifferentiated intuition. Here too, myth and language are seemingly inseparable: they constitute two modalities of one and the same impulse toward symbolic expression. Myth is language, but also religion: mythology encompasses the original qualities of both speaking and believing. In the belief that provides the basis for the unity of its experience, mythology is religious thought, or at least potential religion. In mythical experience religion is already totally present. Mythology, concomitant in language and religion, finds itself assigned a central function in theory regarding the human mind. It constitutes the native soil of all symbolic forms. Right from the start it linked practical consciousness, theoretical consciousness, and the modes of knowledge, language, art, law, and morality, including fundamental models of community and of the state. Virtually all forms of culture are rooted in mythical thought: "They are all as it were clothed and enveloped by some figure produced by myth."

Myth, Ritual, and Society

Neither Durkheim nor Cassirer embarked on an interpretation of myths based on their reflections on "mythical thought." But others, without the same theoretical ambitions, did devote themselves to interpretation. In 1890 James George Frazer began to publish what became the twelve volumes of *The Golden Bough.* It constitutes an immensely wide-ranging interpretation of myths from all over the world, and allots a prime place to mythical tales drawn from the Greek and Latin authors, which are then compared to those of primitive peoples. Frazer certainly notes all the similarities, paying scant attention to the differences, but his inquiry proceeds along two different paths of investigation. On the one hand, he concentrates on ritual: it was the gestures and practices of ritual that lastingly fashioned cultures, the social subconscious, and the memories that underlie all the major festivals of the human race. On the other hand, he pursues the power and models of transmission, especially the relations between symbolism and power. Frazer sets out to show that human societies develop in three stages: first magic, then religion, then science. He does not regard mythology as the particular province of a type of thought with an autonomy of its own.

For sociological historians in France, such as Marcel Granet and Louis Gernet, the analysis of myths in China and in Greece seemed to open up a splendid approach to different forms of thought. Both subscribed to the hypothesis, theorized by Antoine Meillet and Emile Benveniste, that language conveys concepts and thereby itself imparts form to institutions. Vocabulary is not so much a lexicon as a conceptual system; it is organized around concepts that refer to institutions—that is to say, to the guiding schemata that are present in techniques, modes of life, and the procedures of speech and thought. Granet and Gernet, while regarding "institutions" as a kind of historical subconscious, concentrate upon the mode of thought that they call now mythical, now mythico-legendary or mythico-religious. In the civilizations of both China and Greece, mythical thought, the depository of the fundamental frameworks of ancient thought, can be apprehended only through remains, fragments, vestiges: the vestiges and remains of a unitary and all-encompassing thought that finds expression only in certain myths, not in the mythical corpus that is accessible, at least in Greece, in "mythographic" forms. Like the China of the Warring States period, archaic Greece reveals itself as one of those places in which the inquiries of sociological historians can uncover mythical data in which "much of the social subconscious" is deposited. The investigations of Gernet, so innovative in the Hellenist studies of the first half of the twentieth century, revealed mythical data associated with the traditions of both ancient royal houses and peasant phratries. In the course of about thirty years, Gernet's "attentive reading" centered upon traditions of sovereignty, along with images of gift-giving, challenges, treasures, tests, and sacrifices, and also upon a whole rural fund of beliefs and practices amid which people celebrated, feasted, entered into marriage alliances, and confronted one another in competitions. In those particular fragments at least, Greek mythology seems to offer the sociologist access to a real society whose image is reflected clearly in myth, while at the same time it presents the historian of "prehistoric patterns of behavior" with a whole store of religious and legal notions that were to be deployed within the space of the future city.

On the Place of Greeks and Abstraction

Through their inquiries, and thanks to the very nature of their field, Greek scholars have revealed that the investigations into mythology and mythical thought carried out by Tylor, Durkheim, and Cassirer all have a common horizon. When Gernet, in his essay "The Origins of Philosophy," showed how important it is to define what "mythical concepts, religious practice and the very forms of society contributed to the schemata of the emerging philosophy," he was referring explicitly to the Greek context. It was in archaic Greece, not in Oceania, some African city, or even China, that western observers noted how myth and mythical thought had come to be overtaken. For Tylor, Frazer, Durkheim, Cassirer, and all the rest who turned to mythology as a unique form of thought, Greece was the exceptional place in which there occurred what Hellenists call, quite simply, "the transition from mythical thought to positivist abstract thought" or, more snappily, "from myth to reason." Since the thought of the eighth century B.C. at least, the Greeks had occupied a strategic position, for they were in command of the frontier between fable and religion, between myth and philosophy. The Greeks represented by Homer and Parmenides look down upon the narrow defile in which myth was overtaken by philosophical thought. They are, indeed, totally identified with both that landscape and its conceptual description. Cassirer, being a philosopher, understood better than others to what extent the data and the formulation of the problem are Greek and are indissolubly linked.

Today, even after the advances made in comparative studies of Greece, China, and India, no historical or intellectual configuration seems so forcefully to present the spectacle, almost unchallengeable in our eyes, of this emergence of philosophy: a new kind of philosophical thought against a background of mythology and mythical traditions. Neither in ancient China nor in Vedic or Brahmanic India does there seem to have existed first such a contiguity, then such a distance, between the major recounted myths and forms of abstract or positivist thought as is to be found in archaic Greece. On that account, perhaps, divergent interpretations have been produced not only among Greek scholars working on close analyses of forms of rupture and continuity, but also among the sociologists, philosophers, and anthropologists activated by how thinking changes. As Durkheim saw it, an "engendering," in the form of a demystification, took place: thanks to the Greeks—that is, to the philosophers of Greece—mythology gave birth to a universe of concepts. Cassirer, who is more attentive to local configurations of thought, spoke of a "misunderstanding" of mythic consciousness and emphasized the aspect of overtaking and new understanding: "a true overtaking of myth must be spurred by an understanding and recognition of it."

On the Overtaking of Myth

Overtaking, abstraction, emerging: all these metaphors are applicable in this frontier area. In his *Mythologiques*, Claude Lévi-Strauss describes mythical thought as moving toward abstraction and strong enough to contemplate "a world of concepts in which relations are freely defined." By 1966 he had converted that "being overtaken" into "a withdrawal." A frontier was reached, and "mythology *withdrew* in favor of philosophy, which emerged as the precondition for scientific thought."

For Lévi-Strauss, as for Cassirer, the situation was more complicated than one simply of overtaking or discreetly withdrawing. For mythology to be understood and its essential elements recognized, what was needed was the intellectual mastery of the Greeks, above all the Greek philosophers, who were the first to set about interpreting this "pre-historical" thought. To Lévi-Strauss, the Greek paradigm seemed so meaningful that, faced with various readings of Greek myths that he himself had inspired, he remarked that the ancient Greeks "seem to have perceived and thought through their mythology in terms of a procedure that was to some degree analogous to that followed today by ethnologists attempting to discover the spirit and meaning of the myths of illiterate peoples." The primacy of the Greek example was now fully acknowledged: their culture presented the spectacle of mythical thought that, reaching beyond itself, acceded to a logic of Forms on the basis of which Greeks, equipped with concepts, set about thinking through their mythology and interpreting it. Now that, from Tylor down to Lévi-Strauss, the Greek paradigm has been recognized, let us return to those ancients whom the founders of the science of mythology claimed as their immediate precursors: those "pious and thoughtful" men of Greece at the time of beginnings, such as Xenophanes of Colophon and Plato. For it was they and others like them who were the first to "try to find explanations for beliefs closely linked to religion yet which seemed a negation of both religion and morality." Those were the terms in which the contemporaries of Max Müller and Tylor spoke of mythology: stories described as beliefs, which oscillated between religion and irreligion. Moderns seem to imitate the ancients and to find in their ways of proceeding the best of reasons for acting as they did and agreeing to call certain stories myths—stories that, once collected, are referred to as mythology, if not mythical thought itself.

We shall return to this point later, in connection with analytical procedures, so at this point it suffices to remark, as Lévi-Strauss did at the beginning of his long and admirable voyage of discovery, that "throughout the whole world a myth is perceived as a myth by all its readers." For surely it must be useful to show the interpreters whom we all are the extent to which, even among the Greeks themselves, the category of "myth" eluded the kind of simple and positive definition that we might expect from those who were apparently the first to set about thinking through their own mythology (if that is what we decide to call it).

CHAPTER TWO

What the Greeks Called "Myth"

As suggested in chapter 1, the interpretation of the great stories of the Greek tradition began in the sixth century B.C., with the earliest philosophers. If we are to reflect upon *interpretation* in its earliest form—in ancient Greece, at least—we must first distinguish it from *exegesis.* Exegesis may be defined as the ongoing commentaries that a culture produces on its symbolism, its behavior, and its practices—everything that constitutes it as a system in action. Exegesis proliferates from within. It is speech that nurtures the tradition to which it belongs. Interpretation, in contrast, begins at the point where an external perspective develops—when, in a society, some people begin to argue about the tradition and criticize it, distancing themselves from the stories of their tribe. The process of looking with an outsider's eye at what is accepted by everyone else may take at least two different forms. In Greece, one form, which was minimal, began with the prose writing of those whom the fifth century came to call *logographers.* For the past century already, they had been arranging, within the new space created by writing, traditional accounts and stories ranging from genealogies to long, heroic epics. But, in parallel to that discreet and silent distancing procedure produced solely through the operation of writing, a second process was developing, in a form that made a major impact. It found expression through new modes of thought that were inseparable from writing, such as the early philosophy of Xenophanes of Colophon and the conceptualized history of Thucydides: modes of thought that radically called into question a tradition now condemned as unacceptable or no longer credible, for it made no immediate sense and did not seem to have any deeper meaning.

The Initial Interpretation

In the way that myth was interpreted, a new concept of myth was formed, and the image of mythology, in the Greek sense of *mythologia*, in all its specificity, emerged. In the history of the period between the sixth and the early fourth century, a series of landmarks help to define how the territory assigned to *mythos* was organized. In about 530 Xenophanes, in the name of the fledgling philosophy, forcefully rejected the whole collection of stories about Titans, Giants, and Centaurs, including those purveyed by Homer and Hesiod. They constituted a pack of scandalous adventures that set on stage gods or superhuman beings and featured all that was offensive and deplorable in the world of human beings, such as theft, adultery, and deceit. Xenophanes rejected all traditional tales of that kind, assigning them a twofold status: in the first place they were forgeries, *plasmata*, or pure fictions; and second they were barbarian stories, tales told by "others" (F. 14–16 Diels). But the word *mythos*—which, ever since epic, had been part of Greek vocabulary, speech, or language—was not yet mobilized to designate the discourse of others at which philosophy, barely established yet already scandalized, was pointing the finger and which it was so insistently denouncing. Very soon, however, a poem by Anacreon of Samos gave the term *mythos* a new meaning. Between 524 and 522, the party of the Samian rebels who rose up against the tyranny of Polycrates was known as the party of the *mythiētiai*. As the ancient grammarians explained, these were factious men, troublemakers, or probably, to be more precise, people who spread seditious talk (F. 21 Gentili). *Myth* thus meant revolution, *stasis*, the opposite of the *eunomia* advocated by Polycrates. Then, in the course of the fifth century, this semantic development, to which Anacreon's poem happens to testify, took a more precise turn in the vocabulary of Pindar and Herodotus, where the word *myth*, still used quite sparingly, came to designate simply such discourse of "others" as was illusory, incredible, or stupid. In works such as Herodotus' *Histories* and Pindar's epinicians, which seem to accommodate a large number of what we should be tempted to call "myths," the occurrences of the word *mythos* can be counted on the fingers of one hand: it appears only twice in the nine books of Herodotus' *Histories* (II.23, 45) and three times in Pindar's *Odes* (*Nemean*, 7.23–24, 8.25–26; *Olympian*, 1.27–59). When Pindar sings the praises of a victor in the Games, he is pronouncing a *logos;* myth only makes its appearance with *parphasis*, the speech of illusion. It is rumor that engenders *mythos.* It flourishes with deceptive accounts, with twisted words that are seductive but violate the truth. Fashioned like one of Daedalus' statues, *mythos* is detectable from its motley of lies. It creates appearances that fake credibility and constitute a shameful betrayal of the manifestation of "what is." But myths are always stories told by "others," by those who have usurped the renown well deserved by Ajax but now credited to Odysseus, or those who spread abroad a scandalous version of the banquet of Tantalus, in which the gods are represented as having feasted greedily upon slices of Pelops' flesh.

Herodotus makes the same distinction. His own accounts are always proper discourse, *logoi.* And when referring to particularly holy traditions, Herodotus always calls them sacred *(hieroi logoi).* The famous "sacred discourse" that *we* would call "myths"—particularly as the traditions are often associated with ritual actions and gestures—is never referred to as *mythoi.* As Herodotus sees it, when people try to explain the flooding of the Nile by blaming the immensity of the river Ocean that surrounds the earth, that is a myth, for it is a fiction pure and simple, which excludes any kind of rational argument and can accommodate no empirical observation. And when Greeks claim that Busiris, the king of the Egyptians, tried to sacrifice Heracles, that too is a myth, for it is stupid and absurd: how could the Egyptians, the most pious of all men, even dream of committing such a grave impiety?

To speak of *myth* is a way of evoking scandal and pointing the finger at it. *Mythos* constitutes an extremely convenient word-gesture, the effect of which is to indicate stupidity, fiction, or absurdity and, at the same stroke, to condemn it. But as yet *myth* is still something vague, something distant and ill-defined. Not until the very end of the fifth century did it come to designate a more or less autonomous discourse or form of knowledge. At that point, both the stories of the ancient poets and all that the logographers had been writing swung over onto the side of *mythos.* One of the contexts in which this division took place was the history written by Thucydides, for he defined the field of historical knowledge by excluding the fabulous, or *mythōdes,* from his conceptual territory and assigning it to a separate domain that took over a quite different way of recounting and recording things.

The Choices of Thucydides

The logographers set tribal stories down in writing. Herodotus aimed to provide the city with a new store of memories. Thucydides, for his part, set out to construct a model for political action, an understanding of future possibilities, with the historian regarded as an ideal political leader. He aimed not to recount what had happened, but to convey the truth in discourse made up of arguments so well constructed that, more effectively than any other means, it indicated how best to behave within the space of the city, both in the present and in the future. However, a history of present times, such as *The Peloponnesian War*, is bound to tackle problems posed by memory and the oral tradition. Thucydides does so in what is now known as an *Archaeology*, in which hearsay stories are criticized. Memory is fallible, for there are holes in it; besides which, it interprets, selects, and reconstructs, and the more troubled the times, the more marvels proliferate, and the more everything becomes credible, the more unreliable it is. In Thucydides' view, all that circulates orally, all that is *akoai*, is fundamentally erroneous on account of the absence of a critical spirit on the part of people who recount or report what happened yesterday or in the past, even in their own land where they could become better informed, could check out and correct their stories. Traditional memory is judged guilty of accepting ready-made ideas and of credulously spreading unverified information that swells the flood of *fable*. Poets and logographers are included among the accused in the charges brought against hearsay, for rumors, ready-made ideas, which in any case fall into the category of what is incredible, are no longer at all believable when the poets turn them into stories, endowing the events with splendors that make them more impressive, and when, in parallel fashion, the logographers set about combining several ready-made ideas with the idea of pleasing the ear rather than establishing the truth. With Thucydides, the distinction becomes cut and dried: on the one hand, there is tradition, which continues to express itself even in the public recitations and pronouncements of the late fifth century; on the other, writing, now sure of itself, which rejects pleasure and marvels, and is aimed at a silent, solitary reader. The author of *The Peloponnesian War* is convinced that anything that is passed on by word of mouth inevitably degenerates into fable—that is to say, into all that tends to block the efficacy of discourse conveyed by abstract writing and designed to reinforce action of a political nature.

The Mythology of the City in Plato

Alongside Thucydides, and contemporaneously, the overarching thought constituted by the philosophy of Plato proceeded, with even greater rigor, to separate out what Plato and his contemporaries labeled, on the one hand, *mythology*, and, on the other, *archaeology*. The radical critique, aimed, through the poets and craftsmen of *logoi*, at the entire tradition, singled out the mimetic character of *mythology*—that is to say, modes of expression with formulary, rhythmic, and musical aspects that catered for the needs of memorization and oral communication but that, for a philosopher, constituted irrefutable evidence of belonging to the polymorphous world of all that appealed to the lower part of the soul, that separate realm where passions and desires run riot. Not only was the discourse of mythology scandalous—and the *Republic* listed all its obscene, savage, and absurd stories—but also it was dangerous, on account of the misleading effects created by hearsay whenever it eluded surveillance and control. However—and this constituted the major difference from Thucydides—while it was easy enough, in the ideal city, to ban the ancient beliefs and to get rid of the poets by dint of censoring the traditional stories, the Platonic plan to reform the crisis-stricken city made it necessary to invent and fashion a different, new *mythology*—a fine, useful lie, capable of ensuring that all and sundry freely did whatever was right. Plato's *Laws*, in particular, contains an intuitive and spectral analysis of what constitutes a "tradition": rumor that ranges from malicious gossip repeated by others all the way to discourse inspired by the gods; oracles or eulogies that generate great reputations; genealogies constantly evolving; tales about the foundation of cities in the inhabited world; stories that go as far back as Deucalion and Phoroneus; nursery tales, proverbs, and sayings; all the kinds of discourse that get repeated over and over again and everywhere win acceptance. No sooner was it liberated from the ancient beliefs than the city strove to recover the secret unity of tradition. For a society, even when conceived and governed by philosophers, needs the only thing that can hold it together: namely, shared and implicit knowledge, thanks to which—as is stressed in the *Laws* (664a)—a community seems to be of one mind throughout its existence, both in its songs and in its stories. By the beginning of the fourth century, as a result of the combined action of two types of thought—the one philosophical, the other historical—what had furtively been called *myth* was wiped out, melting away into a new landscape, now known as *mythology*, where mythographers, already professional figures, were to deploy their writing skills.

It was undoubtedly with good reason that the founders of the science of myths recognized Xenophanes and the thinkers of ancient Greece as the initiators of a distinction that they themselves, scholars of the nineteenth century, were happy to ratify. Plato and Thucydides, long before them, certainly were the first to manifest the scandalized reaction that mobilized F.-M. Müller and Lang once it became clear that the language of mythology was that of a temporarily demented mind. But there was a downside to that prescience, for neither in the nineteenth nor in the twentieth century did any of the shapers of the new science realize quite how strange this "mythology" was: this concept that had stemmed from that ancient attempt at classification and that, ever since, has continued to prompt the most diverse of questions.

CHAPTER THREE

Mythology, Writing, and Forms of Historicity

Plato provides a helpful definition of *tradition* in the most common sense of the term: it is that which hearsay holds to be true, that which the ancients have handed down. And the word that Plato uses for anything that has been transmitted and seems to have been believed forever is *mythology.* Plato identifies those whom he calls "the collectors" of this mythology in Greece—that is to say, Hesiod and Homer, and also those who are simply curious, men with the leisure to research into the ancient traditions. In Greece, the transcription of stories and traditions gradually gathered pace and took a variety of forms, but in some other societies the transcription of myths took place suddenly, with distinctive effects on their types of historicity, if not on the transition to historiographical thought.

Transcription in the Japanese Manner

Japan presents an extreme example of how traditions came to be written down. In the eighth century A.D. a series of changes, breaks, and foundational new departures took place over a period of ten to fifteen years. A central power emerged, established a fixed capital, imposed written laws, took censuses, introduced cadasters and new ways of measuring time, and, finally, created two commissions charged with setting down in writing "the facts and accounts of the past." Japan defined itself in opposition to China. Its written records of tradition (cosmogonies, stories about the gods and Japan's first sovereigns) took two distinct forms, one of which was certainly autochthonous. The other, however, was Chinese, for China, with its long tradition of a literate administration and written annals, loomed large in the early times of Japan. The first records of the Japanese tradition were written in the Japanese language and entitled *Kojiki*, "Accounts of the Ancient Times." They were compiled by an official of middling rank who set out in writing what was "recited" or "read" to him by an individual who was not even a court official. Once set down in writing, the *Kojiki* seems to have been deposited in a chest where it lay, undisturbed, until the eighteenth century, when it reappeared to counterbalance the Chinese domination of Japan. In contrast, the second set of written records was produced by Chinese literati. It was known as the "Annals of Japan," or *Nihonshoki.* The Chinese writers, trained in an annalistic culture, chose to carry the history of the Land of the Rising Sun right down to the recent past, but they also chose to cite all the variants of the mythical accounts. While the *Kojiki* was conceived as a closed work that set tradition apart, deliberately avoiding dates and references to the present of eighth-century Japan, the Chinese *Annals of Japan* takes the form of an open-ended book in which events are dated, a book that is oriented toward the ongoing progress of a society bent on producing annals and keeping them up to date. There are many emphatic markers that point to the historicization of the tradition and that repeatedly underline the uniqueness of the imperial lineage descended from the gods. The *Nihonshoki* even works back from the present, using historical events authenticated by dates to fill in the temporal gap separating the eighth-century present from the time of origins. It introduced new historicity and at the same time a new kind of historiographical thought, in the Chinese manner.

Transcription in the Kanak Manner

Here is another example of writing that profoundly altered oral accounts, bestowing a different status upon them and switching directly and deliberately to historicity. In this case, however, the process was more gradual and resulted from private initiatives. In the Kanak region, as almost everywhere in Oceania, stories, whether major or minor, only made sense, indeed only existed, when they were insistently recited, chanted, or recounted in specially designated places and in the appropriate circumstances. Designed as they were to be told on certain special occasions, they took a narrative form that could not easily be accommodated in writing. Those accustomed to retail them orally no longer even recognized them once they were seized upon and fixed in writing, and made no bones about rejecting them. The early administrators, who carefully noted down the stories they were told when people challenged or laid claim to certain rights, were understandably deeply shocked by the newly transcribed versions. It was round about the 1930s that, in New Caledonia, ethnologists introduced, among other modern customs, that of writing, and even of self-reflexive writing, or writing about oneself. This had long been customary practice for western cultures both Catholic and Protestant, but in Kanak areas it was diffused by Protestant pastors, such as Maurice Leenhardt, who were also colonial ethnologists. Attracted or converted by these pale-skinned visitors, the Melanesians took to noting down their own stories. Soon they were putting together "mythology notebooks," and in this way they brought the local stories they recounted to a general readership. Discourse that until then had been of a strictly deictic nature was thus made generally available by the Protestant intellectuals of New Caledonia, and as the years passed, they put together the first version of a common mythology, though one that was centered upon the people who now became known as "the Kanaks." These intellectuals, now "mythographers," were committed to the movement working for independence, and in the 1970s they set about forging the identity of the Kanak people, unified thanks to the decolonization movement. Under the charismatic influence of Jean-Marie Tjibaou, these twentieth-century Melanesians sorted out the major themes of their tradition and also created a new mythical figure: the autochthonous Kanake, the first man, the primordial representative of all the Kanaks. Before our very eyes, a history, composed partly of myths, partly of memories, was invented—a history analogous to that which the still tiny France of the fourteenth century had created for itself, thanks to the efforts of monk-scribes and various figures in the royal court.

Rome and the Annalistic Tradition

Traditions, orality, and writing are means of transmission. In many societies it is possible to see how a mode of fixing those traditions that is more rigorous than memories or pictographic records may to varying degrees transform what is transmitted. Seen from this point of view, writing does not constitute a simple, familiar concept that is obviously the one to adopt. In contrast to an oblivious Japan, China seems not to have produced a large body of records in the early days of its history. The purpose of the first written Chinese texts that constitute an essential part of the ancient tradition was to record phenomena relating to sacrifices and to interpret them in accordance with a rich divinatory system. Later, a more elaborate form of writing, placed at the service of the imperial authority, was used for the *Annals*, but still in accordance with the procedures of the modes of thought of that rich system of divination. In fact, the first "annalists" were known as "diviners." Whether they were historians "of the Left" or "of the Right," the "annalists" were inseparable from the lordly or imperial household to which they were attached. They devoted themselves to keeping a meticulous day-by-day record of the circumstances and doings of their lord or prince, and of all the "events" that happened to occur. The distinguishing feature of this circumstantial history was that it aimed to establish what each event might reveal concerning the meaning of the general evolution of the world and also what meaning the general evolution of the world conferred upon each and every event.

Rome presents a different picture, in which tradition, mythology, and writing were all mobilized to produce a temporal model. Historians of archaic Rome openly confess to their perplexity: where are the great myths of Rome to be found? Are they implicitly conveyed by the oral and figurative traditions, or have they, as some believe, been transposed into the most ancient annalistic tradition? The distinctive feature of Rome and the tradition that it created for itself seems to lie in the decision to keep written records of all important events that affected the political community. The role played by magistrate-priests in the public domain seems to have been crucial. The pontiffs were priests who enjoyed considerable liberty of movement and initiative. From up on the Capitol, at the beginning of each month they publicly proclaimed the "nones," the ninth day before the "ides." This official proclamation involved the "king of sacred affairs," the second-highest religious figure in the Roman hierarchy. He it was who, on the nones, was responsible for announcing all the religious events for the coming month. The pontiffs not only were in charge of future time and all that it inaugurated, but also held responsibilities where the past was concerned. They safeguarded the memory of certain of the facts and events of the past: exemplary military expeditions, successes, disasters, and sacrifices; prodigies of all kinds; and signs sent by the gods. The *pontifex maximus* seems to have adopted the habit of fixing to the walls of his dwelling, at the end of the year, a tablet recording its outstanding events—a kind of update on the existing relations between the gods and human beings. These partly ritualistic, partly historiographical activities of the pontiffs, at the juncture of either two months or two civil years, seem to have prepared the way for the writings of the first annalists and then for historians such as Livy. Rome witnessed the beginning of a historiographical operation that was destined for a fine future: it involved recounting a nation's great happenings for better or for worse, without reference either to tradition or to "accounts of ancient times."

From Myth to History among the Amerindians

In the Roman context, the history that was written down certainly did not refer directly to myth. But even in the absence of explicit references to the mythology of Rome's beginnings, attentive analysts, the most perspicacious of whom was Georges Dumézil, have detected in the histories of Livy and others mythical models that affect their narration of the high deeds and history of the great men of the Roman world. At the beginning of the twentieth century ethnologists—especially Americanists, such as Franz Boas—engaged in collecting autochthonous myths were recording accounts of a mainly historical nature. Claude Lévi-Strauss pointed out that the mythological corpus of an illiterate people generally takes two contrasting forms: either a mass of disparate pieces, each with its own individual characteristics, or else collections of interrelated stories oriented toward what seems to be the recent past. The latter variety are the kind that, in recent decades, have been directly mobilized by the native peoples of North America to affirm their rights over certain territories (such as James Bay in the province of Quebec, or British Columbia) and in a history bent on challenging the white invaders. In the context of these self-identificatory mythologies, literate native peoples—like the Kanaks and certain African peoples—have produced literature that combines major, carefully ordered accounts with others selected with a view to justifying their territorial or even economic and political claims. This constitutes a field where we may make a rewarding study of different ways of creating histories and new and probably unprecedented forms of historicity, contrasting them to those with which we are familiar from our own western history. Lévi-Strauss has followed up the effects of what he calls the degradation of myth into history. He notes the disappearance of stories relating to the creation of the world and also of those describing the exploits of the trickster-deceiver, and the appearance of events spaced out diachronically that serve to found the name, rank, and privileges of some figure who comes to occupy a central place in this history. This adds the new dimension of written history based on the oral traditions of several families whose ancestors all lived through roughly the same events.

The Transcription of Traditions in Greece

Any careful observer of Hellenic ways of transcribing "the traditions" can today see that Greece certainly did not favor selecting a single version of events for which Herodotus or some other figure provided irrefutable evidence. Those who were known in Greece itself from a very early date as "logographers"—that is to say, transcribers of speeches and stories—wrote genealogies and engaged in inquiries in no way commissioned by the cities; some, such as Hecataeus of Miletus, produced comparisons of the various versions of a story. But they did not fully commit themselves to writing of a past radically separated from the present. Even if they distanced themselves critically from certain traditions, they certainly did not triumphally usher in a new regime of historicity. However many successive and important changes took place in the collective life of the Greeks, they did not suffice to trigger historical thought of a kind to set about organizing the "present absence" that is constituted by the past of any group. In Greece, the major obstacle blocking the recognition of a break between the past and the present was certainly Homer: for a very long time, and even for Thucydides, the Homeric epic constituted a memorial and account of the past, a heroic past filled with the unforgettable exploits of the people of earlier times. The Greeks regarded the Homeric epic now as mythology, now as history of the ancient times. For Plato, Homer offered a collection of the best known myths, while Thucydides turned to the Homeric poems when he wished to reconstitute the state of civilization prior to the present, the only subject worthy of the attention of a historian. One of the most decisive moves toward the development of historical thought was made by Herodotus, who strove to separate the history of the gods from the history of human beings as distinctly as possible, leaving to Homer and Hesiod the heroic past mixed with stories of the gods, while he began his own inquiry with the Persian Wars, recording "the astonishing achievements both of our own and of the Asiatic peoples." He made the first break between a recent past, different from the present, and the mythical and heroic traditions, which were traced back to Hesiod and Homer.

CHAPTER FOUR

The Practices of Myth-Analysis

Between 1958 and 1964, in France and primarily at the École Pratique des Hautes Etudes (Sciences Religieuses), Claude Lévi-Strauss embarked upon a radically new reading of mythical stories. Some hasty interpreters soon produced a handful of formulas in which they summarized the implicit philosophy. These, swept up in the fashion for structuralism, almost immediately blocked the development of any thought on the actual procedures followed in this very new way of analyzing familiar stories. The ignorance and vanity of those who, amid confusion, proclaimed themselves to be poststructuralists created such misunderstanding that today it is more helpful to speak of the practices adopted in the analysis of myths, rather than to become bogged down in arguments over signs and texts.

Since Hermann Usener and Marcel Mauss, mythology, as generally understood, has been perceived as an inevitable kind of social thought, but on a subconscious level. For Mauss, mythology could be reduced to combinations: "A myth is one stitch in a spider's web." Lévi-Strauss, for his part, was from the start more interested in the spider and its instinctive understanding of geometry. Mythical thought, the savage mind, mythology believed to be universal consists of a manifold of forms from the oral tradition produced by a particular kind of mind, "a mind that refuses to accept a partial answer and seeks explanations that incorporate the totality of phenomena." On the one hand, there is a "mind" faced by a single problem; on the other, a way of proceeding that involves considering that problem to be homologous to other problems that arise at other levels—cosmological, physical, juridical, social, and moral—and accounting for all of them at once. That is one way of defining mythology, which stresses the multiplicity of levels of meaning, but does not pause to consider the diversity of contexts that any analysis must address. However, it by no means excludes another definition that Lévi-Strauss would be happy to endorse: it is a native definition produced by an Amerindian teller of myths: myth is "a story of the time when men and animals were not yet distinct." A time before, a cosmogonic state, a story from before the beginnings, which, however, is not frozen in prephilosophic discourse.

There are, then, two ways of perceiving mythology and, it would seem, of analyzing it: either as a system of representation that always goes beyond the narrative genre devoted to one particular aspect of the mythology, or as a narrative genre, a domain organized by certain modes of narration. The latter model seemed at first to have triumphed with the idea, so quickly accepted and unreservedly appropriated, that "myth is language" and that a myth must be broken down into mythemes, the distinct units that make up this language, units from which a semiotic analysis of the myths will soon produce a narrative grammar. It seems to me that Claude Lévi-Strauss's initial proposition in his *Mythologiques*—namely, that "throughout the whole world, a myth is perceived as a myth by all its readers"—is tenable, provided one avoids the pitfall of a "narrative genre" and the "mythemes" of a natural metalanguage (to borrow the formulas of A. J. Greimas).

Relations, Transformations, Contexts

Yet the first of those two ways of perceiving mythology seems to have won out, following those experiments in semiotico-linguistics, thanks to the analytical procedures developed by Lévi-Strauss in works ranging from his *Geste d'Asdival* to the last of his *Mythologiques* volumes, *La potière jalouse (The Jealous Potter)* and *Histoire de Lynx (The Story of Lynx)*. Three concepts may help to define this type of analysis: relations, transformations, and contexts. The first hypothesis concerns relations: terms considered in isolation never convey an intrinsic meaning. Meaning stems from how they are opposed to one another;

it depends upon interrelations. The second proposition is that the analysis of a myth involves studying the transformational relations among the various versions of the myth and between that myth and others related to it. In other words, neither one single version nor a synthesis of several versions constitutes an adequate subject for study. The third principle, which may in truth be a more modest form of the first hypothesis, is that this type of analysis requires an understanding of the ethnographic context—an ethnographical context that is *independent* of the mythical material itself and that embraces the whole collection of objects, values, and institutions that constitute the culture of the society in which the myths chosen by the analyst are recounted. Plants, animals, customs, geographical data, ecological systems, astronomical phenomena, techniques: the interpreter-decipherer of myths needs to acquire knowledge of all these in the manner of a native encyclopedist. For beneath such a wealth of details, some curious, others unremarkable, the analyst will discover the multiple levels of meaning that make up the thick fabric of the mythical account. The analyst must mobilize all the different registers of the culture in question—its plants, animals, foodstuffs, hunting methods, fishing techniques, astronomical calendars—and must do so in as many societies as seem necessary, judging from a comparison of closely related or contrasting myths.

Contrary to the perceptions of those who have neither practiced it nor understand it, the structural analysis of myths involves not only the myths themselves but also an understanding of the concrete circumstances of the relevant societies and experimentation with their intellectual structures, sometimes in a limited local context, sometimes in a wider one. The analyst needs to work using several levels of meaning; at each level, latent properties may be extracted from the domain under investigation that allow it to be compared to other domains.

Although such analysis combines many elements, it is not necessarily interminable. Like all forms of interpretation, the structural analysis of myths accepts certain constraints and sets itself certain limits—in the first place, those affecting the particular culture in which the myths circulate. The said culture may well, thanks to the richness of its myths and the wide range of their different versions, present a field vast enough to allow the analyst who has selected certain abstract schemata (which another analyst may well leave aside) to reconstruct an organized semantic context and to interweave elements that seem to belong to the same configuration. It is a procedure that certainly enriches the myths rather than diminishes them by reducing them to a small number of skeletal oppositions. And if the analyst chooses to limit the inquiry to the parameters of one particular society, he or she may have reason to hope, by restricting the field of comparison around one constellation of myths together with their distinct versions, to discover more possible differences and distinctions, and thereby to enrich the culture with a new set of qualitatively different relations.

Mythology as a Framework and Mythology as Lore

This type of analysis, which pays attention to the correspondences among several semantic levels and chooses to open up each mythical account to other related traditions and stories, is not content merely to discover the odd conceptual mechanism here or there. It suggests that mythical stories are transformed as they are passed on. The hypothesis of "the mythical" introduced by Lévi-Strauss perhaps makes it possible to move beyond the idea that mythical thought thinks itself. Let us assume that each story that is told is the work of one individual. No sooner does it emerge from the lips of its first narrator than it enters the oral tradition or, at least, is tested by the mouths and ears of others. To explain how the story becomes "unforgettable," Lévi-Strauss suggests drawing a distinction between structured levels and possible levels: the former, which rest upon communal foundations, will remain stable; the latter, which depend upon approbation, will manifest an extreme variability, which stems from the personalities of their successive narrators. Put another way, in the process of becoming part of the communal memory, whatever each individual narrator is responsible for—through his way of adding certain details or leaving others out or of expanding certain episodes and omitting others—is different in nature from that which roots the story in the tradition that produces it and that it, in turn, produces. In the course of oral transmission, as the continuous chain of narrators unfolds, the possible levels clash, are worn away, and progressively separate out from the mass of the discourse what might be called "the crystalline parts"—that is, the parts that confer a more regular structure or "a greater symbolic meaning" upon a traditional story. As Lévi-Strauss says in the conclusion to *L'Homme nu* (1971) (*The Naked Man*, 1981), "The individual works are all potential myths, but it is their collective adoption that, in particular cases, actualizes their *mythism*."

Once "the mythical" is recognized as one of the major phenomena of memorability in cultures of the spoken word (rather than call them "traditions that remain oral"), "myth" begins to be considered a literary genre in itself or a narrative of a particular kind. This leads to the discovery of the diversity of the works that preserve memories: proverbs, tales, genealogies, cosmogonies, epics, and songs of love or war. Myth comes in many registers, and each society is free to choose particular ones and to theorize about them. In each of those registers variation is at work through repetition, and each is subjected to a similar process of selection. Just as, from this perspective, it would be illusory to suppose that any myth is immediately recognizable as a myth, the mythology of a society does not necessarily immediately coincide with what appears to be its mythology, nor with what the society, left to itself, calls "mythology." A structural analyst, in quest of the concrete elements that will make it possible to penetrate the levels of meaning of accounts possibly belonging to very different genres, knows perfectly well that certain proverbs, nursery songs, or episodes in sacrificial ceremonial are, in many cases, essential for a detailed understanding of what has become an exemplary story or for the construction of a conceptual schema that will reveal the interactions of two versions of the same narrative.

Plato, an observer of man better known as a philosopher, was well aware of the full range of what must be called "mythology" in Greece itself, the place where mythology—the whole collection of stories about gods and heroes—had become a particularly Greek category, thanks to the mediation of those soon to be known as "mythographers," who set about composing collections of those stories, keeping them quite separate from other traditional pronouncements. Given that it was Greece that provided the rest of the world with the category of "mythology," we should point out that in the home of Plato and Pindar two types of mythology coexisted: mythology as a framework and mythology as lore. Mythology as a framework consists of a system of thought that is revealed, or rather *reconstructed*, by structural analysis—that is to say, the more or less complex, all-encompassing system that extends throughout Greek culture, with all its beliefs, practices, and different types of accounts (among which those of Hesiod and Homer are simply better known than the rest). Meanwhile, mythology as knowledge, prepared by "native theologians," was written partly by the early "logographers" or historians, partly by the authors of the mythographic works that culminated in the *Library* attributed to Apollodorus that, in about 200 A.D., was revealing the full cultural richness of mythology in Greek society over a period of seven or eight centuries.

The more these ways of analyzing myths are developed, the better we shall come to understand some of the mental mechanisms that underlie cultural competence—that is, the body of representations that any individual, as a member of a society, must possess in order to think and to act. Furthermore, anthropologists studying polytheistic civilizations will discover even more of the secret complexity of the systems of gods and the representations of supernatural powers that are so often built into the architecture of the myths and the great, unforgettable narratives of so very many societies.

Part II / Does Mythology Have a Sex?

CHAPTER FIVE

The Danaids among Themselves: Marriage Founded upon Violence

A family affair.[1] It begins with a band of boys harassing their female cousins. There are insults, blows, violence, all the makings of a drama. Thanks to the vigilance of the archaeologist Ludwig Curtius, who salvaged a fragment of a broken vase,[2] we find ourselves confronted with the image of a naked man lying on a bed while a woman, clearly one of Danaus' daughters, stands over him, sword in hand, about to commit her unforgettable crime, a crime as terrible for Greeks to remember as that perpetrated by the women of Lemnos, who drowned every single member of the masculine gender in a sea of blood. Even worse, when we consider that it was on their wedding night that the daughters of Danaus pitilessly slaughtered their young husbands when they fell asleep. It is hardly surprising that so black and scandalous a tale should have forcefully affected modern interpreters, whose own family histories have made them particularly attentive to ancient conflicts that, not so long ago, were ignored, unless they were perhaps mentioned in obscure proverbs like the one about the famous bottomless barrel.

To be sure, the affair of the Danaids is a drama of violence between blood relatives. But in that reciprocal violence in which males and females clash head on, what is essentially at stake is power: power in both senses of the word *kratos* —namely, might and authority. The context of that clash—a crucial one for the civilizing order of Argos—is the sovereign conjugality that is enforced in this territory by Hera of Argos, the poliad goddess who knows better than anyone about the rights of the marriage bed. We should thus recognize right from the start that this is a story woven around the invention of marriage, the institution of a new way for the two antagonistic races to live together, sharing the same bed, without violence and with each partner respectful of the rights of the other. Such a story is not common in the Greek memorial tradition. Certainly, the tradition incorporates numerous stories that recur in one city after another about the appearance of the first woman or the first mortal, the emergence of civilized life and a human society following a long period of connivance with the gods, or a more or less paradisiacal state, of pure animality. In every city and every village there were also stories about the Sons of the Earth or the first Autochthonous Woman, Euboean Chalcis and Theban Melia, and a whole profusion of tales and myths about the first sacrifice, accidental bloodshed, the disturbing similarities between murder and the deaths of sacrificial victims, and about what one should eat and what one should not if one belonged to the human race. In contrast, silence surrounds the subject of sexual reproduction, conjugality, and monogamous unions, a silence that seems to coincide with an institutional void manifested by the Greek language's lack of a word to designate the union of a man and a woman. It is a state of anonymity that Aristotle notes in the *Politics:* there was no legal form of union, no institution of marriage.[3] It was amid that silence that a rumor grew concerning an episode of violence that took place in Argolis but was heard of throughout Greece. Fifty girls had been pursued and harassed by fifty boys intent on possessing them by force. The story had been told in the seventh century, set out in an epic, the *Danais,* and it became one of the tales that the Greeks continued to tell and that everyone accepted. In other words, it was a myth, in the Greek sense of the word, as understood by Plato in the *Laws.*[4] Everyone in Greece knew how, in Argos, one episode of violence tended to lead to another in the war between the sexes.[5]

The story of the Danaids tells of a bloody war that escalated in a society whose members were related by blood: two groups of first cousins, one male, the other female. And on the horizon there can be glimpsed a space in which, for the first time, a social contract would be founded upon the conjugal relationship—a contract that would be supported by many ritual gestures and religious practices designed to guarantee particular ways of behaving, and that would constantly be safeguarded by the divine powers called upon to convert open hatred into a necessary alliance.

At the heart of the plot lies a paradox. The daughters of Danaus, who have been the victims of aggression, slaughter the males at the first opportunity, on their wedding night, in the nuptial chamber. Yet those same Danaids, spattered by the blood shed in an abominable murder, are then established in Argos itself as the priestesses of Hera, the sovereign goddess of Argos, who holds sway over the conjugal bed and legitimate sexual unions and who rules over the contract that binds a husband and wife together. And every year the blood-spattered Danaids in the service of the goddess, who have become the providers of fresh water, in the name of the women of Argos perform all the ritual gestures of water-carrying, decency, and the wearing of a woven veil,[6] without which no woman could achieve fulfillment nor could there be a matrimonial pact or a consecrated alliance between the male and the female. What is so strange about the daughters of Danaus is that they are dispensers of pure water as well as shedders of blood; they introduce the sword and murder into the heart of the home, but also appear as initiators for the Demeter of marriage, instructing women in the ritual of the Thesmophoria, the essentially political festival of legitimate wives who congregate together, as women, for three whole days, keeping all intruders away: a feminine city within the city. How is it possible that violence of the bloodthirsty kind, in response to the violation to which the women were subjected, can authorize and introduce the ceremonial of a contract that binds the two opposed sexes together? How can these same daughters of Danaus, marked by the horror of a crime without equal, perpetrated in the very marriage chamber, appear—in the tradition familiar to Herodotus' listeners—as the women from Egypt who came to Greece to teach the initiatory ceremonies (*teletē*) of Demeter and her holy Thesmophoria to the wives of the Pelasgians?[7] No interpretation of the double orientation of the destiny of the Danaids can ignore the puzzle or deny the tension.

It was certainly war between Danaus' daughters and the suitors who pursued them. But this was no regular, chivalrous confrontation in which rival groups engaged in fictitious battle and were then reconciled, forgetting their hostility amid the festivity and joy of banquets. This war between males and females was shot through by desire and fear, gripped by hatred, and spurred on by a killer instinct. Everything about the suitors testifies to their lack of moderation: they behave like insolent brutes; filled with impious fury, like aggressive dogs, they are deaf to the voice of the gods; they behave like lascivious, sacrilegious beasts;

they are rapacious, predatory hunters of women, who fall upon their prey like a flight of kites, birds so horribly thieving and so cruel as to devour the flesh of other birds. These males are determined to seize the Danaids despite their resistance and despite the wishes of their father. And as they pursue the women intent on remaining free from any yoke, they speak of them as slaves, claiming to be their masters, boasting of their right to seize them, declaring that they will mark the bodies that belong to them with a red-hot brand, yelling that they have the power to sever heads and make blood flow.[8] The marriage that fills the Danaids with such horror is described in the Argive story as a limitless war, fueled by destructive sexual desire, in which the right of males is imposed by the naked violence with which a predator treats its prey or a master his slave. It is pure physical violence, perpetrated by physical force, and made even more extreme and unbearable by the very proximity of the partners, who are parallel cousins, blood siblings: blood kin who make their own blood flow.[9]

But however excessive this violence that invades the conjugal domain may seem, it is not completely alien to it. In the first place, it is inherent in the constraint that forces marriage upon girls who are allowed no way of fulfilling themselves outside the married state: a girl has to be married, precisely in the passive sense implied by that linguistic construction. Marriage is compulsory, there is no escape from it. But there is more to it than that, as was conveyed by the gestures of the man, who took his bride, and the woman, who was led away, in a fashion that was both legally and ritually correct, since in ancient Greece marriage was patrilocal and implied moving from one household into another. In its pietist version, the ritual prescribed that a wife should never be hounded or treated as prey or as a slave, but, on the contrary, should be shown all the respect due to a suppliant placed under the protection of the hearth, and should be led by the hand into her new home.[10] Caring and respectful though that gesture was, it was marked by the power to take, to seize, and, in that movement, to unveil the bride, publicly stripping her of the veil that signified that she was a marriageable virgin.[11] There is in all this an element of Violence that seems inseparable from the Necessity of marriage. Those were the two powers that were considered as kin in a sanctuary where nobody was allowed to enter, at the highest point of Corinth, close to the altars of the Sun. Here Violence (Bia) reigned as the sister of Necessity (Anangke).[12] In even the most legitimate forms of authority there was, according to Greek thought, an element of brutal coercion reminiscent—through vivid metaphors invoking yokes and spurs—of the modes of action of a shepherd, driving his flocks.[13]

And there is yet more to the situation. In the course of the struggle between the Danaids and their cousins, the race of women affirmed its own warrior violence when confronted by the race of males. In the epic that bears their name, the daughters of Danaus seize their arms and do battle against the sons of Aegyptus.[14] And when they arrive in the land of Argos, the Danaids are women with a strange appearance, their skin tanned by the sun and the wind: they look like Amazons,[15] women who delight in warfare and love to chase their quarry through exotic landscapes, steering their chariots through forests filled with aromatic odors.[16] It is impossible to tell whether they are girls or boys. They have the same kind of disturbing beauty as the huntress Atalanta, the girl who, out of horror at the idea of taking a husband, fled into the mountains, where she amused herself beheading the suitors whom she outstripped in the chase and then tracked down like terrified beasts. The Argive tradition on the daughters of Danaus confirmed their warrior vocation. It did so first by proclaiming the virtue of warfare in the *polis'* festival for Hera, in which the city's shield was offered to the winner of the running race before the entire assembled city; and then again on the Day of Immoderation (Hybristika), by reminding the city that the women of Argos should wear masculine clothing since they, like the Danaids in the old days, had taken up arms to defend the city against the threat of Sparta.[17] The martial Danaids who went off to cast the severed heads of their aggressive husbands into the waters of the Lerna were commemorated in the essentially folkloric use of the little false beard that the young brides of Argos would fix to their chins on their wedding nights, so as to be in no way inferior to the men with whom they shared their beds, within a matrimonial setting established entirely on the basis of the long since legitimized violence of the daughters of Danaus.[18]

Both upstream and downstream marriage is the target of reciprocal violence that is both a war between blood relatives and also a battle to the death between the male race and the female. Marriage is the only kind of social relationship that figures in the story of the Danaids and the founding of a new kind of city. According to the mythological tradition, from Hesiod down to Apollodorus, the daughters of Danaus did not penetrate the territory of the city of Argos represented by Aeschylus in his *Suppliant Women*, with its ramparts, its king, and the murmurs rising from the assembly of citizens voting on their decisive decrees. The territory of Argolis that the Danaids discovered when they landed at Lerna, not far from the sanctuary of Poseidon,[19] was a land in a state of total drought, lacking all sources of water. It was a land transformed into a desert, the sight of which was all the more striking, given that the stories about its early days told of times of moisture when the river-kings Inachus, Asterion, and Cephissus held sway. These were powers thanks to whom Argos enjoyed a prime position in relation to Ocean, under whose authority it had existed since the earliest times—old Ocean, the father of gods and the original principle of all beings, "from whom came all rivers, from whom the entire sea was born, and all springs and deep wells," sweet water and salty alike, whether visible or subterranean.[20]

The history of Argos unfolds under the sign of water, as is confirmed by the action of the Danaids, summed up succinctly by Hesiod: "Argos had no water. They provided it."[21] But in between the disappearance of the water and its restoration, which places the daughters of Danaus at the hub of this story, the tradition, which entered into written form at the end of the sixth century, introduces other important actors: younger gods, Olympians such as Hera and Poseidon, and also a First Man, Phoroneus. Phoroneus seems to open up a different path that leads toward fire, with its civilizing power, and toward the emergence of a society in which the first signs of a city can be detected. The most remarkable aspect of Phoroneus, one well worth analyzing, is that he represents failure and impotence at a time of beginnings that seemed extremely promising for Argolis, beginnings that, had they succeeded, would have led to an altogether different destiny. Through both his ancestors and his descendants, Phoroneus seems an ambivalent figure. His parents were Inachus and Melia (an ash lady who belonged to the same family as Ocean),[22] but Phoroneus himself was known as the "Father of the Mortals,"[23] and his tomb, where annual sacrifices were made, testifies to his interest in the human condition.[24] However, some of his descendants, his granddaughters, gave birth to offspring "with long life": mountain nymphs who ranked as goddesses, the cowardly breed of good-for-nothing satyrs, and also the Couretes, fine dancers who loved to enjoy themselves and who likewise ranked as deities.[25] But it was through fire and its importance that Phoroneus acquired a place in mythology, for in his role as the bringer of fire he rivals one of the most famous Greek figures. When Pausanias visited the sanctuary of Apollo Lykios, founded by Danaus, the people of Argos were still insisting that the inventor of fire was not Prometheus but Phoroneus.[26] In Argos this was said to be proven by the fact that fire, the first fire for mankind, fell from the sky and landed right there.[27] This was not stolen fire, taken by cunning and deceit from the dwelling place of the Olympian gods, nor was it a technical fire, given along with the means of producing it and continuing to use it.

Phoroneus' claim to have discovered this fire from the sky was justified by his birth and inheritance from his mother Melia, the ash lady. For he was thereby connected with the company of the nymphs of the great trees, the trees that carried amid their lofty branches the fire of the sky,[28] the dazzling lightning that, according to the *Theogony*, Zeus gave to men "by means of the ash trees," long before (although, admittedly, in another story) fire obtained by trickery took the place of those indefatigable celestial flames.[29] Through that same Melian connection of his, Phoroneus could lay claim to be the father of mankind, for in several traditions the ash tree produced the human species as its fruit, either in the form of the fragile human beings of the earliest days[30] or in that of the men of bronze, born from the Melians and armed with the "murderous ash tree," a javelin of hard wood that provided them with a shadowless double.[31]

Phoroneus, a legitimate dispenser of fire, was invested with the powers that went with his mastery of it: he produced a panoply of arms for Hera,[32] set up the first cult to her,[33] and was the first sovereign of the land of Argos.[34] All these inventions, one leading into the next, stemmed from the appearance of the fire that was, so to speak, Phoroneus' natural attribute. But at no point did the first man claim to be a blacksmith or one of those alarming inventors of weapons of war and death. Nor did his Melian fire inaugurate the ceremony of sacrifice that set the seal on the break with the world of the gods and bestowed upon human beings an inferior identity. The fire of Phoroneus simply fostered sacrifice, just as it spontaneously produced a warrior panoply. But as king, albeit fleetingly, Phoroneus dreamed of acting more directly as a founder: he built a town and set up a law court; it was said that he brought together human beings, who until then had all been dispersed, living separately, as nomads, knowing nothing of social life until, under Phoroneus, a common space took shape and was marked out. On this spot where people assembled, the "city of Phoroneus" appeared and was simply declared to exist.[35] In this roughly planned urban settlement, a disorganized version of a city, Phoroneus hastened to establish a court of law about which we know only that its mandate was to pass judgment on "the people of his race."[36]

But this court designed for people all of the same blood never actually sat, for before it had time to do so, another, emergency assembly took place at the request of the irate gods. It was at this point that the Olympians conceived a desire to take possession of the cities and their territories so that each of them could receive the sovereign honors that were reserved for poliad deities. The land of Argos, which Hera coveted, was also claimed by Poseidon. The river gods were asked to decide, solely among themselves, between the two rival claims and to declare who was to take possession of Argolis.[37] The decision was to come from the powers that had always been the guardians of Argos. There was no mention of Phoroneus, nor did it occur to him to intervene in such an affair. Inachus and his two co-assessors took the risk—a serious one for river gods—of provoking the anger of Poseidon by denying him sovereignty over their territory and instead favoring Hera, even though she seems to have been far less close to those river powers of the early beginnings of the world. Faced with their reformist choice, the master of running waters and bubbling springs immediately put a brutal stop to the circulation of water: all the rivers dried up, the springs failed, and, along with them, the beginnings of organized life that Phoroneus had set up were consigned to oblivion amid the indifference of the ancient gods.

At the same time as the age of Ocean's waters passed away, so too did the tentative, barely sketched-in forms of the beginnings of a continuity, when the immortals had seemed to be dissolving into the first mortals and the human race was still a shadowy category apparently unaffected by hunger and other physical desires. Phoroneus, with his fragile inventions, was a transitional figure, not a mediator. He presided over still-born innovations, the most spectacular of which was the fire that was carefully preserved in the sanctuary of Apollo Lykios amid archives of a past that was alien to the new world of Hera and the Danaids. For it was a fire that had fallen into such disuse that it was not even required in the only two festivals in Argos in which fire played a role. In the Lerna festivals, which used to require a new flame, the Argive people went to fetch it from Artemis of the Red Hair (Artemis Pyrōnia) on Mount Crathis, on the frontier between Achaea and Arcadia.[38] And the Festival of Torches, in Argos itself, commemorated the fire signals exchanged by Lyncaeus and Hypermnestra, the first human couple to reject murderous, sexual violence, who inaugurated the time of shared power, when a wife had rights of her own in the conjugal bed.[39] Festive Argos was illuminated by a flame that bore a message of love, ushering in an age entirely alien to Phoroneus and quite separate from the time that had preceded the clash between women and men.

Like an inverted deluge, the disappearance of water decreed by the incensed Poseidon wiped out all traces of what had gone before in the land of Argos. The Danaids, arriving by sea, introduced into Argos the first human beings of flesh and blood: everything began with them and with their violence. In this landscape of death the appearance of life was marked by an action at once ordinary and inaugural: a search for water.[40] It was a quest that was indispensable in order to begin a sacrifice addressed to the local gods, but also in order to take possession of the land and to root in the vicinity of a spring the disturbed and violent life of this race of women. The meaning of this search for water needs to be explained, although there are other stories that tell of it differently. Water, carried by girls known as *hydrophoroi*, was the first ingredient used in the liturgy of sacrifice, even before the cereal grains that were tossed over the animal victim.[41] Water prepared the way for the blood that would be shed on the altar and for the fire by which the meat would be cooked and the gods' share would be consumed. The water in the ewers within the sacrificial space represented both nourishment for life and the lustral element—that is to say, the liquid sprinkled on the heads of the sacrificial victims. Water was thus purificatory but at the same time a liquid of anguish, in which the knife would be reflected: this water evoked the blood that was to be shed when the victim was slaughtered.[42] In the Argive tradition, in which the fire of Phoroneus, along with its fleeting sacrificial importance, at this point disappeared, water and the Danaids now took over the leading roles in this story of beginnings. The sacrificial use of water for founding purposes, which at first motivated the search for it, was now eclipsed by what water, purely through its own virtues, instituted: a first social contract, the strength of which stemmed from a whole series of ritual gestures designed to get an abundant flow of water, the first of all riches, which purified and brought fecundity, to circulate both through the group of human beings present and throughout the city's land. The quest for water, originally motivated by sacrifice, led to the invention of an alliance between the female race and the male, a contract between woman and man, expressed in ritual terms.

At this point the story picks out two particular figures from the homogeneous group of Danaus' daughters. These two, distancing themselves from their sisters and rejecting murderous violence, set out along separate but parallel paths that lead them to discover a mode of social relations in which brute force is at last exorcised. The story of the forty-eight Danaids (fifty minus two)[43] is now diverted into two strands. The first recounts the adventures of Amymone and is set in the domain of the gods. The second tells how, in the world of men, Hypermnestra rejected and distanced herself from her sisters who were unanimously bent on shedding the blood of the males. The progress of Amymone, to whom it falls to seek out water in this land stricken by drought, begins with a hunting expedition.[44] Clearly, the Danaids' destiny to be carriers of water coexisted with their warrior propensities. Amymone, like her sisters, was used to hunting in the woods. She set off in pursuit of a doe, but her javelin missed its mark and instead aroused a far more daunting beast: a forest dweller, half-horse, half-daimon, humanoid but with bestial physical features that betokened a huge sexual appetite. This satyr lost no time in living up to his mythological image. No sooner had he laid eyes on the Danaid than he threw himself upon her. A third figure intervened and put the aggressor to flight: Poseidon, the lord of the deep waters, chased the violator away and reassured Amymone, speaking to her gently in a manner quite the reverse of bestial desire and violence. The god hidden in the depths of the woods, where his anger blocked the flow of all springs and rivers, now behaved in the most courteous manner. With loving, tender, and ardent words, he set about winning over the Danaid, persuading her to submit to his desire and agree to become his wife. His words of love were followed by a declaration of commitment. For Amymone, Poseidon invented the formula for a contract that linked the two partners in a bond of mutual respect: "Your destiny is to be married, mine to be your husband."[45]

Upon becoming the first, unprecedented wife, the Danaid laid aside her warlike violence. As a gift to her, Poseidon released the waters, and she became the *hydrophoros*, thereby inaugurating Hera's reign with the complicity of the master of the underground waters who, in the joy of his marriage, did not hesitate to sanction his rival's sovereignty over the land. From that time on, the name of Amymone was given to two springs, one within the city, the other on the edge of the territory. The recovered water sprang forth near Lerna, on the seashore, where fresh water still springs today. Poseidon decreed that Amymone's spring should always produce a regular flow of water, in summer and winter alike; it was fed by underground courses that carried water upward from the depths of the earth.[46] The water from Lerna, on the territory's frontiers, guaranteed continuous fertility for the land of Argos; meanwhile, at the center and heart of the political space, the other Amymone spring gave rise to a liturgy that sanctioned the regular power recognized to be possessed by married women and that inscribed within this confirmed contract a series of rituals placed under the approval of Hera:[47] she who, of all the deities, was the one most committed to reciprocal rights in a contractual marriage, one that endured throughout every stage in a woman's life, beginning with the nubile girl and lasting through to old age, taking in the woman giving birth to children and the fulfilled matron. That series of roles was reflected in the list of Hera's religious titles, all of which would be evoked in the course of the Argive marriage ritual, over which Amymone presided, just as she did over her springs of life-giving water, which purified and confirmed the pacified virtues of the women of Argos.[48] The whole of social life was constructed around the relationship of a man with the woman whom he married.

The shortcut taken by Amymone, who proceeded from sacrificial water straight on to the springs of nuptial water, was matched by the course followed by Hypermnestra, the only other daughter of Danaus to reject murder on the wedding night.[49] She too avoided repaying violence by violence, by sparing the life of her partner in bed, apparently because he alone of all the suitors in pursuit of the Danaids likewise renounced violence, respected his Danaid's fragile body, and recognized her essential rights, first as a suppliant and then also as his partner of equal rank. It was by mutual agreement that murder and violence were thrown out, and the change that thus took place thanks to Hypermnestra and Lyncaeus, cousins of opposite sex but no longer enemies, was all the more dramatic in that it was brought about by two human beings standing in isolation against the generalized violence. Because she had dared to transgress the law of intestine and endless warfare, the rebel Danaid was arraigned before a court. The legal body before which she appeared was not asked to declare for what was lawful rather than for vengeance, but simply to decide whether or not the accused had been right not to shed blood.[50] It was at this point that Aphrodite, taking over from Poseidon and his persuasive words to Amymone, came to the aid of Hypermnestra with all the power of her own beguiling speech. On the very spot where her trial had taken place, Hypermnestra, upon her acquittal, consecrated a statue of Aphrodite coupled with one of Hermes, for it was Hermes who prompted brides with words of love and whispers that led into the pleasure that the woman and the man then afforded each other. As well as being closely associated with Aphrodite, Hermes presided over sexual intercourse and desire, and the bodies that lovers offered each other without reservation. In Hypermnestra's case, as in Amymone's, persuasion triumphed over violence, and the alliance of the couple stood as a paradigm of social order, an order in which power was shared as it should be, just as Hera declared and willed herself to be "equal in rights" *(isotelēs)* with Zeus, her bedfellow.[51] For what the Argos court had, against all the odds, granted to Hypermnestra was her right—regardless of the authority of her father—to decide for herself who was to be her husband, choosing freely and without any kind of constraint. Her acquittal made her a "subject with lawful rights": of her own volition she could link herself with the man of her choice. Then and there the mutual trust between Lyncaeus and Hypermnestra seems to have founded the pact to which Aeschylus refers in the *Eumenides*, a pact "guaranteed by Zeus and Hera, the goddess of marriage."[52] It thus prefigured a type of marriage by *auto-ekdosis* that did not become legally recognized practice until the Hellenistic period.[53] Here, in the Argive tradition, this was established amid the silence of a city still in the process of emerging, and with no reference at all either to the definition of citizenship or to the founding of a legitimate line of descent. The purpose of the marriage of Hypermestra was not the production of children whose legitimacy would be recognized. For it was not a matter of bringing to an end a time of confused sexuality and unions that resembled those of the animals, but simply of putting a stop to violence and to the war between enemy sexes.

In the Argolis of the daughters of Danaus, everything began with marriage. And it was Hypermnestra, even more than Amymone, who, with this matrimonial pact, inaugurated the reign of Hera in the Argive land and the royal line of the mortals who ruled the territory protected by the Heraion, the sanctuary where Hera was enthroned in majesty, scepter in hand, with at her feet a conjugal bed flanked by the Charites and a large shield.[54] Hypermnestra was truly the first priestess of the Hera of Argos. And the kings of Argos were descended from her and Lyncaeus:[55] Hypermnestra engendered the royal line. In the semicircle of the rulers of Argos consecrated by the Argives in 369 B.C., after the founding of Messene, her statue stands in front of that of Lyncaeus and immmediately behind that of Danaus.[56] In Hypermnestra,the exercise of royal power seems inseparable from the confirmed rights of the marital bed and from the power, the *kratos*, which she obtained in the name of the daughters of Danaus and the women of Argos.

The disciplined warrior band composed of the other, anonymous daughters of Danaus was left to take responsibility for the violence and to suffer the remarkably light defilement of bloodshed from which, however, they purged themselves as discreetly as they had got rid of the severed heads of their husbands, which they had consigned to the bottomless depths of the waters of Lerna.[57] Then, following in the steps of Amymone, they too entered into marriages that gave them full power over the lustral and nourishing virtues of water. But the much-traveled Danaids were also destined to pass beyond the frontiers of Argos and open up the legal limits of Hera's domain, moving in the direction of Demeter's realm. For it was they who introduced all the women of Greece to the initiatory festivals of Demeter known as the Thesmophoria, in which, to be sure, legitimacy was de rigueur and the powers of the female body were exalted, but at the same time the race of women, recovering autonomy even within marriage sanctioned by the *polis*, constituted a closed city, an acknowledged and redoubtable gynocracy. The reason why this was redoubtable was that inside the precinct of the Thesmophoric sanctuary, formally off limits to all males, the ritual of Demeter invited the women, quite exceptionally, to shed sacrificial blood.[58] As a result of this action, from the depths of the city's memory of the alliance concluded between men and women, what resurfaced was the unforgettable, murderous violence of the daughters of Danaus. By instituting the Thesmophoria for totally legitimate wives, with its ritual of anguish that cast a shadow over the festival, the Danaids showed that, while the social contract of marriage could exorcise the blood and warfare between those who were closest and most similar to one another, the union between a man and a woman nevertheless remained characterized by violence, and would forever be founded upon it.

CHAPTER SIX

A Kitchen Garden for Women, or How to Engender on One's Own

Not for the first time did the goddess Hera set off to visit Ocean and Tethys, but the journey to the end of the world was a long one. So, before reaching the great river of sweet water in the endless circle that was the home of the first couple, Ocean and Tethys, brother and sister born from the same mother, Hera, feeling tired, decided to break her journey in the garden of Flora.[1]

The banks of Ocean were doubly familiar to the wife of the master of Olympus. Part of her childhood, which had lasted several centuries, had been spent close to her primordial grandparents, who had raised her in secrecy and silence. And it was also on the banks of the river Ocean that there stood the nuptial chamber in which she had become Zeus' legitimate wife. That position had given her the keys of marriage, upon which the privilege of her sovereignty over the marriage ritual was founded, a sovereignty so unassailable that, in the festival of the deities' marriage, the Zeus who was invoked was called the Zeus of Hera.[2] This journey of Hera's was thus a return to herself, to her own identity. On a previous occasion, recounted in the *Iliad*, she had returned there, she claimed, as a go-between, to persuade Ocean and Tethys to put their quarrel behind them and be once more united in love.[3]

Now, however, she was full of rage and had come to complain of the behavior of her husband. Not about the kind of infidelities that sometimes angered her, for this time the matter was more serious. As a result of swallowing Metis and, with her, all the world's cunning intelligence, Zeus had become pregnant with a motherless daughter and had himself given birth to Athena. He had become a father with no help from his wife. Hera had been dispossessed of her essential power: that of the legitimacy of the conjugal bed. Athena's unusual birth challenged Hera's sovereignty over that royal couch. She would get her own back without delay. Hera thus decided that she, in her turn, would give birth to a child; she would reproduce herself without letting her husband touch her or even come near her. The voyage to the world's end brought her to a land that was marked with all the signs of her outraged power: "I will try all the drugs in the wide world, and I will explore the seas and the depths of Tartarus."[4] In order to become both a father and a mother, Hera needed to invent a new drug. And Flora, in a corner of her garden, was cultivating the secret means for her to do so.

"I, who am now called Flora, was formerly Chloris."[5] Once a nymph in the land of the blessed, Flora, who had been ravished by the West Wind, was now the mistress of a many-colored garden, where she reigned over the flowers. Flowering begins with young, green growth, and everything flourishing belonged to Flora: the wheat, the vines, the wine in the cellar when its surface bubbles and froths, and the green years, too, when youth is in its flower and bodies are vigorous and ardent. Nothing in the process of growth was alien to Flora. But the Flora of Ovid's *Fasti* also had greater powers. She enriched the catalogue of flowers and plants by producing new species. Strange seeds came from her garden. They were of two kinds. On the one hand, there were the flowers that sprang from the blood of handsome youths struck down by fatal wounds. Some of these—narcissus, crocus, hyacinth—kept the names of the living boys destroyed in the flower of their youth.[6] Another, the anenome, born from the vital blood shed by Adonis, evoked the vanity of that which can be carried away by a puff of wind.[7] And right next to that patch of flowers grew a single, anonymous, precious bloom that came from the land of Olene. A mysterious figure had given it to Flora, and it had the power to make anyone who touched it fecund. No sterility was proof against it. In contrast to the narcissus or the anenome, whose stems were formed from blood that had been shed, the flower of Olene engendered life and new blood.[8]

Hera had found what she was looking for: seed that would enable her to engender a child without any contact with another body. Flora's hand detached the flower from its stem, moved it toward Hera, and touched her gently with it. She immediately became pregnant. The child born from the flower of Olene was Ares, the god of war. The mere touch of the nameless flower made Hera pregnant, bypassing all sexual relations. By entering the estate that lay close to the river Ocean and not far from the orchard of the golden fruits that symbolized the ritual marriage contract, Hera, without abdicating her status as a wife, moved from a shared garden to another in which her sovereign power over conjugal legitimacy was confirmed and manifested its autonomy. But once was not enough for Zeus' wife. She returned for more, once again to a garden, but this time to its vegetable patch. By eating a lettuce, she conceived a sister for Ares: Hebe, or Youth. Although this tale has only come down to us through the genealogical jumble of the mythographers,[9] there are good grounds for its authenticity, for it fits in with a whole series of myths that begins with the births of Hephaestus and the dreadful Typhon, and that goes back to Hesiod's *Theogony*.[10] In anger and in defiance of her husband—to whom she arrogantly refers as her "bed companion"[11]—Hera engendered Hephaestus "without being united in love." Was the absence of desire a drug insidious enough to become a substitute for the flower of Olene? There can be no answer to that, but at any rate the child Hephaestus is supposed to have emerged from Hera's thigh, just as Dionysus did from Jupiter's after the latter had plucked him from the womb of Semele, when she had been struck by his lightning.

Hephaestus' skills as a blacksmith were manifested by his twisted feet and bandy legs, visible marks of his power with fire and his mastery of the art of metalwork. But soon the daughter who sprang from the head of Zeus made Hephaestus' mother dissatisfied with the offspring she herself had produced. She decided to do better. To spite Zeus and to seize his heavenly fire, Hera determined to conceive a dazzling son, more powerful than his father. She appealed to Earth and Sky, and the Titan deities were also invoked. A heavy, open hand struck the ground, and a shudder ran through Gaia, the giver of life and nurture. Nine months later, the sinister Typhon made his appearance, the product of Hera's and Gaia's complicity, for Earth had carried within her the fruit that was engendered with the aid of the great powers activated in accordance with Hera's will.[12]

Another, less well-known version of the story confirms the solidarity that developed between Earth and Zeus' wife. The war against the Giants is over, and Earth, vexed by the massacre of her sons, has confided her anger to Hera, setting her against Zeus and his despotic power. As in the Ares story, Hera sets out on a long journey. She goes to find Cronos, at the edge of the world where the powers of the past sleep. The father of Zeus gives her two eggs smeared with his own seed, telling her that she is to entrust them to Earth, burying them beneath Mount Arimon in Cilecia.[13] The seed of Cronos, the womb of Earth, and a couple of eggs: that was surely enough to create a monster more daunting than Hephaestus, a rebel so timid that he ventured only to take the side of his mother.

But in a version of the story taken from Lucian's ironic *Dialogue on Sacrifices*, another link is suggested between the brothers with curved limbs, both of whom are masters of fire and wind. The link is provided by an orb of living matter, the egg that plays its part in the genesis of both Typhon and Hephaestus. Lucian's *Dialogue* refers to Hera as a mother who gives birth to children without sexual union, and describes Hephaestus as a "child of the wind," playing on both senses of the Greek word *hypēnemios*.[14] One is that an infant carried by the wind can only be a vain and inconsistent being. However, the term also has a technical sense that is applied to wind eggs—that is, eggs that are unfertilized, such as are produced by certain domesticated birds, and which some biologist contemporaries of Aristotle considered to prove that females could produce seed without any intervention from males.[15] The marginal Hephaestus of Lucian is a child of the wind, just like the desirable Eros of the Orphic cosmogony, of whom we are told in Arisophanes' *Birds*. Here, black-winged Night first produces an unfertilized egg, which she places in the limitless womb of Erebus, and out of it comes a god who resembles the gusts of wind, the power of Desire, in person.[16]

Both Flora and Night are female, and in her desire to conceive on her own, Hera reproduces the works of the most autonomous of the feminine powers: Earth, who never forgets that she was the first to carry new life, and black-winged Night, who knows of no power greater than her own. Of the four offspring of Hera produced with no father other than their mother, only the daughter named Youth does not seem to belong explicitly to the primordial setting that is suggested both by Hera's journeys to Ocean and to the castle of Cronos and also by the role that is played by Gaia, a mother before ever there was a couple, who began to produce children on her own before the appearance of Desire and, along with him, erotic pleasure. While Typhon, a fiery creature of interlaced snakes and tentacular violence, reproduces in hugely magnified form the stigmata of his elder brother Hephaestus, Youth, born from the lettuce eaten by Hera, seems simply to constitute a feminine being corresponding to Ares, who was produced by a unique flower.

Zeus no doubt had reasons enough to detest the tempestuous energy of the god of irrepressible warfare,[17] but this son conceived by Hera in no way exceeds the acknowledged power of Flora. With his swift legs and arms, he is a masculine embodiment of the qualities of youth, continuing the Homeric tradition according to which the peak of a warrior's strength was reached in the flower of his youth. In parallel to Ares, his sister, Youth, testifies through her very name to her floral nature: in the vocabulary of biologists and doctors, Hebe was the sign of adolescence, the nubile age, when the pubis came into flower and was first covered with down.[18] In the ancient city of Phlius, Hebe was the feminine counterpart to the handsome Ganymede—whose name likewise evokes the dazzling, vital brilliance of a young body—and, alongside the cupbearer carried off by the eagle, she reigned over the festivity of the Olympians, dispensing wine at the banquets at which the gods with their ever youthful limbs enjoyed themselves.[19]

But into the harmony of the pair formed by brother and sister, a jarring note is introduced by the vegetable through which the beautiful Hebe was born. The lettuce that made Hera pregnant was no stranger to Flora's garden. It was implicitly present there, in the secret corner reserved for new kinds of seed, behind the anenome whose fleeting life ended amid the blood from Adonis.[20] In the *Metamorphoses* the death of Aphrodite's lover is placed under the sign of a flower, all of whose qualities converge to negate seduction: shallow-rooted and excessively light-petaled, hardly has it pushed up than its head falls, torn off by the wind after which it is named. The anenome is a rose without perfume and, although it somewhat resembles a pomegranate flower, it is fruitless. So, on the vegetable level, the anenome resembles a horticultural plant associated, ever since Sappho's poems, with the downfall of Adonis and his pitiable death from the goring of a wild boar. That plant is the lettuce, the cold, damp lettuce growing in the vegetable patch toward which the handsome seducer at bay rushed, seeking refuge—unless it was his mistress who, in a fatal, foolish lapse, sought to hide him there. For the lettuce was regarded as food fit for the dead and, above all, was believed to produce impotence in all who ate it.

Within the close space of this garden for women, a strange contrast is detectable between Hera's daughter and Aphrodite's lover, both of them adolescents of dazzling beauty, but one of whom dies amid the plant that produces the other, its golden fruit. But the real connection lies elsewhere, not in the contrast between the two adolescents, but in the contrast between the austere Hera, who gives birth to Hebe as a result of eating lettuce, and Adonis, stripped of his sexual potency as a result of touching that same vegetable. On the one hand, Hera, who is both a father and a mother; on the other, Adonis, the seducer who is no longer either male or female but is felled by impotence and dies.

The explanation why one and the same vegetable species produces such contradictory effects, within the same symbolic system, is not that the plant is ascribed different positions in myths that are distinct and differently oriented. No, the reason is to be found in the qualities that the Greeks themselves ascribed to the lettuce. There was a fundamental distinction between men and women that is also detectable in connection with the agnus castus plant used by women assembled together, and also the anenome. The distinction is associated with a whole series of beliefs about the bodies of women and their relation to sexual pleasure and about the sexual desire ascribed to each of the genders.

In the Greek world, the correct way of using lettuce was determined by a whole set of rules that, to us, may be somewhat disconcerting. Men, for their part, were all agreed that lettuce should not appear on the dining table. To eat it would be to deprive themselves of erotic enjoyment with women. The disciples of Pythagoras, who would solemnly chew lettuce leaves during the dog days of high summer, *a contrario* confirmed the non-Pythagoreans' rejection of lettuce. As for women, their dietary behavior with respect to lettuce was dictated by the salutary effects that salad was believed to have on the way their bodies worked: it was excellent for their periods and crucial for the flow of the menses. What was considered bad for men was considered good for women, and it is not surprising that nobody thought to say anything about the pleasure that the wretched vegetable denied to women, for inequality between the masculine and the feminine underpinned the entire institutional system. Sexual enjoyment belonged by right to the males, who indulged in it among themselves or with courtesans. As for legitimate wives, their job was to produce children as much as possible like their fathers. An identical view of the role of women dictated the symbolism of the agnus castus plant, branches of which were used to make the mattresses upon which the legitimate wives slept when they gathered together under the patronage of Demeter Thesmophoros, with no males present. On the one hand, this plant was believed to favor the continence of women and deter them from any sexual activity during the time that this ritual caused them to spend away from their husbands; on the other, it was reputed to facilitate the flow of their menses and also the production of their milk. The ritual framework of the Thesmophoria festival, centred on the city's reproduction of itself, helps to explain the bases of the role played in the city of women by the agnus castus: it rid their bodies of all sexual desire and prepared them for their sole function, namely, reproduction.

But although the agnus castus and the lettuce were assigned the same role, their targets in the negation of desire were different. In the case of the agnus castus an absence of pleasure was produced in the female body until such time as the woman was reunited with her husband. In contrast, although the lettuce killed desire in both sexes indiscriminately, its effect upon the male body was more particular in that it not merely induced sexual apathy but imposed upon the male partner positive impotence followed by violent death. Aphrodite's lover was thus left bloodless and dead. Nor is it surprising that Hera found herself pregnant at the touch of the plant that so bitterly disappointed the mistress of the excessively handsome Adonis. After all, it was the wife of Zeus who savagely punished Tiresias for daring to declare that in lovemaking the woman felt nine times as much pleasure as the man. Hera could not bear to be confused in any way at all with the smiling and curvaceous Aphrodite.

All we need to discover now is the connection between Hera's seminal lettuce and the lettuce that promotes lactation and menstruation in wives. The functioning of the female body provides a model of vital flows, which stem from the transmutation of the various humors—flows that range from milk and blood to seed and menses. Medical thought and the thought of biologists—in particular that of Aristotle in *The Generation of Animals* and *The History of Animals*—is permeated by a whole alchemy of the body. The reason why the production of milk is so closely linked with the flow of menstrual blood is that milk is a product of the sanguine humor.[21] Milk is of the same nature as the secretion from which every living creature is born, because matter that nourishes is identical to that from which nature proceeds to generate new life. In living creatures with a blood system, milk is thus formed from blood. Aristotle explicitly states that milk is blood that has been submitted to a perfect coction. But if the origin of milk is blood, then according to the *Generation of Animals*, it follows that the nature of milk is the same as that of the menses.[22] The same goes for semen. Seminal liquid, which is a residue from nourishment, can only be blood or some product that stems from blood, but it is distinguished from it by the degree of coction that it has undergone: sperm, produced in the vital region of the diaphragm, is blood that has been treated to the highest degree of coction. Experimentally, this can be verified by venereal excreta:[23] sperm that has undergone insufficient coction takes on a bloody appearance; it is in danger of becoming no more than a discharge of the same nature as the menstrual blood that escapes from the female body, in the coldest and wettest part of the month, when the waning moon is about to disappear.[24]

The connection between the phenomena of lactation and menstruation was thus an accepted feature in the physiology of the body, but within the context of a hierarchy that comprised, starting from the top, semen, milk, blood, and menses. The radical distinction between males and females was made by the first and the last terms of this hierarchy—semen and menses—but for a more precise definition of the power that was credited to each of these, it will be useful to introduce another element that appears in the ancient Greek representation of the body.

Some animals of the female sex produce not only milk and menses, but also eggs, described now as "wind eggs," now by the name of the fertilizing West Wind—that is to say, as "Zephyrean."[25] Conceived spontaneously, with no intervention from any male, these eggs are produced especially by birds of heavy flight, which have at their disposal an abundant residue not required for the creation of claws or feathers. Such birds belong to species in which, when the males are burning to cover the females, the latter emit an abundant material that does not flow away as menstrual blood. An example is provided by the female partridges that were used as lures: as soon as they set eyes on a male or heard its cry, they were filled with eggs, which they immediately laid.[26] This phenomenon serves as the basis for two different interpretations. The more authoritative of the two, established by Aristotelian discourse, emphasizes the vanity of these autonomous products from the female, and cites, as a prime example of the congenital inadequacy of anything produced by females left to themselves, eggs that are Zephyrean. According to this interpretation the female, who is colder than the male, is incapable of cooking all the elements that she absorbs and so can emit no more than imperfect seed in the form of menses or wind eggs. Her "sperm" is never sufficiently cooked; the female is bad at cooking.[27] This proves that she is, by nature, simply a mutilated and sterile male, inevitably characterized by deficiency.[28] For other interpreters, who adopt a position contrary to that of Aristotle, this very phenomenon shows clearly that the female is no way inferior to the male, and that she too can produce seed that, qualitatively, is no different from that of the males. The behavior of certain species of birds, the female of which, in the absence of her mate, is willing to be covered by one of his peers and then lays eggs, can only be interpreted as a desire to ejaculate her own seed, just as a male does when he enters into sexual relations with a man. This was the theory that predominated in the pre-Socratic tradition. In the view of Anaxagoras, Empedocles, and Diogenes of Apollonia, the woman or the female of the species provides her own contribution of semen. Each of the genitors secretes a seed, either a male one or a female one: so women, as well as men, are capable of producing seed of either sex.[29] It is here, in the pre-Aristotelian tradition, that an image of the female body was created according to which there was no separation among menses, milk, and seed. The woman was not marked by the "menstrual" inferiority that was later foisted upon her by the Aristotelian view. This limited the production of seed to males, and it seems to have been the ideology best suited to a society in which the female species, excluded from political activity, was denied any form of existence in the public domain.

Hera, with her offspring ranging from Youth to Typhon, is positioned in polar opposition to Aristotle's theory. Not only does she refuse to share seed equally with a male, but when her choice falls upon the lettuce, Zeus' legitimate wife lays claim to autonomous procreation even more radically than when she adopted other means. On this occasion, she does not go off to request seed from Cronos, the ancient male at the world's end. Instead, she finds that the milky sap of a lettuce growing in a vegetable patch is seed that, for her, is all the more fecund because, for men, this very vegetable means impotence and sexual death. Perhaps these stories of women, whispered among women, are the source of the bizarre prohibition recorded by Plutarch, according to which women should never eat the heart of a lettuce, the part where the sap of the plant is concentrated.[30]

As for Hera, her position is clear. It is not just that she rejects the male, but that her desire is stilled. Hers is a body without delight, which identifies only with the determination to produce other bodies, albeit meanwhile still claiming its sole right to the space of legitimacy: Hera, the wife, but also the father, is nevertheless still wedded by unbreakable bonds to the conjugal bed.

CHAPTER SEVEN

Misogynous Hestia, or the City in Its Autonomy

An alternative title for this essay might be "Misogynous Hestia, or Sharing within the City." If we take an overall and admittedly somewhat cavalier view of the Greek world over the twelve centuries that separate the sacrificial banquets of Homer from Porphyry's reflections on different ways of eating and observing the cult of the city gods, this could be understood in two different ways. The first interpretation seems to blaze its way straight to the crux of the practice in which the actions involved in consuming meat and in offering up sacrifices are confused and totally identified with the elementary forms of sociability. To understand this, we should investigate the blood sacrifice of edible victims, following the line of questioning of a city philosopher that was adopted by Porphyry in the third century A.D., when he rediscovered the injustice and violence involved in eating meat and endeavored, though without undermining the laws of society, to claim for philosophers a place that would set them aside from a world in which to eat was to kill and no line could be drawn between murder and sacrifice. Along with the sages, the lovers of wisdom convoked by Theophrastus, we need to make straight for the god of Delphi, Apollo, and the murderous violence that kept his altars bespattered with human blood, even in the sanctuaries where, in their piety, the most just of men sang the praises of the purity of that deity. Following in the footsteps of Gregory Nagy, let us consider Delphi at the moment when Neoptolemus, the son of Achilles, was slain there by the priests of Apollo, on the occasion of a sharing out of sacrificed victims that turned into a bloody quarrel. From there, let us move on to the altars and holy places where that same Apollo required the blood of the animal known as the plowing ox, and surrounded himself with butcher-companions who wielded the large knives—or at least did so whenever the god himself did not take over, brandishing a *pelekus* (a double-edged axe) or a *machaira* (a sacrificial knife).[1] All these images reveal a violence that puts paid to sharing even as it inaugurates apportionment. Both upstream and downstream they introduce limits that reveal the precarious nature of the always equal—or more or less equal—meals, the peaceful liturgy of which the cities delighted to tell, a liturgy of sacred laws that continued, in unchanging fashion, to become sanctuary rules throughout the long, for the most part uneventful history of the commensality that accompanied sacrifice in the polis.

The other way to understand sharing within the city limits is resolutely to take up position within those meat-eating cities, amid the altars, tables, and banquet halls—in other words, to examine the sacrificial system in its most *political* dimension, at the extreme point in the process of apportionment and distribution. That extreme point comes when regular distributive practices are disrupted and the customary repetitive procedure is bypassed by a concept that goes beyond sharing out, a more extreme political idea that involves a precise extension of the *koinon*—that which belongs to the community, that which is common to all. To put this more clearly, in order to see, from the concrete gestures performed, what abstract figure now comes to dominate the procedure of sharing out, why it is necessary to investigate that figure, and what it symbolizes, let us first broadly sketch in the institutional scene in which it makes its appearance.[2]

In the background to the Greek city, the warriors constituted the foremost social group. They were linked to one another not only by family ties and territorial loyalties, but also by contractual relations. They were all molded by the same educational techniques and by the kind of behavior expected from those whose vocation was to die in battle, and they were recognizable to one another from various strongly institutional practices in which they all took part. Simplifying somewhat, it could be said that from the armed society of epic down to the leading citizens of Sparta, the warriors as a group constituted a company of men who were all *the same:* they were the Homoioi, they made up a community composed of equals. That sameness, with its egalitarian shadow, was expressed essentially in two major practices: the sharing of booty and the sharing of food. The distribution of booty adopted a spatial model that was both circular and centered, in which the median point represented what was held in common, collective property, that which was placed at an equal distance from each man, in a relation of abstract equality.[3] Just as the division of captured booty took place in the middle, so too the distribution of meat within the warrior group took place in an egalitarian fashion in the banquets for "equals," in the *dais eisē*[4] that was a feature of Homeric society. The two practices are represented as closely linked in a story in which the Dioscuri conclude a warrior alliance with the Apharetids, Idas and Lyncaeus. The booty from one of their raids consists of large herds, and when it comes to sharing them out, one of the Apharetids chooses an ox, prepares it for a sacrificial meal, and divides it into four portions, laying down the rule that the first to eat will take the first share of the booty, and the second to eat, the second share. But the rule is immediately flouted when the organizer grabs the first portion for himself, seizes the second, and makes off with the booty,[5] to the great indignation of the Dioscuri, a highly egalitarian pair who naturally had a right to expect that each portion of *moira* would correspond to a share of the booty. That the meat of a sacrificial victim would be divided equally—whether on a geometrical or an arithmetical basis—was a fundamental assumption founded on the isonomic model of cities in which commensality always involved cutting up the meat into portions of an equal size and weight.[6]

The warrior group's commitment to egalitarianism found expression in sacrificial meals in which all the portions were equal, and from that tradition stemmed a whole series of rules, models of thought, and social and institutional practices, known as *isomoiria*, *isokratia*, and *isonomia:* the equal division of land and the equal division of rights, rights that were already of a political nature. It was definitely within this context that the ideal of a human world in which "those who take part in public life do so on a basis of equality" originated.[7] This insistence on equality in every domain—meals, the law, land ownership—imposed an almost tyrannical rule on the city that was the very epitome of sameness in Greece: the archaic Sparta of the Homoioi, the city of those who were all the same. In its entrenched camp, Sparta offered a spectacle of absolute commensality, with its equal meals, called *syssitia*, eaten together, the men seated elbow to elbow, each with an identical dish, the same broth, all uniformly the same, day after day. But the most remarkable thing of all about this military mess the size of a city was that when the Spartans ate together, they consumed products to which all had contributed, products from their own plots of land. Their monthly contributions of barley flour, pork, cheeses, figs, and wine were all placed in common, then immediately redistributed, shared out in the most egalitarian fashion between all the members of the community of equals.[8] This was an extreme warrior state in which sharing was the order of the day at every level—for meals, for land, for politics—a huge open-ended machine wearing itself out in the task of redistribution. Sparta represents an example of a city engaged permanently in redistribution, in which, truly, the sharing out was endless and an end in itself. In contrast, other societies (and they were in the majority) preferred to bypass such a situation. They did so by elaborating from within the sacrificial data an abstract figure that represented the central point, the common middle in which the efficacy of equal shares was rooted. With such a perspective, how was the process of transcendence organized, with the principle of sharing reflected upon itself? And by means of what symbolism did the city, tearing itself away from the fascination of sameness ad infinitum, create a space in which it could think itself through?

The figure known to the Greeks as Hestia provided the city with one means of exercising and building up its own autonomy.[9] Her name was commonly understood to mean "fire," the fire in the hearth or the fire on the altar, which was connected both with eating and with sacrifice: with sacrifice because it marked out the fixed center of a cult, rooted in the earth yet at the same time a human construction, the work of an architect. But for this hearth or altar to become the Common Fire, Hestia Koinē, it was necessary for it to absorb the values developed from the idea of the equidistant center and focal point of fair distribution. Various practices and new liturgies, creating a whole new ceremonial, were evolved to proclaim the special powers of Hestia.

First, we should note how Hestia, a power who belonged to the world of the gods, differs from the rest of them. She personifies fire and is a goddess of the same standing as Athena or Hera, but she is, as it were, distanced from the intrigues of mythology. Her career is marked by no anecdotes and is quickly summed up. She was the first of Cronos' children, but also the last, because her father, who swallowed her first, when drugged regurgitated her last.[10] Instead of marriage, insistently urged upon her by both Apollo and Poseidon,[11] both dieties rightly known as founding gods, *themelioi*,[12] Hestia opted for total, unalterable virginity, a singleness that set her apart from the desire of her suitors. Once she had made that choice, her lot was to take possession of the fat offered up on the *hestia*, the hearth positioned at the center of each home, and, by the same token, to have a cult devoted to her in the temples of all the other gods, wherever a sacrificial fire was lit:[13] the first libation was for her, as was the last.[14] All this information suggests a highly abstract figure. Already in the *Homeric Hymns*—the first text to break the silence that surrounds her in both Hesiod and epic poetry—she is an idea, a pure form of something that incorporates both the end and the beginning, ubiquitous yet with a fixed center, an idea that imposes order on all the space that surrounds her. Artemidorus' *Onirocritica*[15] imposes upon this semi-geometrical figure the formulas of a symbolism that is explicitly based partly on the interpretation of dreams, partly on a collection of textual and epigraphic references. Throughout the monographic history of Hestia those two elements are mutually supportive. For those who took part in public affairs, the *politeumenoi*, the sight of Hestia as herself and as represented by her statues, her *agalmata*, meant the city council, the Boulē, and also the place where the city's wealth was stored, the public treasury. For ordinary individuals, *idiotai*, Hestia represented the fact of living, life itself. And for a king, *basileus*, or a governor, *archon*, she was power, the *dunamis* of his own power, his *archē*. The symbolism extended from the individual life of each separate household's hearth to the collective and public power personified by Hestia in the three manifestations of her single being: the city council, the public treasury, and the power of authority itself. The political Hestia, who was linked through her power to the life of each individual, established around her a space for the exercise of her autonomy, a space that took the material form of not only the Prytaneion, the home of the magistrates in power, but also her altar and her particular attributes.[16] The "first" Greek democracies[17] were set up under the sign of Hestia. In Chios, on a stele dated to between 575 and 550 B.C., on which is engraved one of the first laws promulgated by the *demos* after consultation with the entire community and one demarch, Hestia is invoked at the beginning of the inscription as the deity of the hearth of the city.[18] It was also she who inspired the first attempts, in the sixth century, to place power "in the middle": it was thus in the Prytaneion of Athens where Hestia's altar stood that the laws of Solon were made public, laws that covered two domains, the civil and the sacred, setting out the rules for sacrifice alongside the first laws of the polis.[19]

Traditionally, Hestia dwelt in the Prytaneion, where the archons resided and the city held open house for visiting foreigners and for some of its own citizens, and also where certain forms of justice may have taken place.[20] Several indications suggest that important magistracies may have begun and ended with a sacrifice to Hestia, as certainly happened in Miletus. Here, it was performed by the leader of the College of Singers, the Molpoi, who were gathered around the Delphinian Apollo in the sanctuary where, from 525 B.C. onward, the direction of political life was entrusted to the arbiter, the eponymous Aisymnetes.[21] Quite often, Hestia performed such opening and closing functions in the company of Hermes and Aphrodite,[22] both of whom would be honored in the dedications made by the outgoing magistrates,[23] and who appear to have helped Hestia in that they combined the complementary values of space that was open and space that was closed, values that Jean-Pierre Vernant has detected in the partnership of Hermes and Hestia.

Not only did Hestia on special occasions receive sacrifices, which testified to her connection with the Prytaneion, as at Tenedos, as Pindar's Nemean Ode records,[24] but also the fire of the polis presided over sacrificial commensality in the form of a quasi-liturgy offered by Hestia to those who derived the power of their authority from her altar. Demosthenes[25] tells us that during each prytany the magistrates, who together formed a college, each day shared salt, libations, and a common meal. At these, they offered up communal sacrifices from which the city, through Hestia, fed those who held power in the name of the rest.[26] But this was also a public table at which the obligatory commensality of the small number of magistrates took the place of the daily collective meals in which all citizens took part if they were born Spartans. In Athens, the practice of eating together was delegated and subject to regulations that obliged each citizen to eat once a month in a public meeting-place, thereby entering into commensality, *to parasitein*,[27] that is to say fulfilling, in the service of the city, the function assigned to the ritual "parasites" who were active in many sanctuaries dedicated to Apollo, Heracles, Athena, and Hera, where they were known now as *hierophagoi*, now as *paredroi* (attendants) or *symbiotai* (companions).[28] With Hestia and in the space devoted to her at the center of the city, commensality functioned as an exercise of *isonomia*, a political duty carried out in the sight of all those who, each in turn, were invested with power and authority. In the Prytaneion, the dining table constituted an extension of the altar where Hestia affirmed her right to preside over the communal, public sacrifices, the *thusiai koinai* which, as we learn from Aristotle's *Politics*, covered all sacrifices that the law reserved not for the priests but for the magistrates who derived their *timē*, their authority and honor, from the Common Hearth—that is from the power of Hestia.[29] The magistrates who presided over these public sacrifices through which the city affirmed its identity were the Prytaneis, the Archons, and the

Kings or Archon-Kings, men for whom a dream about Hestia meant coming face to face with the full might of power. Such dreams were for citiizens[30] who were already familiar with the abstract idea of the principle upon which a city was founded.

But more specifically, how did Hestia acquire her autonomy? By what process did the Common Fire come to represent the idea of the city? Aristotle's reference to common sacrifices merely spells out the fundamental identity of the political Hestia and the sacrificial fire. But a study of the sacrificial rituals and procedures reveals the way in which the sovereignty of the fire of all citizens was established. In the first place, it is worth considering the proverbial tradition of the *Paroemiographi graeci*, in which thought about the very idea of sacrificing to Hestia finds expression. Offering a sacrifice to Hestia symbolized everybody eating from the same *kanoun*, or basket, banqueting together without stint, for everything was expected to be consumed on the spot and nothing was supposed to be carried away at the end of the meal.[31] But at the same time, sacrificing to Hestia evoked eating covertly, a way of eating alone that bordered upon avarice or at the very least conjured up the image of someone not inclined to give to others.[32] As is well known, Hestia was an active fire, constantly needing to be fed with new fuel. In Callimachus' account of the consuming hunger of Erisichthon, accursed by Demeter, when the famished wretch had emptied the cowsheds and even devoured the mules unharnessed from their great chariot, his last meal of meat that was generally acceptable consisted of a cow that his worthy mother was keeping secretly for Hestia,[33] after which he moved on to consume a race horse, a war horse, and even the cat that kept the mice away. Around Hestia's fire, the circle of people eating together was always closed upon itself, and on her altar Hestia, for the sake of her guests, kept a firm hold on both ends of the sacrifice, in exemplary fashion exercising her power over the beginnings and ends (she was both *prōte* and *prymatē*).[34] The two extremes in both time and space traced the closed circle of a sacrifice turned inward upon itself—a kind of ritual of self-sufficiency, designed to promote the growth of the virtues of centrality, around a deity of fire who in herself exalted the identity of all those who gathered to eat together, seated in a circle around her.

Alongside sacrifice of this kind, reduced to the zero degree, which was perhaps its purest form, two rituals in particular may help us to understand more about Hestia's roles and what she symbolized for the polis. One is from Cos, the other from Naucratis, the Greek city established in the Nile delta of Egypt. In Cos, in a complicated annual ceremony regulated by a sacred law dating from the fourth century B.C.,[35] Hestia was paired with Zeus, a city Zeus known as Polieus, while she herself was called Hestia Hetaireia,[36] the deity of all the groups of male companions whose origins stemmed from the military structure of a society organized into three tribes and nine sections, each comprising one thousand men.[37] The city festival of Zeus Polieus, which provides a fine example of the forms of egalitarian sharing, also helps us to define the powers of Hestia when confronted by the god who was not only the first of all the twelve gods, but also one of this city's particular deities. A whole series of differences between Zeus Polieus and Hestia is discernible within their common framework, the city space and its political center, the agora, the public square with its "communal house" in which the priest of Zeus would spend the night before sacrificing the victim that was eventually selected.[38] The public space shared by Hestia and her accomplice was affected by a double movement, one part of which was centripetal. This, by means of the sacrificial victims, drew all the various distinct components of the social body toward the center, where Hestia's altar stood.[39] It was followed, as if by a backwash, by the process of dividing up and distributing the sacrificial victim, a single animal, which was cut into pieces under the sign of the poliad Zeus. Hestia, for her part, presided over the intermingling and coalescence of disparate elements, what—on the analogy of Anaxagoras' cosmological model—might be called a *panspermia*, the term used for a ritual offering of many different types of grain that became indistinguishable when cooked over a fire.[40] To be more precise, when one particular animal had eventually been selected from among the oxen paraded in the procession, the unificatory process that followed was centered upon the figure of Hestia: this was a ritual in which the victim was put up for sale and, in order to belong fully to the whole city, had to be purchased by all the citizens of Cos together, the price being paid not by the poliad Zeus, but by Hestia, the figure who thus most strongly affirmed the unity of the members of the social body.[41] Only then was the priest of Zeus, who kept his distance from Hestia, expected to officiate with his acolytes, moving between Hestia's communal dwelling and the altar of the Polieus deity.[42]

Hestia's mode of intervention thus opens up a distance between herself and the poliad Zeus, a distance within which other differential features are also discernible. In the first place, the sacrifice offered up to her precedes the sacrifice to Zeus Polieus.[43] Second, Hestia's victim, instead of being chosen by a jury, designates itself with a single gesture, by *lowering* its head.[44] Finally, Hestia's altar is tended by the chief magistrate responsible for public sacrifices, not by a priest.[45] We should perhaps turn to the history of Cos that is contemporary with this ritual to discover why, at the level of political symbolism, a hierarchy was elaborated in which Hestia's position was higher than that of Zeus Polieus. For in the mid-fourth century, after a period of troubles, a new city of Cos was founded, bringing together all the island's inhabitants.[46]

In Cos, ritual found a way of formulating an extremely abstract idea of the city itself, without dispossessing Hestia of her attributes as a religious power. The process of abstraction used the concept of value, *timē*, value in terms of the monetary economy. In Cos, Hestia was seen as the "treasurer,"[47] one of the meaningful figures listed in Artemidorus' *Onirocritica:* for those who took part in public affairs, Hestia stood for "the collection of revenues," "the depository of the common wealth."[48] It was the notion of a state treasury, evoked by the symbolic gesture of depositing money at Hestia's feet, that placed the Common Hearth a degree higher than the idea of the city conveyed by Zeus Polieus.

Where wealth was concerned, the public treasury seems to have played the same role as did the Prytaneion at the level of eating. An inquiry into the forms of collective property in Greece, begun by Kurt Latte in 1947,[49] on the one hand, revealed the importance of the mechanisms for the redistribution of the collective wealth; on the other, it showed how very slowly the need for public funds, radically separate from the citizens' private possessions, came to be recognized. In some Cretan cities, the product of fines and certain taxes was regularly divided among all the members of the community;[50] likewise, since the city naturally owned whatever lay underground, the profits from mineral resources were redistributed among all the citizens. A similar procedure was followed in Siphnos,[51] but was discontinued in Athens from the time when, in 483, Themistocles halted the customary distribution and redirected those resources into the construction of a fleet.[52] In Sparta, meanwhile, private and public wealth continued to be confused. Thucydides reports that one of the Spartan kings remarked upon this at the beginning of the Peloponnesian War.[53] In Sparta, which was committed to absolute commensality, the continued practice of redistribution may also explain the absence of any public treasury or Prytaneion.[54] It could likewise explain why the only trace of Hestia on Spartan territory was to be found in the small sanctuary of the Fates, or Moirai,[55] which also accommodated the Zeus and Athena of hospitality, who were confined there along with the goddess of the hearth, in this remote holy place, well out of the public eye. Their exile can be accounted for both by the two Spartan kings' traditional privilege of performing all public sacrifices[56] and also, at a deeper level, by Sparta's refusal to abandon its model for the redistribution of all wealth.

The traditions of Naucratis[57] express the autonomy of Hestia even more clearly than those of the city of Cos. It is strongly reflected as much in sacrificial ritual and the alliances concluded in its Prytaneion as in the inventive rivalry into which Hestia was drawn by other powers of a political nature. In Naucratis, where the excavations of British archaeologists have dated the earliest Greek presence to between 615 and 610, a philhellenic pharaoh called Amasis ceded the town of Naucratis to Greeks who wished to live there; to others, who did not wish to settle but who spent some time there in the course of their maritime trading ventures, he offered sites where they could set up altars and sanctuaries for their gods. The project thus involved both rebuilding and also new foundations.[58] Greeks who were entirely committed to trading with Egypt and its neighbors built themselves temples and altars on the land ceded to them, where the archaeologists have found sanctuaries for Aphrodite, the Samian Hera, and the Milesian Apollo, and also one consecrated to the gods of Greece, "the Hellene gods."[59] A short distance away, in the new Greek city of Naucratis, Hestia reigned, probably on the agora, in a Prytaneion over which she herself presided. Thanks to the erudition of a mythographer of rituals who wrote a treatise on the Apollo of Gryneion, we know of an account of the festivals celebrated in Naucratis and also of a portrait of the Hestia Prytanitis.[60]

The first tradition to note is the celebration of Hestia's anniversary. The first of the three festivals recorded honored the day of Hestia's birth but, given her insistence on being known as Hestia of the Prytaneion, coupled with the paucity of her personal mythology, in all likelihood her anniversary was really that of the city—that is to say, of the founding of the Prytaneion. The second relevant tradition is the rule governing banquets. It was very rigid. The menu was fixed and unchanging, and it was strictly forbidden to introduce any other foods. The fare was certainly copious, but it was restricted to this particular celebration within the confines of a closed circle, as befitted the deity for whom a sacrifice meant that everything should be consumed with nothing left over to be carried away afterward. The two rules associated with the Hestia of the banquet were thus that nothing was to be introduced from outside and nothing to be taken outside. The third factor to note is that in the Naucratis Prytaneion, where everyone wore white clothing—a Prytaneion uniform, as the native Greeks called it, that was compulsory—two other deities also had the the right of entry, a privilege sanctioned by the honors reserved for their respective priests. Dionysus was celebrated here on the occasion of the Dionysia, as was Apollo, for his *panegyria*. This was Apollo Kōmaios, the Apollo of the banquet and of the *kōmos*,[61] who, in Naucratis, was also a Pythian Apollo, for it was in Delphi in particular that these two deities were intimately related. This symbiosis between Dionysus and Apollo was further emphasized by the favors enjoyed by their respective priests, who received double rations of wine and double shares of everything else, too. In that she welcomed into her dwelling the couple formed by a Dionysiac Apollo and a Dionysus so close to Apollo, Hestia, born to be "of the Prytaneion," was certainly innovative, boldly enjoying the liberty that appeared to be afforded her by the new Naucratis and the political space of the Prytaneion.

The autonomy of the Hestia determined to personify the ideal city was reinforced by an unusual prohibition: no woman was allowed to enter the Prytaneion except, it is true, those who played the "double flutes" that were de rigueur at festivals held for Dionysus and the Apollo of banquets. This exclusion of women, ordered by a deity who did not conceal her preference for a masculine personnel of high-ranking magistrates,[62] accentuated the distance that separated the Public Fire, personified by the flames on the altar,[63] from the deity with a woman's body who, for her part, dwelt at the heart of private homes, in the twofold guise of a virgin and an old woman.[64] In order to be unquestionably political, the Hestia born to be a city magistrate seems to have wished to reject all collusion with the feminine world. One explanation for Naucratis' radical creation of a center where Hestia left her other self behind may be that this new town fostered the kind of experimental conditions that, in about 610, led about a dozen or so cities in this part of the world to create for the first time a vast sanctuary known as a Hellenion, which was open "to all the gods of the Greeks," the deities whom the Greeks claimed to share when they thought of themselves as a group of Hellenes, transcending their respective individual cities, each with its own idiosyncratic pantheon.[65]

CHAPTER EIGHT

Even Talk Is in Some Ways Divine

How to detect false rumors: that is an important problem for historical criticism, as is clear to everyone, even if not everyone immediately appreciates the practical difficulties involved. Some societies, such as the former Soviet Union, managed to eliminate "gossip columns" officially and to eradicate false rumors or "talk" almost completely. But, as is well known, in the West historians have been paying careful attention to "talk" ever since their discipline determined to be rigorous and scientific—that is to say, ever since the late nineteenth century. Any scholarly assessment of what history calls its "sources" necessarily makes room for the rumors that well up mysteriously and are then diffused in a clandestine fashion, constituting a genre that, according to Emile Bernheim's "introduction to the science of history," consists neither of anecdotes, nor of proverbs, nor even of myths.[1] It is in the domain of orality and traditional societies that this historical inquiry has proven its worth. Faced with communities whose pasts appear to be disseminated throughout the present and dispersed among a whole crowd of witnesses, historical ethnologists set out to gather together all those who can or should provide information regarding traditions, which are assimilated to the necessary past. Aware that their duty is to authenticate the facts and rediscover the real importance of the events of the past, ethnological historians school themselves to be suspicious; they are mistrustful of each and every witness, constantly imagining reasons why they might be falsifying the evidence.[2] For such societies, always in thrall to the powers of hearsay, exist under constant threat from uncontrollable information, unfounded speculation, anything that may attract the ear. These are defenseless peoples, totally at the mercy of "talk" or rumor.

Not surprisingly, to "detect false rumors" amid indistinct voices, flurries of speech, volleys of words, and sidetracking stories, ethnohistorians, true to their critical instinct, may resort to methods akin to those of police investigations. The people of Athens certainly once did just that in their efforts to track down a rumor. This was in 413 B.C., when the military might of the Athenian empire was about to learn of the Sicilian disaster, the destruction of its fleet, the death of its generals, the decimation of its army, and the survivors' incarceration, in chains, in the Latomia. Plutarch tells us that a barber in Piraeus was the first to hear of all this from one of the few slaves who had escaped. The humble shopkeeper at once rushed to town, where he spread the news. Panic ensued. The people gathered in an assembly where "they tried to get to the root of the rumor *[phēmē]*." The barber, who was summoned, did not even know the name of his informant. He ascribed the rumor to "an unknown and anonymous person." At this the people grew angry, declaring that he was a storyteller and a troublemaker. He was subjected to torture, which continued until the official news arrived, confirming that the war had indeed been lost.[3] The stricken populace dispersed, lamenting, leaving the shopkeeper, still bound to the wheel, to meditate alone on the folly of those who insist at all costs on routing out false rumors.

The Athenian barber, through his misadventure, at least created a kind of image of rumor, characterized by its power to spread and the untraceability of its origin. The only clue was the voice of the slave, who for his part was all the more insignificant because his face was unfamiliar and his name unknown. An anonymous figure had thus pointed to a shadow even before the rumor acquired a life of its own and was then swept along by an impetus that magnified its impact and immediately drove it beyond the reach of the investigator, with his vain attempts to trace its origin. As both the barber and the general population of Athens knew full well, "even Talk is in some ways divine."[4] Rumor was a goddess with an altar of her own, a cult addressed to her, and sacrifices offered up to her, and she was surrounded by a little pantheon of powers that included some major and minor psychological phenomena: Fear, Forgetfulness, Modesty, Quarrel. Once she received recognition in this way, Rumor clearly made the would-be detectors of false rumors seem derisory. Without a doubt she ensured that, wherever truth or falsehood might lie, the philosophers of ancient times as well as the sociologists of today should ponder upon her extraordinary power to foster belief and to mobilize public opinion and the masses, thereby getting the diverse city to acknowledge her secret, mute identity, acclaiming it in unison, as with a single voice.

In the Greek tradition, rumor flourished in a setting in which premonitory words echoed oracular sounds and whispers, and the recognizable voice of the gods, whether soft or alarmingly loud, would burst through the babble of human beings—rambling old men, spellbinding bards, and chattering nursemaids—and the malevolent gossip that is whispered in asides.

On the ramparts of Troy, voices are raised. Priam and his old men are in session in the Council of Elders. It is an assembly of fine speakers, "the leading men of the Trojans, like cicadas, which settle on a tree in the woods and pour out their lily-soft song." They see Helen coming up toward them, and a muttering of winged words arises: "She is fearfully like the immortal goddesses to look at."[5] The murmurs of the Trojans are undisturbed by any reference to the ominous implications associated with the name Helen: Helen, the femme fatale, the destroyer of ships *(helenas)*, the slayer of warriors *(helandros)*, the ruination of cities *(heleptolis)*.[6] However, a dense volley of such images is let loose by Aeschylus when he hears what Gorgias, in his *Encomium to Helen*, calls "the rumor of a name,"[7] alive with memories of wars and dire misfortunes.

The old men's covert whispers are the voice of a city that dreams of the departure of Helen, yet declares that such perfect beauty must surely signify the presence of a divine being. And what the whispers that float from the ramparts and carry from one door to the next are really proclaiming to all and sundry is the glory of Helen. When Odysseus and Ajax argue over which of them more deserves to be allotted the arms of Achilles, the Greeks send out spies to listen to what the Trojans have to say about the matter. In the *Little Iliad* we are told that they overhear a conversation between some young girls who are discussing the respective merits of the two Greeks. One of them, inspired by Athena, sings the praises of Odysseus so convincingly that the Greeks forthwith declare him the winner.[8] They do resort to the opinion of others, but at least in this case it is the fresh voices of young girls, speaking unselfconsciously and truthfully, that prevail.

When set out in an epic poem, the double strands of Trojan rumor point to the ways adopted by the speech of the poet or Homeric bard who has the lips of his heroes praise his own unforgettable speech. Aeneas thus says to Achilles: "We both know each other's birth, and we know each other's parents, from hearing the tales that mortal men have long made famous."[9] Fame—a renowned name and lasting glory—is fueled and fostered by the rumors of epic, which, referring to Penelope, declare: "The glory of her virtue will not fade with the years, but the deathless gods themselves will make a beautiful song for mortal ears in honor of the constant Penelope. What a contrast with Clytemnestra, the daughter of Tyndareus, and the infamy she sank to when she killed me, the husband of her youth. The song men sing of her will be one of detestation. She has destroyed the reputation of her whole sex, virtuous women and all."[10] Praise of the faithful wife is inspired by the gods, while blame directed at Clytemnestra exudes from the earth like a voice of loathing.

In such memorialization, in which the fame of a man of good reputation is so closely associated with eulogistic, anonymous "talk" or rumor, the poet, who is the agent of memorability, may himself be called Phemius, "the man of rumor." One such is a bard in the *Odyssey*, claimed to be the most famous of them all, but who must in truth have resembled a court poet, forced as he is to sing for the masters of the day and at the behest of the audience. Dutifully he sings before the banqueting suitors of the death of Odysseus and his impossible journey, and later, also of the hero's return, when the table and the sonorous flagstones are soaked with the blood of the banqueters.[11] The very name of Phemius the bard holds out the promise of power for the single yet multiple voice that bestows fame and glory. The Greeks called such glory *kleos*, "rumor that spreads." It is a word that is semantically close to *klēdōn*, which means "a name proclaimed by voices." In this form rumor, socialized rumor, is confined to oracular practices in which arresting sounds and floating voices become portents and appear to prolong rumors that have originated with the gods.

A few steps away from Phemius, in the darkness of the palace, Odysseus, with uplifted hands, cries out to Zeus: "O Father Zeus, if it be true that after all your persecution you gods willed to bring me home over dry land and sea to my own country, let someone in the palace where they are waking now utter a good omen *[phēmē]* for me and let some other sign outside the palace be given." No sooner has he spoken than the glorious skies of Olympus are filled with lightning. This is a sign that the god is answering him. Then, from somewhere in the palace, close by, comes the wail of a woman exhausted by her task of milling barley and wheat for the table of the insatiable suitors. The palace servant prays that this will be the day when the suitors feast for the very last time. Odysseus immediately turns her wish for their death into a sign *(sēma)*, speech with the power to make things happen.[12] That unknown voice, penetrating the night, becomes a prophetic pronouncement *(klēdōn)*, as it were, a human version of the voice of great Zeus, sounding forth in counterpoint to the divine lightning.

In this case the sign takes the form of a whole sentence. In others it comes as a single word, often a name, one that bodes well but must be acted upon immediately. Take the example of the embassy of the Samians who come to persuade the Greeks to enter into alliance with them against the barbarians. The delegation is headed by a man known as Hegesistratus, "army leader." One of his interlocutors abruptly asks him, "What is your name?"—perhaps either because he hopes to find some omen of success in his reply or because he is inspired by a god. And how could one possibly ignore the implications conveyed by an ally who declares himself to be "leader of the host"? As Herodotus puts it, "the bird is received," for an omen is a winged word: the fragile sound of a name leaves the trace of a wing in the sky.[13] Furthermore, oracular rumors are sometimes allotted a place of their own or even their own sanctuaries. In Thebes, there was an Apollo known as Apollo of the Ashes, because his altar was composed of the ashes of cremated sacrificial victims. For this, the most prophetic of all gods, divination took two forms. Prophecies were conveyed either by ashes or by voices: at the Theban altar of the deity known as Apollo of the Ashes, you came to hear not the imperious speech of the Lord of Delphi, but sudden bursts of words, fleeting sounds, words borne away by the wind. Likewise, outside the walls of the city of Smyrna, many dispersed voices were summoned and collected in the sanctuary of Divinatory Voices.[14] To consult this oracle of rumors, the procedure was probably similar to that customarily followed at Phara, close to Patras, in a place consecrated to Hermes and Hestia. The god of the public agora, bearded and carved from a rectangular piece of stone, stood opposite Hestia's immovable hearth. One whispered one's question to him, then hurried away from the agora, blocking one's ears. Once beyond it, the first voice heard was an oracle from the god.[15] Hermes was a god of murmurs and whispered words, just as Demeter was a goddess of sneezes, the oracular importance of which was supposed first to have been pointed out by Demeter herself.[16]

To whoever knows how to listen, all rumors are portentous. One particular voice is suddenly uplifted, like a single atom of manifold Rumor itself which, passing from mouth to mouth and spreading from ear to ear, is transformed into an already formal story, in which each teller adds something or omits something, in a process that is quite unconscious but nevertheless contributes to a multiple creation. If an individual who comes to consult Rumor is able to give a particular meaning to a single voice picked out from the humming swarm of sounds, that is assuredly because the gods are constantly providing human beings with signs, sending them dreams of flights of birds that are at once messengers and oracular voices. All rumors thus stem from the god who rules as sovereign over the heavens and is called "the master of voices," the Zeus of portents, who is known by the name Phemius, just like the bard in the palace of Ithaca.[17] And at Zeus' side stands a docile, ready messenger—Rumor, a power known as Ossa, whose name is associated with a type of divination that uses sounds *(otteia).*

Rumor can lead a whole crowd, such as the mass of Achaeans on their way to the assembly, "as when a mass of bees comes swarming out from a hollow in the rock in a never-ending stream: squadrons take wing this way and that, and they fly in tight clusters to settle on the springtime flowers." Rumor (Ossa), Zeus' messenger, is there, "blazing among them, urging them on."[18] Leading the crowd to the assembly, Rumor proceeds in silence or murmuring in undertones, but in the last book of the *Odyssey,* she is garrulous and runs through the town "with fateful news of the suitors' hideous death."[19] Now another crowd swarms up toward the palace of Odysseus, for bloodshed cries out for vengeance. And on the horizon there hovers the monstrous figure of Fama, the Rumor of the *Aeneid:* "Small at first, through fear, she mounts up to heaven and walks the ground with head hidden in the clouds." During the daytime she remains on the watch, perched high on the house roofs, but at nightfall she takes to her wings, moving from the sky down to the earth, and her strident news fills the shadows: "At this time, exulting with manifold gossip, she filled the nations and sang alike of fact and falsehood." Her monstrous nature is manifested by her dappled body, which is wholly covered by tongues and feathers, and bristles with ears and mouths: "a monster awful and huge, who for the many feathers in her body has as many watchful eyes below—wondrous to tell—as many tongues, as many sounding mouths, as many pricked-up ears."[20]

This is a figure that seems to have sprung from a nightmare or been dreamed up for the canvas of a surrealist painter. But in the Greek world its force as an imaginary representation is submitted to a spectral analysis by Plato, the philosopher of the *Laws*, who was probably the only person to understand that Rumor was a goddess unlike any other. He saw how very puerile it was for the people of Athens to set up an altar to Rumor just because, on the day of some general's victory in a distant land, the entire town entered spontaneously into a bout of festivity. These people seemed to think that the sole achievement of the deity of Phēmē was suddenly to transmit good or bad news from somewhere several days' sail away.[21] Admittedly, in the *Republic* Plato initially imitated the Athenians of 413, who fancied that they could put an end to rumor by arresting any creator of fables found guilty of spreading false rumors. Those were policing methods reinvented in the past by well-meaning historians, but which the Guardians of the Republic applied with a totalitarian stupidity, boasting of eliminating all fabricators of myths, stories, news that did not correspond to the official line or to the "mythologemes" of the state mythology.[22] It was in the *Laws*, and in the course of the implementation of his plan to rethink tradition and culture as a communal memory, that Plato realized that "public opinion has a surprising influence, [so that] there is no attempt by anybody ever to breathe a word that contradicts the law."[23] He was able to speak of it only by using images that evoked its almost meteorological nature: in the education of the young sent to pasture in a meadow that had to be faultless, rumor was the breeze that was blown there from salubrious regions, the effluvium or breath of the earth and the waters, which made its way into human beings by way of their eyes and ears. It was a kind of public voice that was the most subtle element in the surrounding air, whose essential quality lay in the quasi-silence of what Plato calls "a little tiny word." It was, for each individual, an unwritten law that did not need to be enunciated, either because not the slightest incestuous desire ever arose—given that everyone by common consent regarded such actions to be totally impious, odious to the deity, and the extreme of infamy—or, in a more positive mode, because it was a matter of uniting with the party that best served the city rather than with one that an individual secretly preferred. In Rumor, and in it alone, lay the secret of deep unanimity, unspoken beliefs held in common, a city's total adhesion to particular principles and founding stories: what Plato called a "mythology."

The *Laws* themselves, which tell of the philosopher's dream city, set in Crete, both begin and end with good rumors: first, the oracular voice dispensed to Minos, the model of past legislators, in the cave to which, every nine years, he repaired to meet with his father Zeus, the master of voices;[24] and later, the humming rumor of laws[25] that sing in the ears of the children, infiltrate the nursery rhymes, and slip into conversations as people make their way from the agora to their homes.

When it comes from the gods, as it does in the case of the *Laws* passed by Minos, rumor demands the ceremonial that is its due. Three choirs, corresponding to three different age groups, aim their songs at the souls of the citizens. The first choir consists of children consecrated to the Muses, who sing of great maxims before the assembled city. Next, those under thirty years of age invoke Apollo Paean, calling upon him to testify to the truth of the city's great principles and to dispense to the young his grace and persuasive power. The third group of choristers are men of ripe years, between thirty and sixty. But the most important role falls to the elderly, those of sixty and over.[26] Because singing is too heavy a task for them, they recount stories of fine behavior and great principles.[27] These old men are the consecrated "mythologists of the city," dispensed from singing but with a mission to enchant their listeners by allowing rumors inspired by the gods to filter through to them. The truthtellers, who are dialecticians of silence, harmonize the three choirs, imbuing them with "one and the same voice" in which the community recognizes itself as it has been throughout its existence, expressed through its songs, its tales, its discourse.[28] The mythologists, who are the depositories of the city's founding rumors, are the very incarnation of *euphemy*, the impeccable movement of the lips of those who restrain their voices when silence signifies control and a plenitude of breath. The utopian image of Plato's model is completed by a vision of the myth-tellers transformed into white-haired children. It is as if the old men, bewitched by their own voices that tell such fine and wonderful stories, become just like the children who listen to them and are carried away by their words. It is a way of dismissing time and wiping out the hazards of becoming. But it also inspires a conviction that rumor, far from making minor changes to reality, is a great subterranean power, an essential part of what is held to be true, and that its modalities of transmission and diffusion, which bring into play learning through one's ears and mouth, constitute means, "conspiring and constant" *media*, than which nothing in society could possibly be more certain.[29]

Part III / Between the Labyrinth and the Overturned Table

CHAPTER NINE

An Ephebe and an Olive Tree

In the myth of the origins of Athens, the olive tree is represented as a gift from the gods. In the course of the altercation between Poseidon and Athena over the possession of Athens, Athena made the first olive tree spring from the ground.[1] In competition with Poseidon's manifestations of sovereignty, which took the twofold form of a salt lake with sterile water and a rearing, untamed horse, Athena's olive tree signified the advent of civilized life and the establishment of a social group in a land that could thenceforth provide for its subsistence. All the mythical qualities of this primordial fruit-bearing tree are summarized by the chorus in *Oedipus at Colonus:*

> Our land has a thing unknown
> On Asia's sounding coast
> Or in the sea-surrounded west
> Where Agamemnon's race has sway:
> The olive, fertile and self-sown,
> The terror of our enemies,
> That no hand tames or tears away—

The blessed tree that never dies!—
But it mocks the swordsman in his rage.
And now it flourishes in every field,
Most beautifully here!
The grey-leafed tree, the children's nourisher!
No young man nor one partnered by his age
Knows how to root it out nor make
Barren its yield.
For Zeus the fateful smiles on it with sage
Eyes that forever are awake,
And Pallas watches it with her sea-pale eyes.[2]

Its supernatural origin, its evergreen foliage, its warrior as well as nutritive aspects, its special relations with the Fateful Zeus, Zeus Morios, and Athena, the poliad and warrior deity, all go to make up the olive tree's politico-religious image. Several of the qualities of the olive as a species of tree seem to have played a determining role. Alone of all fruit trees, the olive tree never loses its foliage. It belongs to the *mē phullorhoōnta* species.[3] Its leaves remain green and its foliage continues to flourish in all seasons; the olive tree never withers: it is *akēratos*.[4] Plutarch remarks upon the olive tree's evergreen nature and draws attention to its political significance: "As the first [leaves] are shed others are growing in their place: like cities, each is ever-living and continuous."[5] Throughout antiquity the evergreen tree was reputed to enjoy a fabulous longevity: some said two hundred years, others claimed over a thousand.[6] Certain techniques used for propagating the olive tree help to account for its reputation of immortality. In Book XVII of his *Natural History*, Pliny the Elder explains how it is that olive trees live "in a sort of everlasting sequence: when they begin to get old the shoot next for grafting is put in, and so another young tree grows out of the same one and the process is repeated as often as is necessary, so that the same oliveyards go on for centuries."[7] This process of reproduction is the same as the Provençal *souquet* method, in which fragments of the root or the stump are propagated.[8] From this technique and from the observations of the ancient naturalists, we learn of an astonishing feature of the olive tree: even if the trunk dies, the tree stump goes on living. Modern botanists, in their turn, have often described the amazing spectacle of a young and vigorous shoot springing up amid a heap of blackish roots from a stump with a positively mineral appearance. It is in this context of a combination of fabulous antiquity and inexhaustible youth that we should no doubt set the story of the miracle of the olive tree on the Acropolis, a cubit-long shoot of which appeared growing from the stump of a tree destroyed by the Persian fire, on the very next day after the disaster.[9] However, perhaps the miracle of the Acropolis cannot be totally accounted for by a purely botanical explanation, since the sacred olive tree of the Pandrosion, placed under the double protection of Zeus Morios[10] and the Athena of the fascinating gaze,[11] was an immortal, fateful tree on which the destiny of Athens and the lives of the Athenians depended.

The consubstantiality between the group that made up the polis and the olive tree is confirmed by the determination with which the city of Athens set up institutions to ensure the protection of the olive tree and, in return, to benefit from its powers. In Athens, the twelve Moriai of the garden of the Academy,[12] twelve offshoots from the sacred olive tree, were placed under the direct control of the Areopagus,[13] a council of the ancient type, traditionally responsible for repressing public and religious crime and all misdemeanors that directly threatened the community. In the archaic period, to cut down a sacred olive tree was considered to be a crime of treason and was punishable by death. The Areopagus was also responsible for the olive harvest from the sacred olive trees. The harvest was collected in ritual fashion, in accordance with very strict regulations, and the oil produced from it was reserved solely for victors in the Panathenaean Games. Certain figurative representations show Athena in person supervising the olive harvest, in which several figures wearing victor's crowns are taking part.[14] Originally, the oil was presented exclusively to the athletes who were victors in the most ancient and important contests in the Panathenaea,[15] especially that of the Apobates, the *hippikos agōn*, founded by Erechtheus and modeled on Athena's battle against the Giants.[16] The product of the sacred olive trees thus rewarded the victory that, more than all others, conferred upon a citizen of Athens the religious attributes assumed by Athena Nikē, the Athena who vanquished the Giants and who, with the aid of other gods, then instituted the organized world, the *cosmos* designed for the gods and men, within the framework of the city. To borrow an expression used by Aristides the Rhetor in one of his speeches devoted to Athena, the olive tree was the *pharmakon hugieias*,[17] the sign and instrument of a vital power and of the good health to which a victor of the city Games testified by the brilliance of his triumphant efforts.

The political status of the Athenian olive tree is manifested not only by the role played by the Areopagus, the council that acted as the city's seeing eye, but also by the relations that were maintained between this species of tree and the various masculine age groups that made up the social body. The winner of the athletic contest reserved for fully grown citizens, adult men, received, along with his prize of olive oil, a crown of olive twigs;[18] the elders of Athens chosen to be *thallophoroi*[19] took part in the Panathenaea carrying olive branches, the political significance of which was underlined by the opposition between these and the oak tree branches[20] that were carried, in this same festival, by freedmen and other "barbarians" in the city. And in the age group that was the opposite of the elders, each male infant at his birth received an olive branch that would then be fixed over the door of the house.[21] At each of these three phases of his life, a citizen of Athens thus confirmed his solidarity with the olive, the tree that was explicitly described as the city tree. Athena's olive tree was known as *astē elaia*,[22] "the city's olive tree": not only was it the tree that grew in the *astu*, the town, as opposed to the flat countryside round about, but it was also the tree that belonged to the whole group that made up the *astoi*;[23] it belonged to all the citizens.

The various religious and political representations of the city's olive tree, the *astē elaia*, confirm its role as a political symbol designed to express the religious relationship that existed between the whole group of citizens and a particular portion of cultivated land. It was through the olive tree on the Acropolis that the city was rooted in the soil of Athens, and that the citizens were placed in a symbiotic relationship with the cultivated earth.

For a fuller understanding of the relationship that obtained between the olive trees and the citizens, let us take a closer look at some of the religious representations that form the background against which the political myth of the Athenian olive tree should be read. Among the mythical representations of arboriculture, one collection of stories is outstanding in its richness and scope: the traditions recorded in the epic of Meleager,[24] the hero of the Calydonian Boar Hunt.

In the epic, Meleager's role seems to be principally that of a hunter and a warrior. But the stories about his birth suggest that this image requires modification on several important points. In all three of the accounts that have come down to us, Meleager is endowed with a conditional immortality: he will live as long as some object, which is another form of himself and which incorporates his true being, survives. This external soul of Mealeager's is of a different nature in each of the three versions. In the first, that of Phrynicus and the tragic poets,[25] seven days after Meleager's birth,[26] the Fates, or Moirai, appear and tell his mother that her child will die as soon as the log, *dalos*, burning on the hearth is consumed. Althaea immediately snatches the burning log from the flames and shuts it away in a coffer, which she conceals. In the second version, known to Tzetzes and Malalas,[27] Meleager's fate is linked with an olive sprig, *thallos elaias*, which is produced at the same time as the royal infant by his mother. In the third version, recounted in Plutarch's *Moralia*, Meleager's double is not a burning log or a cutting from a fruit-bearing tree, but a wooden spear, or a hunting spear.[28] All three versions belong with a whole collection of myths in which royal legends centered upon arboriculture correspond to warrior traditions associated with the spear.

The myth of Meleager's birth is inseparable from other mythical accounts in which a royal child is born from the flames of the paternal hearth. In Clytemnestra's dream,[29] probably the most evocative myth of a royal birth, Orestes is a vigorous twig, sprouting from Agamemnon's scepter, which is planted, like a young tree, right in the middle of the hearth. The wood bursts into bud, then grows so fast and reaches such a height that its shadow covers the entire land of Mycenae. There are many layers of symbolism here. First, life is engendered from dead wood:[30] from the soul of the royal scepter a new sprig sprouts. Its appearance is as surprising as the growth, in a single night, of a cubit-long branch from the stump of the sacred olive tree burned down by the Persians when they set fire to Athens, on the eve of the battle of Salamis. Second, Orestes' roots reach deep into the royal hearth. He is a child of the hearth—*pais aph'Hestias*—as is Demophon, the infant of Eleusis whom Demeter hides in the flames as if he were a half-burned log, *dalos*, an amazing log, for it shoots up in a single surge, *hos prothalēs*.[31] Finally, those two factors are superdetermined by a third: the tree casts its shade as far as the frontiers of the land of Mycenae. Two other royal dreams are immediately evoked: those of Astyages and Xerxes. Astyages thought he saw, emerging from his daughter's sexual parts, a vine cutting that grew until it covered the whole of Asia. The interpreters of dreams who were consulted were categorical: the child to be born would take over the sovereignty from Astyages.[32] The second dream came to Xerxes: before setting out to conquer Greece, it seemed to him that he was crowned by a leafy olive wreath and that the branches from the wreath grew and grew until they covered the whole earth.[33] All these mythical images underline the connection between the royal figures and fruit-bearing plants, in particular vines and olive trees. For a whole tradition that considered a fruit-bearing tree to be a precious object, an *agalma*, it was also a sign of power: a vine stock of pure gold won Hypsipyle's recognition for the grandsons of Thoas;[34] a golden cluster of grapes was handed down from one heir to the next in the Dardanid family;[35] an olive, tattooed on the shoulder, was the distinguishing mark of male descendants of Pelops.[36] The first appearance of this theme of magic royalty is in the *Odyssey:* "some illustrious king [rules] a populous and mighty country with the fear of the gods in his heart, and upholding justice. As a result of his good leadership the dark soil yields its wheat and barley, *the trees are laden with ripe fruit*, the sheep never fail to bear their lambs, nor the sea to provide its fish."[37] Through his own virtue, a sovereign encourages the fecundity of the earth and the flocks. He is a nurturer, and his power is felt at both the pastoral and the arboricultural levels. As a royal heir, Meleager is a sprig from the olive tree that flourishes on the land of his father,[38] Oeneus, the "man of the vineyard." Young Meleager brings with him the promise of an olive tree destined to cover the entire Calydonian land with its foliage.

This first aspect of Meleager, the royal child born from the flames in the hearth, the son of the king, who is associated with fruit-bearing trees, is counterbalanced by another, antithetical, aspect: the Meleager associated with the spear, both a hunter and a warrior. In the story of the son of Oeneus, the wooden weapon, whether the spear of a hunter or that of a warrior, which figures as Meleager's double, is neither an isolated feature nor one introduced at a much later date. A whole section of the legend of Meleager is dominated by the image of the spear. When games are held in honor of Peleas, it is with his spear that Meleager triumphs over his rivals;[39] it is again with a spear that Mealeager triumphs over the wild boar that he then consecrates in Sicyon, in the temple of Apollo, who himself had similarly triumphed over the Python snake.[40] The image of the young Meleager, whose external soul is the wooden shaft of a fighting or hunting spear, refers back to a whole corpus of myths about men born from ash or oak trees, trees never cultivated, types of hardwood from which the javelins of hunters and the spears of warriors were crafted. The nurturing olive tree is counterbalanced by the ash tree, the wood of which can become a lethal weapon. This association with the spear calls to mind a whole series of warrior myths: the Men of Bronze, the Giants, the Dryopes. The Men of Bronze were born from ash trees, from the Meliai, just as the armed troop of Giants erupted from the earth, each grasping a long javelin of ash wood.[41] In parallel to the men of the ash tree, the Dryopes constituted a band of wild warriors closely linked with the oak tree. Dryops, their leader, a grandson of Lycaon, was suckled by his mother along with an oak sprig, from which he took his name.[42] All were warriors, men committed to warfare: Caeneus, the Lapith who identified with the spear;[43] Parthenopaeus, who swore solely by his javelin and put his trust only in the might of his weapons.[44]

It seems clear from the configuration of his birth and its mystical framework that Meleager's destiny is twofold: as a spear prepared to kill or fight,[45] and as an olive sprig flourishing within the paternal orchard. His story is constructed on the basis of a tragic tension between, on the one hand, the cultivated earth, the world of growing, tended plants, and, on the other, wild nature and the world of hunting and warfare. This polarity orients Melager's genealogical history as well as his adventures.

Two movements are detectable in the epic account of the high deeds of the Calydonian hero: the one leads from wild nature to the land of cultivated trees, the second from the cultivated space into the world of hunting and warfare.

The first sequence starts with Orestheus, the man of the mountains, and ends with Oeneus, the man of the vineyards. The son of Deucalion,[46] Orestheus, has come to Aetolia, to reign over it. In his *Histories* Hecataeus of Miletus relates that Orestheus owned a female dog that produced a litter that included a piece of wood, *stelechos*.[47] Orestheus had this buried in the ground. To commemorate this, he named his son Phytius, the planter; and this planter was the father of Oeneus, the man of the vineyards. The piece of wood, which introduces one of the themes of the story of Meleager's birth, plays a mediating role between the man of the mountains and the man of the vineyards, a role analogous to that of Phytius, a figure linked with the growing of trees,[48] but not yet totally committed, as Oeneus is, to serious arboriculture.

The second sequence leads from Oeneus to Meleager, but in the opposite direction. Oeneus is both a good chariot driver and the master of a splendid vineyard. The image of his sovereignty appears to reconcile the tension between the two activities, which constitutes the mainspring for the story of Meleager. But a moment of forgetfulness soon spoils that equilibrium. When Oeneus sacrifices the first fruits of his harvest to the gods, he forgets to offer Artemis the portion that is her due.[49] Once placed in context, this negligence can be seen to be symptomatic: the Artemis known as Laphria is the major deity of Calydon,[50] the land where Oeneus tends his vineyards and over which he rules. Artemis Laphria is a disturbing goddess whose reign extends over the forests and the wild animals. Each year all kinds of wild animal victims are sacrificed in her honor: deer, wolf cubs, bear cubs, and wild boar are all burned alive in a great brazier. Such a sacrifice stands in absolute opposition to the offerings made by the man of the vineyards, an opposition that expresses the divorce that separates wild Artemis from the king of Calydon. The Thalysia[51] incorporates an offering of the first fruits of the earth to the Earth deities, who are called upon to confirm the fertility of the crops. The Laphria, in contrast, represents a ritual of destruction in which many kinds of victims, mostly woodland animals, are destroyed in honor of the deity who is a patron of the wild earth. The distance separating Oeneus from Artemis is so great that one should not write off the hypothesis, formulated in the *Iliad*, that Oeneus overlooks Artemis deliberately: "Either he forgot, or he ignored her."[52] The antagonism between the sovereign of the vineyards and the deity of the forests of Calydon was all the greater, given that Artemis—who was close to the species of trees, such as the oak tree and the walnut, that although wild, did bear fruit[53]—in her capacity as Koruthalia[54] claimed the right to preside over the growth of young shoots in the same way that, as Kourotrophe, she watched over the growth of young boys, whose name, *koroi* or *kouroi*, "offspring," tended to be confused with *koroi* meaning "the growing offshoots of plants."[55]

It was thus inevitable that the Calydonian wild boar should make its appearance. According to the *Iliad*, this was a solitary creature with very white tusks, "a huge wild boar with white tusks, which kept doing great damage in Oeneus' orchards: it uprooted many tall trees and flung them whole on the ground, roots, ripe fruits and all."[56] Meleager organized a hunt for this beast that was ravaging the cultivated land, and was favored by the help of his maternal uncles, the Curetes. A fight against a wild boar—in Greece always regarded as a terrifying animal and a monstrous beast—was an initiatory test, an exploit that revealed the worth of the adolescent hunter and proved that he possessed the qualities of his adversary: courage and ferocity.[57] The hunt of Meleager and the Curetes conforms to the model of a testing hunt that appears both in the myth of Odysseus[58] and in that of Theseus.[59] But by setting the boar to ravage the vineyards of Oeneus, Artemis, while appearing to be providing Meleager with the chance of performing a heroic feat, was in truth condemning Oeneus' son to the darker side of his personality. Thanks to his conditional immortality, Meleager managed to kill the wild boar, but the warrior frenzy that the hunt aroused in him was to prove his downfall. While the spoils of the hunt[60] were being apportioned, Meleager was drawn into a quarrel with his maternal uncles, and attacked the Curetes. At this point in the story, two different versions arise. According to the more dramatic of the two, to avenge the murder of her brothers, Althaea, Meleager's mother, seized the fateful piece of wood and threw it back on the fire. According to the other version, it was the man of the vineyards, Oeneus himself, who destroyed the olive sprig that contained Meleager's life.[61]

The second version of Meleager's fate is, as it were, anticipated by the image of the wild boar uprooting the fruit-bearing trees and ravaging Oeneus' orchard. That image is itself based on an opposition whose terms are explained in yet another epic episode: the fight between Menelaus and Euphorbus.[62] Euphorbus boasts that he will hand Menelaus' herd to his parents. Menelaus retorts that, although Euphorbus may be a ferocious wild boar, if he steps any closer he will be a dead man. Euphorbus leaps at him, and Menelaus cleaves his throat. Euphorbus' fall is described at length in a comparison to an olive tree: "As when a man nurtures a flourishing olive-shoot in a solitary place where plenty of water wells up—a fine healthy shoot it is, shaken by the breath of every wind that blows, and it blossoms thick with white flowers; but suddenly there comes a wind in a great storm and uproots it from its trench and lays out its length on the earth. Such was . . . Euphorbus of the ash-spear, as Menelaus . . . killed him and set to stripping his armor." In the myth of Meleager, as in the story of Euphorbus, the price to be paid for the ferocious boar is the finest of olive trees, which is uprooted and crashes to the ground. The conflict between land that is cultivated and land that is wild reaches its climax. To defend the crops against wild beasts, Meleager has to become so much of a hunter that he negates the values of the cultivated earth. It is a reversal that takes a tragic turn when Oeneus, the master of the orchard, also swept up in a warrior's frenzy, tears up the olive shoot, thereby destroying the finest tree in the whole plantation.

Two main guidelines run through the whole collection of mythical representations involving arboriculture: on the one hand, the particularly close relations between the ephebe and the olive shoot; on the other, the complementarity and opposition between two kinds of space, land where the trees are cultivated and uncultivated land, wide open to hunting. Several important aspects both of Cretan practices and of certain Athenian institutions manifest the continuity between this mythical level and the way that the city represented the ephebe and his position in the polis. They all help us to understand the social weight carried by the mythical models of the Athenian olive tree.

Within the framework of the city of Athens, the ambiguity that stamps the status of an ephebe[63] inevitably evokes the double destiny of Meleager. Before being integrated into the city and accepted into the hoplite phalanx, an Athenian ephebe was assigned the position of a *peripolos:* stationed in frontier zones, in the *eschatai,* he moved about the territory's periphery, where the wilderness threatened to encroach upon the cultivated land, and where clashes were likely to occur on the common frontiers of two cities. At the end of this trial period, a new citizen was fully accepted into the city territory, which coincided with the cultivated area, as is testified by the oath sworn by the ephebes[64] at the point when they were promoted to the ranks of the hoplites. After swearing to remain in his position in the phalanx, to defend the soil of his city, and to protect the *hiera* and the *hosia*—the people and the gods of the city—every young Athenian male would invoke, alongside Hestia and several warrior deities,[65] "the boundaries of the Motherland, the Wheat, the Barley, and the Olive and Fig trees." That is to say, he would list the powers that presented an image of the city as a land at once cultivated and political, the two being inseparable.[66]

This Athenian oath, which does not distinguish clearly between, on the one hand, the olive trees and, on the other, the rest of the cultivated crops, such as other fruit-bearing trees and cereals, may be complemented by another oath, the one sworn by the ephebes of Dreros,[67] or, to be more precise, by the strange chronicle of the "ancient land of Dreros,"[68] which is engraved under the text of the oath. Behind this concise document, which was addressed to the newly promoted ephebes, it is possible to detect a series of episodes that took place in the initiatory cycle through which boys had to pass in the course of their Cretan education. First, there is a mention of a battle, fought under a new moon, between the troops of Milatus, the closest neighboring city, and the ephebes of Dreros, who were proud to fight for the territory, the *chora* of their city.[69] Next, there is an allusion to a victory won over the *agela,* a troop of young men, in a trial the name of which is not clear. Finally, it is laid down that each man—that is, no doubt, each ephebe—was required to plant an olive tree and display it in bloom, *helaian hekaston phutenein kai tethrammenon apodeiksai.* A heavy fine would be imposed on anyone failing to plant his olive tree.

When referred to the entire body of Cretan traditions known to us, these three episodes seem to mark out three stages in an initiatory ritial. First, a battle of two groups of young men, on the border between their respective cities, under a new moon. Second, a trial in which the members of the *agela* were pitted one against another. This seems to have been the race that, in Crete, founded the status of a citizen, by granting the youths access to the Dromos,[70] the public gymnasium that was a major feature of the urban and political space of Cretan cities. Third, the action of planting and growing an olive tree, which represented the final stage in this initiatory process. R. F. Willetts[71] interprets this action as an economic measure designed to oblige the ephebes to contribute to the production of olive oil, which was indispensable to the functioning of the gymnasium and which at the same time confirmed their rights to the land they stood to inherit and of which they were the legitimate occupants. However, the wholly religious context that surrounds the injunction to plant an olive tree suggests that we should reject this interpretation. The status of *panadzōstoi*, "those without equipment," which was that of the 180 young men called upon to swear the Dreros oath, indicates, rather, that the oath was linked with a festival such as the Ekdusia, celebrated in Phaestus. This was connected with a courotrophic power such as the Leto Phytia,[72] who presided over the transition from the state of a *pais*, who was confined to the feminine world, to that of a young man. The transition was consecrated by the donning of masculine clothing, the equivalent of which, in a hoplite city, was the acquisition of a panoply of arms. We should therefore place this type of ritual planting required of the Drerian ephebe within the framework of similar initiatory tests and with reference to the whole collection of mythical traditions centered upon the olive tree. By planting in the earth of Dreros an olive tree that was expected to grow, each new citizen showed that he was now integrated into the cultivated city space, and did so in a manner that prolonged the ancient solidarity between a human seedling and a fruit-bearing tree, such as the olive.

One and the same model inspired both archaic Athens and the city of Dreros, which subscribed to the same archaic traditions. These were cities where each citizen stood tall upon the territory of the polis, like a fruit-bearing tree and also like a spear with the power to terrorize hostile spearsmen. An ephebe was an olive tree, an olive tree an ephebe.[73]

CHAPTER TEN

The Crane and the Labyrinth

A labyrinth cries out for exegesis, but the network of its crossroads and ramified passages irresistibly draws the interpreter into a thousand and one detours. The fascination exerted by its reputedly universal symbolism is no doubt not unconnected with its graphic nature: it is at once a trail that leads nowhere and the longest path possible enclosed in the smallest space possible. Whether it is on that account or for other reasons that the symbol of the labyrinth is so intriguing, the likelihood is that it defies reduction to a single meaning, both cross-culturally and even within a single culture. And as our imaginary representations of a labyrinth inevitably turn back to the kingdom of Crete and the fate of the Minotaur, perhaps they provide some justification for limiting our internal field of exploration to that marked out by the Greek culture's stories about the labyrinth.[1] The sole aim of our investigation will be to test the constraints of the Greek discourse and discover its procedures (which may also be those that we ourselves adopt) as, locked into the winding ways of the labyrinth, in its efforts at evocation, it assembles within a single culture forms and objects as disparate as a seashell, a monster, a line of dancers, a crane, and a spiral staircase.

In what we, following the example set by Plato, call the mythological tradition, the labyrinth appears as a singularly isolated image. The only story that Greek memories have passed down to us presents the labyrinth as the solitary realm of the Minotaur, the true master of which, however, is Daedalus, who may seem overshadowed by the Minotaur but whose name nevertheless, through its multiple meanings, evokes the innermost secret qualities of the labyrinth. The space where the monstrous form of the Minotaur looms up is marked out by two merging accounts of sovereignty, in which the destiny of Minos and the biography of Theseus cross. Two points of reference are immediately detectable in this narrative. First, the presence of bulls both at the beginning and at the end of the story. Through the lover of his mother Europa, Minos is descended from bull stock every bit as much as is the son of Pasiphae. The resemblance is underlined by the name associated with both of them: Asterius, the starry one, was both the name of Minos' father and a sort of extra name given to the Minotaur. Meanwhile, Theseus' Cretan adventure ends with the sacrificial slaughtering of the Cretan bull, captured at Marathon, then taken in procession all the way to the Acropolis. The second point of reference is the conquest of sovereignty. As a result of his excessive ambition, Minos is a sick king, doubly afflicted in his fecundity. Meanwhile, Theseus, for his part, thanks to his victory over the monster of the labyrinth, the perverse emblem of Cretan sovereignty, claims royal authority in the land of Attica.

The Cretan dynasty began with Europa's union with a god metamorphosed into a seducer-bull with magically fragrant breath.[2] Zeus, the bull, selected a mortal named Asterius to stand in for him. Asterius, the starry or luminous one, acted as nurturing father to the three sons born from the love between Europa and Zeus. The three brothers were soon fighting over the favors of a boy as handsome as Apollo, his father. Minos, when ousted, made war on his brothers, forced them into exile and then, when his own rights to sovereignty were questioned at the death of Asterius, alleged that he had been awarded the throne by the gods, who could testify to his divine roots. But instead of invoking his Olympian father and getting him to use his thunderbolt and lightning in a clear sky in his support, as he does on another occasion in a dispute with Theseus,[3] he turned to the sea, invoked Poseidon, demanding a sign from him and even specifying what it should be: a bull-like creature that would emerge from the waves and that he swore to sacrifice forthwith to the lord of the marine depths. So once again, a bull rose out of the sea, sent by Poseidon. It was an apparition, a *phasma*,[4] in the animal shape of Minos' true father, and it became the talisman of the royalty to which he aspired.[5] For Minos proceeded to appropriate this bull, which he should have sacrificed and returned to the god who had sent it. Instead of doing this, he shut it up in his stables, hiding it amid his herds, and hastened to offer up another in its place.

The sovereign power of Minos had already been shaky, but now it was positively sick, doubly sick, both through the person of the king, who was struck by sterility, and also through the behavior of Pasiphae, his queen. There exists a whole tradition that presents a stark contrast to the image of Minos who, in the better known tradition relating to him, is presented as a just king who enjoyed the trust of Zeus as each Great Year came round and who sat enthroned in the house of Hades, where he presided, gold scepter in hand, over the court of the shades.[6] The opposed tradition includes a story in which the king of Crete is unable to engender any offspring.[7] Minos has been bewitched by his wife, the daughter of the Sun, and now his sad ejaculations produce nothing but venomous creatures, such as snakes, scorpions, and centipedes. His embrace is deadly. Procris, a boyish, exiled huntress, somewhat like Atalanta, heals him of his infirmity either by obtaining from Circe a more powerful charm to counteract that used by Pasiphae, or by resorting to the expedient of a goat's bladder introduced into the vagina of a female partner, to receive Minos' preseminal venomous ejaculation and render it harmless. The curse is lifted. Pasiphae has taken her revenge on the rivals with whom Minos had betrayed her, and the king returns to his wife, who then bears him the children he has so long desired. In this version, the monstrosity is confined to an accidental sexual affliction that befalls the king and is not explicitly related to his wrongful treatment of Poseidon.

In the most widely recorded version, however, Minos' sovereignty suffers through the sexuality of Pasiphae. Denied his promised sacrifical victim, the angered Poseidon strikes back though both the queen and the bull. The animal whose sacrificial vocation inclined it to nonviolence[8] is made wild, and at the same time Poseidon fills Pasiphae with an uncontrollable desire[9] that is eventually satisfied thanks to the skills of a foreign craftsman by the name of Daedalus. Fitted out with a costume of wood and leather that gives her the appearance of a rutting heifer, the queen copulates with the bull, in a repetition of the union from which Minos himself was born, albeit with a reversal of the roles of the sexual partners. Driven by the violent desire that Poseidon kindles deep inside her, the maddened Pasiphae engages in lovemaking as bestial as that of Europa and Zeus was divine, when Zeus the lover took the form of a bull. Led astray by an extreme desire that afflicts her with the most shameful of maladies,[10] Pasiphae's body manifests the sickness that has struck at the fecundity of the king. The offspring that testifies to her limitless desires is called Asterius, after his grandfather, but the new luminous one is a monster, half-beast, half-human.[11]

The Minotaur, a double, hybrid being with a bull's head set on a human body, which appeared in the royal house of Crete, combined in its identity all the signs of a sick sovereignty. Its name reflected the luminous brilliance of the first king of Crete, and this was increased by the talismanic power of the royal animal sent by the gods. But this mixture of a human beast and a bestial man had to be hidden away, to conceal the madness and violence that made it an alien in the king's palace and palace precinct. Again, it was Daedalus who was ordered to find a way out of the dilemma. He created the space best suited to the Minotaur: a labyrinth, a dwelling-place chosen, conceived, and thought out by an intelligence that was unmistakable. To this labyrinth came the young and ambitious Theseus. Theseus is a rival to Heracles, whose fame rests upon a similar litany of exploits and high deeds; he became a member of the pantheon of great men long before Plutarch assigned him a place in his *Parallel Lives*, alongside Romulus.[12] The Athenian stories about Theseus, a hectic accumulation of victories over monsters, great civilizing gestures, and initiatory adventures, compose a long novel in which he qualifies as a hero. In his *Poetics* Aristotle criticizes this *Theseid*, along with—as it happens—a *Heracleid*, putting his finger on what seems to him to be its major defect—namely, the assumption that the plot must necessarily be all of a piece if it has only one hero.[13] He declares that a well-constructed story, a good *muthos*, has a well designed plot, centered on a single but relatively extended action that can be taken in at a glance and that is easy to remember.[14]

The single exploit that is supposed to condense the virtues and perils of the human action and provide a perfectly memorable plot was invented by the figurative tradition long before Aristotle condemned the clumsiness of the *Theseid*. Two centuries earlier, Corinthian vases were displaying representations of Theseus, essentially portraying him as the victor over the Minotaur.[15] That was well before, under the Pisistratids and the Alcmeonids, the figurative tradition, which had become gossipy and as it were incontinent, set about representing the childhood adventures of the hero, his encounters with highway bandits and with countless monsters, and his war against the Amazons. Theseus' defeat and slaughter of the Minotaur already qualified him to assume the sovereignty of Athens. He capped that by overcoming the Marathon bull[16]—that is to say, by his capture of the beast maddened by Poseidon and conveyed from Crete to mainland Greece by the might of Heracles.[17] This was a bull that laid waste the countryside, killing whoever crossed its path,[18] until Theseus sought it out, overcame it, then paraded it, still alive, through the city and sacrificed it either to Delphinian Apollo or to Athena, on the Acropolis.[19] He thus finally led to its destiny the sacrificial Poseidonian animal, which Minos' error had provoked to the limits of savagery, causing the destruction of cultivated fields and the murder of many human beings.

The Minotaur should in no way be confused with the bull of Marathon, whose story incorporates but exceeds that of the Minotaur. The son of Minos and Pasiphae was not a promised sacrificial victim, nor an animal whose behavior alternated between domesticated docility and wild brutality. The identity of the Minotaur is fully conveyed by its dwelling-place: it belongs nowhere but in the labyrinth, with its peculiar topology. In Corinth, the figurative tradition of the sixth century represents the son of Minos and his enigmatic realm by means of two paintings: one of a duel, the other of a dance.[20] Neither attempts to depict the square or circular network of corridors,[21] but both do, in similar manner, symbolize the space of the labyrinth.[22] One shows Theseus striking the Minotaur with his sword while Ariadne, clad in a long robe, looks on, clasping a ball of thread, half unraveled, like a long stem ending in a spiraling flower. The other shows alternating boys and girls, holding hands, performing a dance known as the *geranos* or "dance of the cranes." The dance represents the treck through the labyrinth, just as does Ariadne's ball of thread.

The dance of the cranes, performed by Theseus either on the soil of Crete itself or else before the altar of Apollo on the sacred isle of Delos, enacted the whole dangerous adventure, the perils of which were twofold, as Callimachus' *Hymn to Delos* reminds us.[23] Theseus and his companions escaped from the terrifying bellow of the wild son of Pasiphae and also from the tortuous *(gnamptos)* palace and its winding *(skolios)* labyrinth. The danger is thus double, but it is conveyed by three closely linked terms: bellowing, vibration, sound waves. On the acoustic level these signify confusion,[24] an interlacing of paths, labyrinthine ways through the polymorphic space that corresponds perfectly to the hybrid nature of the monster in whose double being man and beast are confused. To put it more precisely, a labyrinthine topology is expressed by the dance, both through its movements and through the bird after which it is named. The jig known as a *geranos*,[25] after the wading bird, was performed by dancers in single file, as depicted on the François vase.[26] The exegeses produced by ancient Greek commentators explain that the cranes' dance imitated either the escape from the labyrinth[27] or the entry into the Minotaur's lair.[28] The dance itself, as described by the antiquarians, was characterized by two features. First, its major figures were based on the parallax and the spiral (*parallaksis* and *aneliksis*), and it combined in the helixlike patterns alternate movements to the left and to the right.[29] Second, the dance was conducted by two leaders, who were positioned at either end of the line of dancers.[30] The dancers were thus arranged in a continuous line with two heads. It operated as a parade in single file, the tail of which would become the head at a particular point in the course of the dance.[31]

The reference to cranes has muddled and frequently obscured the pertinence of these dance patterns that imitate the intertwining paths of the labyrinth. Some interpreters believe that this was the Spring Dance of the Long-Tailed Tit, which harked back to some ancient agrarian rite relating to some lustratory procedure that had nothing to do with the adventures of Theseus.[32] For others, the bird's name evoked a particular detail in the dance, the triangular shape of a flight of birds[33] or the high-stepping walk of a wader.[34] But in truth, the overall behavior of the crane justified its name being given to the dance that represented and reproduced the labyrinth and the journey through it. Greek bestiaries emphasize the intellectual qualities of the crane. For this bird, the *Ardea grus*, which for some Europeans is the epitome of stupidity and silliness, was famed for its prudence and its wisdom.[35] It presented an example of an animal endowed with reason and the kind of intelligence known as *phronesis*. In the *Politicus*, Plato gives us the crane's point of view.[36] He suggests that an intelligent animal, such as a crane, would classify the whole collection of living creatures by picking out the crane genus and setting it in opposition to all the rest, taking pride in rejecting all the other species and lumping them together as a mass "for which it [the crane] would probably find no other name than that of beasts *[theria]*." In Plato's view, such a taxonomy would be every bit as good as that adopted by man, when he reserves the place of king for himself.

But the prudence of the crane, a wading bird, is revealed by more than its aptitude for dialectics, and especially by its ability to cross the entire expanse of the sky. In the accounts of zoologists, the crane is represented as a marvelously skillful navigator, bold enough to migrate from the plains of Scythia, the coldest part of the world, all the way to the very hottest lands, Egypt, Libya, and Ethiopia.[37] According to Aristotle's *History of Animals*,[38] the crane flies from one extremity of the world to the other, thus linking the two ends of the earth.

The *geranos* performs this exploit, making the most of an expedient so remarkable as to become proverbial. Before setting out on its migration, each crane, in its great prudence, picks up a pebble, a tiny stone that will enable it to tell, from the noise that the stone makes when it falls, whether it is flying over sea or land.[39] It was this trick that made people believe that the migrating bird truly could orientate itself in the immensity of the sky. By taking note of the sounds that carry up to them, the high-flying cranes find the signs and reference points that sailors out at sea seek far above their heads, in the middle of the night, as they navigate by the stars—or so it was claimed by Greek sailors. The proverb "cranes carry pebbles" was appositely applied to those who behaved with great prudence. These large birds in exemplary fashion possess the ability to foresee the future to the point where they seem intuitively aware of the nature of the air, the changes of the seasons—the whole map of the world.[40] How else could they possibly link the farthest ends of the world? Cranes thus constitute a perfect symbol for a journey through a labyrinth, as represented by descriptions of the dance known as the *geranos*. The same prudence that makes it possible for the crane to link the two ends of the earth allows the dancers in the labyrinth to link the entrance and the exit of the labyrinth, making the end and the beginning coincide. In both journeys it is a matter of crossing what is uncrossable, finding the way over a space without visible points of reference, with no fixed directions, in which every exit that seems to be opening turns out to be an insoluble *aporia*, an inextricable knot. The method used by the dancers who successfully pass through the labyrinth is to reverse the leaders of the linked file of people: its tail turns into its head, and the end is identical to the beginning. It is as with two ends of a rope, or the thread that the steps of the crane dance imitate, with its single file of dancers who seem to meander in long detours, yet suddenly return to their point of departure.

Just as the dance finds the exit and entrance of the labyrinth, so too does Ariadne's thread testify to the victory over the Minotaur. Wound into a ball or played out in coils, the thread alternates with the crown of light,[41] the purpose of which is not to bring into the chaos of the labyrinth a brilliance that would fully reveal the construction of blind alleys, but rather to provide a point of reference, one of the luminous marks that the Greeks called *tekmōr*, a "path marker," a point visible on the horizon to which a navigator or traveler can steer.[42] The homology between Ariadne's thread and the crane dance is made explicit by the figure of Daedalus, the inventor of the labyrinth that extends around the Minotaur a net without an opening, made up of a thousand winding detours.[43] It is he who teaches the steps of the crane dance, he who provides Ariadne with the thread that shows the way on a journey, the beginning and end of which he knows so well.[44]

The labyrinth of Daedalus stretches its coils and spreads its ramifications within a conceptual field where a particular kind of progress naturally takes the form of a thread or a linked chain and where, reciprocally, the action of linking in a chain assumes the appearance of a progress or journey that links one point to another. Like the steps of the crane dance, Ariadne's thread indicates the solution to the labyrinthine *aporia*, tying the beginning and the end firmly together. But the stories about Daedalus contain one more episode that lays bare the formal design of the labyrinth.[45] After the famous escape of Daedalus, the craftsman and inventor of the labyrinth, who disappeared into the sky with his nephew Icarus, Minos set off in their pursuit. Wherever he went, the king of Crete offered a reward to anyone who could pass a thread right through the shell of a winkle (*kochlos* or *kochlias*).[46] Eventually, the king of Sicily, Cocalus, accepted the challenge, convinced that it would be child's play for the secret guest living in his palace. And Daedalus indeed took the thread, attached it to an ant and introduced the latter into the shell through a tiny hole pierced at the top. By solving the puzzle, Daedalus revealed his presence, unable to resist the opportunity offered him by Minos to be recognized for his understanding of the spiral.[47] For in its grey, whorled shell, Minos' winkle condensed all the essential features of the labyrinth: the puzzling structure, the *aporia* of the curved detours, and the thread that found its way around the curves. Yet this miniaturized labyrinth was not a small-scale model, not an artifact. It was just a game for which the spiraling shell by chance provided the material. Its essentials lay in the form and the movements necessary to pass through it. In a tragedy by Sophocles about Daedalus and Cocalus, the same seashell is called a *strabelon*, a word meaning "curve," from the verb *strephein*, from which *strabos*, the word for "twisted" or "tortuous," is also derived.[48] On the basis of its curved shape, which combines the spiral and the parallax, the winkle is explicitly associated with the labyrinth in the articles devoted to it by the lexicographers, Hesychius, and the *Suda: labyrinthos, konklioeidēs, topos.* The question that arises is whether this topos in the form of a winkle was not in effect a construction,[49] an architectural space, a three-dimensional creation, such as can be produced by means of tectonics.[50] It is a question that has become more pressing thanks to those who have boldly claimed to have discovered the labyrinth, either in the palace of Cnossos excavated by Evans, or in the grottoes, caves, and underground passages of the island of Crete. But there are also two constructed objects, two artifacts that we must pause to investigate, given that one was known as a "shell," *kokhlion*, the other as a "labyrinth."

The first is carefully described in Hippolytus' commentary on a fragment of Heraclitus devoted to the curve and the straight line: "The circle described by the spiraling part, called a shell, of the tool used by a painter *[graphein]* is both straight and curved."[51] This was an instrument, probably a paintbrush or an etcher's needle, fixed into an apparatus containing a kind of screw that moved forward as it turned. It was probably used to twist and raise the surface of a vase to be engraved or painted. This machine or apparatus known as a "shell" derived its name from its shape and its movement, its *peristrophē*, and from the combination within it of a curve and a straight line. Such spiraling curves also constitute the principle upon which another artifact is based, this time an architectural one that is mentioned in technical terms in the register of accounts for the construction of the temple of Apollo at Didyma: here, *labyrinths* are the staircases positioned on either side of the Chamber of Oracles, Chresmographion, which lead to the upper story and the top of the building. Each of these labyrinth-staircases is composed of a series of curving turns, or *epistrophes*.[52] In other words, these are stairs constructed like screws, spiral "labyrinths." The space is filled with twists and, just as the lexicographers define it, is a place in the form of a spiraling shell, set up vertically, as must have been Archimedes' screw, the famous *konkhlias* described by Diodorus Siculus, which was a machine designed to lift water.[53] Did this type of staircase, known as a "labyrinth" in the vocabulary of the Milesian architects of the Hellenistic period, give its name to the Egyptian "labyrinth" mentioned by Herodotus of Halicarnassus, or was it the Egyptian edifice known as a labyrinth that gave its name to the staircases of certain Milesian sanctuaries?[54] One detail provided by Sophocles favors the former explanation: Daedalus' invention had no roof or ceiling.[55] It was a space full of twists and turns but was open to the sky, as indeed was the winding staircase whose name came from its spiraling design, at once a form and a movement, which obeyed the principle of the endless screw *(apeiros konkhlias)*, one of the five forces discovered by the ancients that are described in the works of Pappus of Alexandria.[56]

Plato uses this same intellectual model to represent a labyrinth in the only metaphor in which he uses this image: it is a kind of *aporia* that is sometimes reached in dialectical discourse. The metaphor occurs in the *Euthydemus*, where each of the sciences turns out to be elusive just at the point where one is about to grasp it: "We were involved in a labyrinth: when we supposed we had arrived at the end, we twisted about again and found ourselves practically at the beginning of our search, and just as sorely in want as when we first started on it."[57] In other words, a labyrinth in which one is trapped, where the twists and turns and curves unfold endlessly, and the *aporia* is confirmed by the elusive *telos* and the impossibility of bringing together the end and the beginning, as is successfully done by Daedalus' dance and by the flight of the cranes.

For this ancient Greek tradition and its ongoing exegesis between the end of the archaic period and the Hellenistic period, a labyrinth is a *cosa mentale*, a space uncluttered by any construction. It is the homologue of the path represented on the Corinthian vases by the discreet indications of Ariadne's spiraling thread and by the line of dancers in single file, although in those two cases the labyrinth is, as it were, already turned inside out, crumbling, disappearing as the Minotaur is put to death. For by the time the dance begins and Daedalus' thread appears, the straight line is already threatening the curves and by its very straightness is linking the end to the beginning. It effaces the twists and turns in the same way as victory over the Minotaur does away with his hybrid form and blots out the memory of his savage violence. This labyrinth was conceived as a path, a passage that hung upon a thread. And it was fundamentally a space without a center,[58] which excluded both what was most concrete and also what was most mystical. It was not a concrete building whose complicated design made it a place of illusions, like the labyrinth of a certain Miletus, constructed by clever builders for the pleasure of people who enjoyed getting lost in it, a place of *apatē* in which illusion became a delight.[59] Nor was the labyrinth an initiatory journey or a descent or way into the other world, toward a center whose religious symbolism coincided with the mystical values of the seashell.

When, with the aid of the Minotaur, the Greeks thought about a labyrinth, they concentrated on the abstract image of a space without issue,[60] leaving to others the task of exploring the significance of the center or the cave. They chose to reflect upon a moving space in which the intelligence of the man who understood the straight line and the curve and the beginning and the end was expressed in the flight of a crane and the spiral of an endless screw.[61]

CHAPTER ELEVEN

The Finger of Orestes

Let us begin with two images of Greek murderers.[1] The one slips in furtively at the end of the *Iliad.* The other, massive and violent, appears during the earliest days of the city. In the first, Hector has just been killed; his corpse is defiled and horribly abused, as every day Achilles' galloping horses drag it three times round the walls of Troy. One evening Priam, Hector's father, can bear the crazy violence and sacrilegious excesses of the spectacle no longer. With Hermes as his guide, he enters the camp of Troy's enemies, approaches Achilles, clasps his knees, and showers kisses upon his hands, the terrible, "murderous" *(androphonoi)* hands that have killed so many of his sons. "As when a man is held fast by blind folly *[atē]*—he kills a man in his own country, and then comes to another land *[patrē],* to a rich man's house, and amazement *[thambos]* takes those who see his entry. So Achilles was amazed when he saw godlike Priam, and the others too were amazed."[2] This unknown figure, who has loomed out of the darkness and is making the gestures of a suppliant, is the father of the defiled corpse, and he throws himself at Achilles' feet. But he resembles a fugitive who, because he has shed blood in his "own country," departs, deliberately exiling himself as he seeks a hearth and a home that will take him in and offer him a new status, far removed from the errors and bloodshed of the past. He comes face to face with Achilles, the slayer of his children, and confronts his "murderous" hands—hands that have shed human blood, but only that of warriors, within a context of bloody death and open warfare.

The second image is that of the Alcmeonids, a houshold of several hundred people in archaic Athens.[3] In about 650 B.C., shortly after Draco introduced his first laws on homicide, the various parties in the city of Athens clashed, and the city was torn apart. An Athenian named Cylon took possession of the Acropolis, to which his opponents then set siege. The city was rent in two. The Alcmeonids promised Cylon's partisans their lives, provided they immediately left Attica. Exhausted and famished, the Cylonids nevertheless refused to leave the protection of the goddess Athena. A strand of wool attached to her statue was supposed to preserve their contact with their protective deity as they made their descent from the Acropolis. But near the Areopagus, which was to become one of the great courts presiding over crimes involving bloodshed, the Cylonids' strand of wool snapped, and they threw themselves upon the altar of the Eumenides, where they were forthwith done to death by the Alcmeonids and their allies. The entire city contracted gangrene as a result of this scourge *(loimos)* and defilement *(miasma)*. The people were assailed by terrors *(phoboi)* and disturbing apparitions *(phasmata)*, and all the sacrificial victims turned out to be deformed. The Alcmeonids were declared to be impure, *enageis*, "surrounded by defilement." They were condemned as Alitērioi of the goddess, sacrilegious people possessed by the anger of the dead who were crying out for vengeance. They had to be ejected, every one of them, including even their dead, who had to be exhumed and whose bones had to be cast out beyond the frontiers of the territory, far from the *chora*, far from the city. A purifier without equal had to be called in. He came from Crete, and his name was Epimenides. He proceeded to effect a veritable refoundation of the territory by reconsecrating its altars and sanctuaries.

Despite their differences, both those scenarios showing the effects of bloodshed resort to refoundations in order to put an end to the defilement. Neither establishes the status of homicide or city institutions designed to deal with bloodshed, but the first one, by focusing on the "murderous" hands of Achilles, prepares the way for the introduction of the technical term *homicide*, while the second introduces into the scene of the drama the Areopagus, soon to become a court of law, and the so-called "benevolent" powers known as the Eumenides. The next major development for the Greek cities, seen as societies with a wealth of rituals to cope with murderers and their victims, was the appearance of courts designed to deal with cases of bloodshed, together with a penal code relating to homicide.[4] The earliest cities legislated first on bloodshed, the murder of a man in the same group, a member of the new kind of community formed of men who all belonged to the same city. Between about 620 and 530, the laws *(thesmoi)* on murder were imprinted in large, colored letters upon stelae set up not only in the longer established cities of the Greek mainland, such as Argos and Athens, but also in the young cities of Sicily and Magna Graecia: if an individual was killed within the city space, the city (polis) itself felt assaulted, so it was the city that ruled on what reparation was due to the victim's relatives and the community. "Civic solidarity took precedence over family discipline and the protection afforded by a patron."[5] "Murder" became a legal category. Under Draco, a murderer, known as an *androphonos*—like the hand of Achilles or a Homeric warrior—became subject to the law. The Draconian law on homicide set about impartially differentiating between categories of crimes, assessing culpabilitiy, marking out its different degrees, and setting up different courts to pass judgment on the various categories. Distinctions were thus drawn between deliberate, involuntary, and premeditated murder *(phonos)*, and also between those and what was called legitimate, justified *(dikaios)* murder. A whole legal code, with public action and popular courts, was elaborated around the concept of an agent, the one who acted, *ho drasas*—an abstract concept, like that of a citizen. The intentions of that "agent" were analyzed, his responsibility was measured, and the degree of his commitment was assessed. In parallel, the city instituted a particular space for the passing of judgment, where the confrontation between the accused, presumed to be guilty, and his accusers took place—a closed space in which the parties present were defined by the new legal terms.

Another innovation introduced by the Greek cities was the creation of a space for warfare. This, too, was autonomous. The city turned warfare into a public affair, directed by magistrates and carried out by citizens in arms. A war was decided upon in an assembly, and was fought in a specially selected space, usually one suitable for a head-on clash of two phalanxes. Raiding no longer had a place in warfare, nor did vendettas, private vengeance, or vengeful expeditions launched by one household against another. Bloodshed in the course of warfare was not homicide. It led to no defilement, required no purification. Nor, for that matter, were Draco's laws concerned with purification or with defilement in general. Once they were subject to the law, murderers seemed to become disengaged from the rituality that tends to surround them in certain cultures in West Africa and the Amerindian world, all of which are marked by a similar archaism. Incidentally, and given the comparativist perspective that we are adopting, it is worth noting that even as the Greek cities testify to a break and a radically new beginning, they simultaneously show just how pervasive socioreligious representations of murderers and defilement were between the seventh and the fourth centuries B.C.: anonymous powers, roused by the defilement of a particular group or even a particular territory, are unleashed; ghastly diseases attack the flesh of a murderer; purifications take place in which the victim's blood is poured over the body of the murderer. Historians, who tend to be particularly alert to changes, are tempted to collect such representations and associate them with the kind of social and religious state that preceded the advent of the city or, to be more precise, the establishment of courts dealing with bloodshed, as an explicit feature of the law.

Nowadays, we are wary of detecting on the horizon behind the Greek cities a form of mythico-religious thought marked by what Louis Gernet, in 1949, called "prelaw," global thought inhabited by myth, which was to fade away in the face of the advance of rationality and juridico-political attitudes.[6] Nor can we follow Marie Delcourt, who in 1959 wrote a remarkable essay on matricide and its legendary representation in Greece. She believed that "ethnology will one day synchronically and diachronically determine the boundaries of the area . . . of beliefs,"[7] such as those that proliferated in the wake of Orestes, who murdered his mother to avenge his father. It is precisely around the extreme figure of Orestes the murderer that the Greek tradition's most vivid and diverse representations of the effects of bloodshed were elaborated: the madness of the murderer, his identification with the victim, his flight and exile, his repeated purifications through blood sacrifices, his founding of altars and sanctuaries, and court judgments that were powerless to put a stop to the wanderings of the murderer and his relentless harassment by the powers of bloodshed. Three-quarters of a century after Draco, between about 550 and 400, Orestes the matricide inspired the richest possible configuration of the links that can bind a murderer to the person whose blood he has shed. In the Greek culture, it is the Orestes file that offers a comparativist anthropologist the best combination of data for an analysis of the effects of murder in the murderer's own body and for setting in perspective a whole series of societies that reserve a special place for murderers and the unmistakable defilement that marks them.

The case of Orestes is an exceptional one that needs to be set in a double context involving, on the one hand, the modalities by which defilement is transmitted in the Greek world, and, on the other, the usual effects of the blood that is poured over any murderer who remains on the scene of the crime. We have already glimpsed the first side in the Alcmeonid affair, for the murder of the Cylonid suppliants as they cling to the altar of the Eumenides, who are the kinder face of the Erinyes, in conjunction with the floods of blood shed on the territory of Athens, unleashes a tide of defilement. This submerges the whole group, the entire Alcmeonid household (as many as seven hundred people); it attacks all the altars and sanctuaries in the territory of Attica; and it affects the roots of the presumably autochthonous group so profoundly that Epimenides, the purifier summoned from Crete, has to set about refounding the community's links with the earth by setting up altars and sacrificing animal victims wherever they choose to lie down, thereby indicating suitable places to consecrate to the powers of the territory, as happens in the foundation rituals of new cities. "A major defilement calls for an absolute purifier," as Jean-Louis Durand puts it.[8] In the fifth century the Hippocratic doctors eliminated from their analyses diseases of the "scourge," or *loimos*, type, rejecting the model of a defilement that could affect every member of a community. Instead, they defended the thesis that each individual afflicted by a disease must personally have come into contact with it. The sick or "defiled" body of an individual was, very early on, considered in isolation from his relation to a territory and independently of his membership of a political community. In this branch of knowledge, as in the legal thought of Draco, but slightly earlier, any representation of a field of defilement covering an entire territory was ruled out, as was that of purification of a religious nature. The introduction of courts for crimes of bloodshed replaced the mythico-religious model of the Alcmeonid affair by a paradigm of a political nature, which prevailed from the time of Draco down to the Greek city of the fourth century B.C.. A murderer had to be kept away from a whole series of sensitive spots in the city space: he was forbidden to approach the basins placed at the entrances to sanctuaries and the agora; libations poured in honor of the gods, of whatever kind; the craters used in banquets, and likewise those that were sometimes set up in the streets; sanctuaries, altars, and all places consecrated to the special relations that obtained between the gods and human beings. The works of Aeschylus, Plato, and Antiphon all contain similar lists: a murderer could no longer live in his father's house, nor could he sacrifice on the altars of his deme or take lustral water in his phratry; he was to be kept away from the *nomima*, the traditional religious places and ceremonies; he was not to "defile" *(miainein)* sanctuaries, the public square, the ports, or any meeting place. He was publicly prohibited from all these, in a solemn announcement. A murderer was politically "excommunicated"; he ceased to take part in anything that contributed to the sociopolitical life of the citizens. Antiphon, or whoever wrote the *Tetralogies*, emphasized the transmission of defilement, using the term "to fill": "the *miasma* fills the innocents at the table at which the guilty one is seated." *Ana-* or *kata-* or *sunkata-pimplēnai* means "to fill by excess or saturation," particularly in the places where citizens eat and drink together, wherever assemblies, sacrifices, meetings, and banquets take place, where the citizens form a more or less homogeneous organism. Wherever sameness, *homoiotēs*, is practiced most actively, there is the greatest pressure from the murderer's defilement, which "fills the political community to excess." It is now a matter of political defilement rather than religious impurity. In the midst of the vicissitudes of his career as a murderer, Orestes, when on Athenian territory, finds himself obliged to drink and eat alone, even during the winter festival of new wine.

Another context in which we can get the measure of the peculiarities of Orestes is when we see the effects of the blood that is poured over the body and soul of a murderer. The Alcmeonids, defiled by the blood of the Cylonids, are soon labeled *enageis:* they are swallowed up by defilement, possessed, seized by its power, a power that is usually anonymous and genetic, but that sometimes takes the form of a daimon or an Erinye. As Plato remarks in the *Laws*,[9] "the tale is this—that the man slain by violence, who has lived in a free and proud spirit, is wroth with his slayer when newly slain, and being also filled with dread and horror on account of his own violent end, when he sees his murderer going about the very haunts which he himself had frequented, he is horror-stricken; and being disquieted himself, he takes conscience as his ally, and with all his might disquiets his slayer—both the man himself and his doings. Wherefore it is right for the slayer to retire before his victim for a full year, in all its seasons, and to vacate all the spots he owned in all parts of his native land." Representations such as this are not superseded by the legislation on bloodshed or by the delimitation of a political space that the murderer cannot share with his former co-citizens. For obscure and terrible links bind together the murderer and his "newly slain" victim *(neothnēs):* a mixture of anger, desire, and maddened fear. The verb *erinuein*, "to be angry," is very much present in the name of the Erinyes, the powers that are aroused by bloodshed. The victim, like the murderer, is *euthumios*, possessed by *thumos*, distressed, tormented by what he has to do or what he has done; he is preyed upon by fear, terror, horror. Not only is he himself driven mad, but in the full force of his madness, he also drives the murderer mad. Once suffered, violence calls out for violence in return. The murderer is engulfed by the very powers of fear and terror that upset the "newly dead" victim. The latter now harasses the one who shed his blood, denying him access to familiar haunts and at every moment invading his memory. If he is not to sink into madness or worse, the murderer must go into exile, desert the places formerly frequented by both his victim and himself, so as to escape the powers of the defilement, the "prostropaic" anger that is turned upon the murderer, taking possession of him and becoming identified with him.

It is worth comparing the Greek traditions and representations of defilements and territories, and victims and murderers, to those of some Amerindian and African societies. Some of these establish a close relation between a type of defilement and a particular social space through the intermediary of a power, in many cases anonymous, that "sanctions any defilement that occurs in its area of jurisdiction." A "field of defilement," to use the formula suggested by Michel Cartry and András Zempléni, seems to be conceived and defined as a physical space that incorporates the bodies of all those who belong to it. In such a case, a defilement is felt to be an attack upon the total social body. By way of reparation or purification of the defilement, the power of the afflicted body demands that its full health be restored through a redefinition of its boundaries. Such a purification or reparation takes the form of an encapsulation—or "enkystage," as Cartry and Zempléni call it—of, for example, the murderer within the group or the segment of space that has been contaminated. Even without developing the comparison on this particular point, a whole series of differences from the Greek world immediately becomes apparent. Among the Greeks no sexual defilement is ever assimilable to bloodshed, not even incest—which, anyway, in Greece is not regarded as a true *miasma*, for the social space of a particular lineage or an earth altar is not homologous to the political space of the groups of solidarity peculiar to the domain of a city. Contamination in the one case corresponds to saturation in the other, and the redefinition of boundaries through the "enkystage" of the murderer stands in opposition to the Greek custom of expelling the assassin, who is thereby invited to carve out a new space for himself, well away from his previous haunts. In a whole series of traditions of a mythical nature, the perpetrator of a murder is assessed, not within his own society, but in an open and alien space that Greek cities tend to regard as virgin, uncultivated, and belonging to no one.

The processes whereby the murderer and the victim are identified seem to offer the most interesting elements for a comparison between ancient societies and certain Amerindian and African ones. Initially, Orestes seems very unlike the image of the matricide that comes to predominate from Stesichorus of Himerus in Magna Graecia all the way across to Euripides' tragedy in Athens. In the *Odyssey* Orestes, determined to avenge his father, kills Aegisthus as well as Clytemnestra. Athena sings his praises to Telemachus, while Orestes, in Argos itself, performs the funeral rituals for his two victims and offers a funeral banquet to the whole community of Argives.[10] There is no mention of matricide, only of vengeance; no purification, no court judgment. The glory that Orestes wins for avenging his father illuminates the destiny of Telemachus and points toward the vengeful actions that unquestionably face Odysseus on his return. But in the mid-sixth century B.C., somewhere in Laconia, a quite different Orestes flees into the night to escape the murderous fury of Clytemnestra.[11] When summoned to Delphi, he is ordered by Apollo to shed the blood of his mother Clytemnestra and her lover. The god of Delphi gives his bow to the avenger, a bow that has already been well tested. Its deadly arrows will respect the Erinye that will rise from the freshly shed blood of Orestes' mother. The Apollo of Delphi knows all about defilement, exile, and terror. Years ago, in Argolis, following the murder of the Python, he was seized by such great terror—in a place "still" known as Terror—that he fled to Crete, to the only purifiers expert in cases of such major defilement. Apollo knows all about the paths that Orestes will have to tread, for he himself has been a murderous god, exiled, even impure; surrounded by the murderers who climb up to his dwelling in Delphi, he knows all about the assassin's horrifying possession by the victim, who surprises him without warning, hissing with anger.[12]

In 474 B.C. Pindar gave that impure, murderous god the name of Ares, the mad warrior, the master carried away by the violence of battle and slaughter.[13] But a little later, in Aeschylus' *Oresteia*, he is again Apollo, "the pure exile from heaven." Orestes, in the company of this god, experiences the threefold trials of exile, in order to wear away his defilement as he journeys; purification, so that the blood of an animal can wash him clean from the murder of his mother; and finally the human court of the Areopagus, on the hill of Ares, in order to regain a place in the city of men.

A whole collection of myths about Orestes, scattered through the Peloponnese, tells of the trials and tribulations of the murderer, the onslaughts suffered by his body, and the penances imposed upon him. In Achaea, in Cerynaea, there was a sanctuary called after the Eumenides, said to have been founded by Orestes in the course of his wanderings. It was a disturbing place, even though it bore the Erinyes' more moderate name: "Whoever enters with the desire to see the sights, if he be guilty of bloodshed, defilement or impiety, is said at once to become insane with fright." This was a chamber that contained all the madness and terrors that had assailed Orestes on the night of Clytemnestra's death, when her killer son leaped about as if possessed by Dionysus, in thrall to a hallucinatory vision of the "Three Virgins Who Resemble the Night."[14] In Arcadia, on the road leading from Megalopolis to Messene, there was another place through which Orestes had passed.[15] Both it and the neighboring countryside were known as The Furies. Here Orestes had a fit of madness during which, as he raved, he devoured part of his own hand, a finger, which he tore off and which was commemorated by a low tumulus known as the "monument to the finger," positioned a couple of paces away from the sanctuary consecrated to the Furies. Facing this first sanctuary was another, known as the sanctuary of Healing (Akē), likewise consecrated to the Eumenides. When the Furies descended upon him, Orestes saw their black faces, but once that fragment of himself had been amputated, the same powers took on a white and luminous aspect. At this sight of them, Orestes is supposed to have recovered his wits and, to ensure his recovery, offered up two blood sacrifices. One was of an expiatory nature *(enagidzein)*, in honor of the Black Goddesses and designed to ward off their wrath. The other, which involved food, was addressed to the White Powers, who were summoned to receive it along with the Graces or Charites. After this, one last sacrifice, known as an offering "of shorn hair," was made, to mark the end of Orestes' madness and the recovery of his wits. This was the sacrifice known as the Coureion, in which Orestes cut off his long, madman's locks, as if he had been reborn and had become one of the youths whose accession to adulthood was marked, in Athens, by a Coureion sacrifice of the shearings from sheep and goats, in honor of boys growing their first beards at the onset of puberty.

Orestes was threatened by dreadful misfortunes, all foreseen by Delphi: "Apollo's oracle . . . spoke of sicknesses, / Ulcers that ride upon the flesh, and cling, and with / Wild teeth eat away the natural tissue, [and] on this / Disease shall grow in turn a leprous fur."[16] Whether Orestes forwent avenging his father or shed the blood of his mother, he was open to attack, and his own body would experience the violence of the death of one or the other of his parents. He would either be one of the living dead, or else committed to an act of self-cannibalism, apparently having to offer a piece of his own flesh to the victim who had invaded his body, before he could return to the socialized form of sacrifice, on an altar, of victims that could once again be shared. In Troezen, in Argolis, a severely tested Orestes was subjected to a long process of purification.[17] Nine citizens set about the task of freeing him from the defilement of bloodshed. During this treatment, Orestes was lodged in a hut built opposite the sanctuary of Apollo (for certainly nobody wished to receive him in his home). The purification seems to have taken place in two phases: first on the sacred stone set up before the temple of Artemis, and then in the isolated hut where the purifiers were keeping him alive until such time as he ceased to be impure. The diet of the murderer was an important aspect of the treatment for, as Pausanias noted, even in his day the descendants of those who had purified Orestes still took their meals there on certain predetermined days. Everything used in the purification was buried close to what was known as "Orestes' hut": the remains of sacrifical victims, and also various kinds of medecines, for it was said that the purifiers had resorted to several procedures, in particular to the use of water from the Horse's Fountain. This was water associated with the power of a horse born from the earth, similar to the terrible water of the Styx, which circulated deep within Gaia: namely, the power of oaths.

When poured over the murderer, blood possessed even greater powers to purify him from the defilement of bloodshed than water did, even particularly potent water such as that mentioned: "Those who are defiled by blood seek to purify themselves with more blood."[18] Heraclitus had no occasion to refer specifically to Orestes in that ironical comment. Orestes was not the only murderer or criminal possessed by a defilement who underwent the kind of purification by blood that certain "charlatans," denounced by the Hippocratic treatises, recommended as a treatment for "epileptics" suffering from the so-called "sacred disease."[19] But in the *Oresteia* the matricide Orestes himself relates how he was purified by Apollo, at Delphi, in the sanctuary of the god known as Phoebus, the Pure One: "My blot of matricide is being washed away. / When it was fresh still, at the hearth of the god Phoebus, / This was absolved and driven out by sacrifice / Of swine."[20] Apollo acts as a purifier, using one of his altars, possibly that reserved for Hestia, the power of the domesticated and the sacrificial fire, which was positioned in the *megaron*, or chamber, of Apollo. Like a priest performing a purification by blood, the god pours over Orestes' head and shoulders the blood of a piglet, the sacrificial victim that produces the most copious flow of the life-giving liquid. A crater now in the Louvre Museum, found at Armento, shows Orestes seated on the altar of Apollo, being showered by the blood of a victim held above him, as if he himself is a living altar spattered by the red lifeblood of the sacrificed animal.[21]

Marie Delcourt pays special attention to these procedures for the regeneration of murderers who, as a result of their exile, have already been transformed into the living dead. She suggests that the position taken up by the murderer identifies him with a newborn child laid beneath the bleeding placenta, *delphus* in Greek, a word very close to that which designates a sucking pig, *delphaks.* She even shows that certain live individuals, considered to be dead following their disappearance or funeral rites conducted in error, were subjected to a ritual of rebirth.[22] Without excluding the possibility that rebirth is explicitly symbolized here, it is perhaps worth also drawing attention to how the Troezen ritual specifically formulates the sacrificial treatment in terms of a commemorative commensality involving both the purifiers and their descendants, a commensality that confirms that a special diet was reserved for the murderer shut away in his hut. The altar duplicated by the scene of purification through the intermediary of blood from a sacrificial victim suggests a similar meaning: the murderer, who is so violently excluded from the circle of those who participate in sacrifice as a Greek social and political ritual, makes his way back to the ritual of sacrifice partly, to be sure, by dint of founding the odd altar here or there and himself offering up special sacrifices that are designed to separate the Eumenides from the Erinyes, but also—and more radically—by himself acting as an altar founded by the blood of a victim shed by a god such as Apollo, the god who is so well known as a founder of sacrifices, altars, and sanctuaries.

Two other ritual procedures followed by murderers anxious to prevent the anger of their victim rebounding against them should perhaps be interpreted within the same sacrificial context. The one involved lapping up the blood pouring from the victim's wounds, then spitting it into the dead man's mouth. In the other, the murderer cut off the corpse's extremities, the hands, nose, and ears, which he then festooned like an oversized necklace, passed under the corpse's armpits, or which he simply placed upon the victim's body.[23] The latter practice was known as *maschalismos*, a term also used for the offering made to the gods in animal sacrifices. This consisted of small pieces of raw flesh cut from all over the body's surface and then placed on top of the haunches set to burn on the altar. These *maschalismata*, already attested by the ancient lexicographers and now confirmed by a sacred Attic law,[24] were the equivalent of the first fruits, *apargmata*, offered by the murderer who lapped up the blood of his victim and then spat it into the latter's mouth. In both cases the corpse was treated as the victim of a sacrifice, not of a murder. Such rituals, which turned the victim's corpse into a sacrificial victim, made it possible for the murderer not to flee the sacrificial space from which the blood shed by a human being would forthwith have excluded him, forcing him into a flight attended by hallucinating horrors, probably into perpetual exile.

Orestes is the focus of the most vivid of the representations of the links forged between a victim and his murderer in the very period that seemed to establish a view of homicide that was liberated from all this welter of defilements, bonds, and purification rituals, which seem to belong to a time before Draco and before the establishment of courts designed to rule on cases of bloodshed within the new space of the city. There is yet another concept that needs to be included in those imaginary representations centered on Orestes: the murderer who, by treating himself, regains his value as a human being. For certain aspects of this figure are detectable in the stories about Orestes, the matricide driven mad. Instead of allowing himself to be caught in the net of terrifying and convulsive bonds from which he would not be able to escape until he had completed a long and dangerous series of rituals, a murderer had another possibility open to him. He could immediately neutralize the effects of the bloodshed by brutally severing all his links with his own territory and social group. He could exclude himself, thereby immediately becoming one of the living dead, a creature with no rights, no home, no possessions, no relations with the gods. By departing from his former territory, such a man left behind him the violence and power of his "newly dead" victim. He was one of the living dead, given respite until such time as he reached the sanctuary of Delphi, an extraterritorial place where he could obtain from the master of the oracle permission to set off in quest of a new territory, seeking a space where he could settle, live, and found a new city, for without one there could be no home or social life for him. In Delphi, and only in Delphi, murderers who chose to exile themselves could meet the god who was himself once a murderer and an exile and who could open up the way for them to find a territory without a past and free from memories of the blood that had been shed and the links that used to bind him. The ex-murderer changed himself, as had Apollo, into a founder who, after his death, was destined to become a glorious Archegetēs whom the new city recognized as its common and immediate ancestor. Such murderers are more imaginary than real (at least in our retrospective documentation), but in the colonizing Greece of the eighth to the fifth centuries B.C., they testify to the inaugural virtues of a murderer who managed to purify himself by separating radically from his earlier identity.[25] He was an individual who refounded himself in a "political" mode, in the Greek manner of an autonomous city that could implant itself on any available spot on the earth's skin.[26]

CHAPTER TWELVE

At Lycaon's Table

The table stood at 4,500 feet, in the heart of Arcadia. It was situated at the top of Mount Lycaeus. So Lycaon, the wolf *(lukos)*, operated on Mount Lycaeus. He was Lycaon, the wolfman of Mount Lycaeus.[1]

No sooner was it set up than Lycaon's table was overturned. It was an unsteady table. Was it even a table at all? Was it not rather a kind of half-constructed, half-natural altar on the top of a hill rising into the sky? And who were the guests invited to the banquet of Mount Lycaeus? The whole affair—for an affair it undoubtedly was—appears to be shrouded in the greatest uncertainty.

It all began with a desire of Lycaon's. I too am in Arcadia, he said.[2] And there, indeed, he stayed, never leaving it. In which respect he certainly differed from another extremely ancient inhabitant of Mount Lycaeus, one whose name was Pan and who, for his part, later erupted into history, in Attica, creating a stir on the eve of the battle of Marathon.[3] The only link between Aristotle's Lyceum and Lycaon's Mount Lycaeus seems to have been a god, a wolf god, namely Apollo, who had characteristics in common with a wolf prowling along the boundaries between one city and another.[4]

Let us first consider Arcadia, and the place reserved there for Lycaon in a genealogical story that is also the story of a particular landscape. Arcadia's antiquity is absolute, its autochthony unrivaled. Pelasgus, the first man to live in Arcadia, appeared there before ever the moon rose into the sky alongside the sun. One fine day, before the startled eyes of Sun, Earth (Gaia) produced that first man, in the leafy mountain woods. He resembled a god *(antitheos)*, which is not surprising, for the race of human beings was born from Gaia, just like the race of the gods. Pelasgus was a contemporary of Cronos and Rhea, the Earth's divine children.[5]

Having become king of the human species, Pelasgus made his mark with a set of decisive inventions: the first dwellings, which afforded protection against both the cold and the great heat, and the first clothes, made from sheepskins. Next, the good king Pelasgus dissuaded his people from eating leaves and sucking roots, some of which could be deadly poisonous, and led them to discover how tasty the precious acorns were, along with all the other virtues of the oak tree: that one tree provided them with both sustenance and roofs over their heads.[6]

In such genealogies, it is customary for the next stage to come as no great surprise: what usually follow are cereal foods, the making of bread, and the weaving of cloth. And all these things were indeed introduced in the reign of Arcas, after whom Arcadia is appropriately named.[7] Before tasting the Arcadian bread produced by that baker king, however, the human race lived through the reign of Lycaon. He was a just and pious king, even a founder of towns, and was also famous for a table and an altar set up in honor of a god as new as himself. But there were some who claimed that Lycaon's table, defiled by human blood, was overturned and that Lycaon thereupon assumed the form of a wolf.[8] The Arcadians discovered, earlier than most peoples, that progress is not necessarily irreversible and that regression is always a possibility in the history of humankind.

In the mountains of Arcadia, ambiguous figures were common enough. One such was Pan, the goat god, a native example of a hybrid in a form partly animal, partly human. Pan was a very Arcadian god, operating midway between hunting and agriculture. His animal laughter would shatter the silent byways; "panic" would take hold of a campaigning army and in an instant disintegrate it; in the full light of day the goat god would appear, his phallus erect. "Panic" was spread by sound coming from nowhere, a bodiless voice, violence, and unpredictability.[9] In the tradition stemming from Epimenides of Crete,[10] this god who dwelled in Arcadia was said to be the twin of Arcas, the baker of bread and the amiable weaver of cloth who was so close to Demeter.

Arcas himself was also an ambiguous figure, for he was the son of Lycaon's daughter, the beautiful Calliste.[11] She was seduced by Zeus while out hunting with Artemis, and was then rejected and transformed into a bear, which gave birth, in the bushes, to a child. Soon this wild child was captured and taken to Lycaon. He was allowed to live in semi-liberty in the vicinity of Mount Lycaeus. One day Lycaon decided to offer up to the newly named Zeus a meal worthy of such a great god, and the child Arcas was carefully cut into pieces and served up to him. But that was not the end of Arcas' story. Zeus put him back together and reshaped him, and he went on not only to become the hero of the life of cultivated wheat but also, in his turn, to provide an example of how difficult it is to identify beings that are hybrid and ambiguous. On another day, Arcas mistakenly entered the forbidden precinct of the sanctuary, while in pursuit of a female bear or a bearlike woman. He even—God alone knows why—tried to seize her and make love to her. Fortunately, however, when Zeus, the master of the sanctuary, so willed it, that prohibited space would steal the shadow of any live intruder, thereby condemning him either to death or to metamorphosis.

Demeter was there to warn the Arcadians of the law that made, for them, a return to an earlier state always possible. At Phigalia, she was known as the Black Demeter,[12] a resentful deity. Clad in dark clothing, she lurked alone deep in her cave, where she lived silently, well apart from human beings and from the other gods. The land withered, famine was rife, and the gods grew alarmed. Only Pan was able to find Demeter's hiding place. Eventually the Fates or Moirai managed to persuade her to adopt a better attitude, after which the cereal crops once again flourished.

In Phigalia, Black Demeter delighted in receiving offerings of the old kind: the fruits of shrubs, grapes, honeycombs, untreated wool still impregnated with grease. Primitive offerings such as these were left at the entrance to her cave, sprinkled with oil. But one day the offerings failed to appear. The goddess was angered by this neglect, and sterility returned. Through the mouth of the Pythia, in Delphi, Demeter informed the people of Arcadia that not only would they revert from being eaters of cereals to a nomadic life, but furthermore she, the Black Goddess, was ready to send them back to a time even before they became eaters of acorns and wild fruits. Soon they would be eating one another and would be devouring their own children. They would revert to tecnophagy or "paedophagy."[13] In the Arcadians' stories of their past, that time of allelophagy threatened by Demeter echoed the misadventure that befell Lycaon on Mount Lycaeus. This episode was an integral part of the official fourth-century B.C. tradition and is mentioned by Plato in the *Republic*, in the passage devoted to tyrannical man.[14] In the town of Megalopolis, the newly built capital of Arcadia, founded in 369 B.C., the Arcadians built a faithful replica of the sanctuary of Zeus Lycaeus.[15]

This is the point at which to introduce a digression on the practice of sacrifice, the ritual that imparts meaning to Lycaon's table manners. When the practice of sacrifice is central to a society's customs, it leads sometimes to interrelations between human beings, sometimes to relations with the supernatural world. Those are the two major purposes of the practice of sacrifice. In the first case, the sacrificial scene leads into social relations, genealogies, marriage rules, ancestrality. That is certainly the dominant model in West Africa. Sacrifice there has to do with birth: the immolation of the victim evokes not murder but parturition, the gesture of the midwife as she cuts the umbilical cord and detaches the placenta, which is considered to be every living creature's twin, the substantial form taken by the "Other," that is to say, the supernatural.[16]

Meanwhile, in Vedic India, the practice of sacrifice gives access to supernatural powers, deities that are identified, mobilized, or even fabricated at the point when, through the offering of a victim within the sacrificial space, relations and links are established between them and the human beings making the sacrifice. Sometimes, indeed, sacrifice is considered to antedate even the existence of the gods and of men.[17]

In the Greek world to which both Arcadia and the drama of Lycaon belong, the practice of sacrifice is oriented by a dietary and sociopolitical vector. The major type of sacrifice, which involves the ritual slaughter of an animal victim, always a domesticated one, is the basis for the distinction between the gods, who feed on savory smells and aromas, and the human species, which feeds on meat. But those meals of meat are divided up according to egalitarian procedures that operate as table manners—manners that are, no doubt, very elementary yet are decisive, since it is through them that each individual belongs to human society and is formally anchored in the political community. The practice of sacrifice thus makes it possible to distinguish among men, beasts, and gods, and it furthermore functions as an egalitarian machine, for the sacrifice of animal flesh serves as a means of expressing the equal rights of all those taking part.[18] In Greece, the place for true civility is elsewhere—at a banquet, in a symposium. Lycaon's table belongs to a time long before the civilities of the banquet became established. Lycaon was famous above all for his table. But Pausanias, who was an expert on Arcadian antiquity, praises the ingenious discoveries with which this son and successor of Pelasgus was credited,[19] of which he emphasizes three in particular. Lycaon founded Lycosura, the city positioned on Mount Lycaeus, known as the "wolf mountain." Also, he was the first to give Zeus the name Lycaeus. And it was he who inaugurated the first Games, those held during the Lycaea festival—panhellenic Games that included a whole series of gymnastic tests. Lycaon, the founder and creator of games and names, marked a definite break from the times of Pelasgus, the age of berry gathering and makeshift huts, when the earliest human beings, although so poor and so helpless, seem not to have been conscious of any distance separating them from the race of the gods. Of Lycaon's three innovations—a space for agonistic competition, the city, and the naming of a god—the last was the most decisive. When he named Zeus, the Zeus of this particular place, Lycaon was designating what, for him, was "the supernatural Other," and at the same stroke he instituted its cult. Lycaon created a separation between human beings and the gods. In this respect his reign was distinguished from that of Pelasgus and is perfectly homologous with that of Cecrops, his Athenian contemporary. Once again Pausanias is our informant.[20] A name creates a form, and from this there develops a particular way of establishing relations with that new form. It was said that the autochthonous Athenian was the first to call Zeus "the highest one," *hypsistos*. Cecrops, prudently, chose to establish the greatest possible distance between Zeus and humankind, and he limited his offerings to the gods to cereals and locally made cakes, which were deposited on an altar constructed specially for that purpose. Lycaon, in contrast, who seems to have decided to give his god virtually the same name as his own, boldly embarked upon the practices of blood sacrifice. He shed blood for the Lycaean god, spattering it all over his altar and even insisting that the first victim to be sacrificed to him should come from the human race. A local child was slaughtered for the purpose.[21] As we know, the consequences were disastrous. In the very place where the ceremony was carried out, Lycaon was suddenly changed into a wolf, or else was consumed in fire sent from the sky, for the Zeus of Mount Lycaeus was a god of the dark heavens, who wielded the thunderbolt.[22]

In another, related, version, transmitted by the historian Hecataeus of Miletus, who was active in the late sixth century, Lycaon and his sons were, right from the start, impious and arrogant people.[23] As soon as Zeus was named the Zeus "of Lycaon," or Lycaean Zeus, he determined to test his arrogant partner. He disguised himself as a day laborer and, seeming to be a poor manual cultivator *(chernētēs)*, knocked at the door of Lycaon's house. The family immediately invited him to lunch with them. In his honor, Lycaon's sons seized a little native boy, slaughtered him, and mixed his viscera with the dishes set on the table, making it a table of horror—which, with a violent gesture, Zeus overturned and there and then consumed Lycaon's family in the flames of his thunderbolt. In yet another version, that of Nicolas of Damascus,[24] Lycaon's own piety stands in contrast to the impiety of his descendants. Here, Lycaon is a just king, who reveres Zeus and also strangers. But his sons want to discover whether the stranger invited by their father really is a god. That is why, in the kitchen, they secretly slaughter a child, cut him into pieces, and mix his flesh with that of an animal victim sacrificed in honor of the guest.

Lycaon is struck down by a thunderbolt, his male descendants are destroyed by fire, and all that remains in the sanctuary of Mount Lycaeus is the vestige of an overturned table.[25] From that time on, each year, following a sacrifice offered in honor of Zeus Lycaeus, one man who has eaten at the secret table there is changed into a wolf. If that wolf abstains from eating human flesh, after nine years it resumes a human form. But the wolves that do eat human flesh remain wolves forever. In this sacrificial space cleared by Lycaon in Arcadia, the human sacrificer always wavers uneasily between being a beast and being a man. In this case, a diet of meat does not have the happy effect of keeping man at an equal and constant distance midway between the power possessed by the gods and the savagery of wild beasts.

Why did Lycaon, the master of the famous table, so boldly embark upon the course of blood sacrifice? Perhaps it was his wolf's instinct that turned him into a born sacrificer.[26] The behavior of Lycaon in his native Arcadia seems to a large extent borne out by other Greek stories about wolves and other canine creatures. Bestiaries, Aesop's fables, and the observations of zoologists, first and foremost Aristotle, all suggest that the wolf is, by nature, the most skillful of butchers and the best of cooks. It uses its powerful jaws like a sharp knife, neatly slitting its victim's throat so that the blood spurts out. And the wolf also knows how to cut the flesh into portions. The sources are categorical on the subject: with its teeth, the wolf tears the meat into pieces all of exactly the same weight. These spontaneously "political" animals are even seen to introduce a social contract, proposing in their assemblies to place the booty from the hunt in common so that each individual present obtains an equal share. So, according to apprentice legislators, famished wolves should no longer be seen as attacking each other in a sad show of allelophagy. The wolf, at once a butcher and a cook, a sacrificer and a political creature, seems to possess all the qualities required for founding an *isonomic* city, opening up a political space based on respect for equal rights before the law.

Yet no sooner have they spelled out the rules of communal life than the wolves violate and transgress them. No sooner do they approach the table of equal and exemplary shares than they abandon it—or else it is overturned. Why is it that—and here again the tradition is unanimous[27]—all the wolf's attempts at sacrifice and commensality are doomed to failure? A furtive word must be said about this, as it were, behind Lycaon's back. Through its very physiological nature, it is impossible for the wolf to envisage being separated from the weapon of sacrifice, for the instrument that so accurately performs the gestures of sacrifice and sacificial cooking is part of its own body. The wolf is consitituted physically in such a way that there can be no separation between "killing" and "eating." Although it is necessary to kill to obtain meat to eat, the murderer and its "knife" must not approach the dining table. Commensality demands that they be kept out of the sacrificial space.

Now let us leave the wolf and return to Lycaon and the table he set up on Mount Lycaeus. With all the authority of a virtually official tradition, in all their variants the texts surrounding Lycaon through a variety of experimental procedures explore the ambiguous aspects of the scene of sacrifice.[28] In the first place, the setting itself is ambiguous: the mountain peak to which Lycaon first summons the form of a god is called Olympus by the people of Arcadia—Olympus, the very same name as that of the home of the distant gods, and one that furthermore evokes a time before sacrifice had been introduced.[29] This was the place of, if not Zeus' birth, at least his childhood, and the Arcadian tradition confirms the Olympian nature of its local mountain when it describes the constant flow from what was known as the "most pure spring," Hagnō, which produced an unvarying amount of water in summer and winter alike.[30] Lycaon took possession of this Olympus and there set up a table that also did service as an altar, which, in principle, was reserved for that "Other" presence upon which he had just recently conferred a name.[31]

Just as Lycaon's Olympus was not really distinguishable from the sanctuary precinct or from a domain in which human beings and the gods kept within their respective limits, Lycaon's altar seemed indistinguishable from his table. On certain occasions the one seemed to merge with the other, particularly in the shadow cast by a priest.[32] However, it was infinitely preferable that the blood of the sacrificial victim should spurt forth onto the altar and not onto the table, and that the place reserved for the commensality of men should be clearly distinct from the altar assigned to the deity. Lycaon's table has the look of a table for experiments. "What is a god?" its master asked. Might a god present himself in the guise of a stranger? How can the ancient commensality with the gods be differentiated from the new commensality of people eating together grouped around an altar? Is a table radically different from an altar and, if so, in what respect? Was it not necessary to put the uncertain form of the "Other" to the test by offering him a living creature, born in the land of Arcadia, a wild child who could grace Lycaon's table just as well as Zeus'?

Armed with his scalpel, Lycaon, at his table, tried to do what Socrates, in the *Phaedrus*,[33] claims that any good dialectician ought to be able to manage: namely, to "divide things by classes, where the natural joints are," as does a competent butcher *(mageiros)*. But Lycaon, in his world of ambiguous forms, failed to distinguish, separate, and differentiate the things that sacrifices everywhere else succeed in distinguishing, analyzing, and delimiting.

In the Greek memories of the archaic past, Lycaon of Arcadia and his secret rituals seem to confirm the impossibility of a radical division among humans, animals, and the gods. Behind the table, Mount Lycaeus is shaken by the deep laughter of Pan.

Part IV / Writing Mythology

CHAPTER THIRTEEN

An Inventive Writing, the Voice of Orpheus, and the Games of Palamedes

According to the Greeks, writing was not only invented but also inventive, for the discovery of that new object that we call the alphabetic system was apprehended, reflected upon, and thought about in a series of stories, fictions, and forgeries, all of them fascinated by the inventiveness of letters, those twenty-four graphic signs capable of visually representing all the sounds and whispers of language. In recent years scholars have pondered the relation between, on the one hand, writing, the alphabetic instrument of the Greeks, and, on the other, their early thought and the great intellectual advances that it made in geometry, philosophical discourse, politics, medical understanding, and legal practice. These investigations, which soon became collective, seem to offer an approach that is valid yet differs somewhat from two others. Of these two, one has in past years encouraged a rethinking about Greek culture before Plato, emphasizing the essential complementarity of orality and writing, and going so far as to suggest that an understanding of oral composition ought to provide the key to an understanding of the written culture: the laws of orality ought to reveal the rules of literary production, in each of its genres. Meanwhile, the other approach, more philosophically motivated, opened up the domain of writing to the voice and to the slightest marks of *différence*, postulating a kind of transcendence for writing, the dazzling light of which threatened to blind us to intellectual operations generated here and there by certain decisive practices of writing.

Today there is one question that seems especially pertinent to the Greek world: namely, the autonomy of writing. Does not writing, *graphein*, suggest not only tracing, engraving, drawing, and inscribing, but also an intellectual activity? And might it not create or invent new subjects for thought, which in return might transform certain ways of thinking? An investigation along these lines might be justified by the specifically Greek formulations that surface in the stories that intermesh around the figures whom the Greeks regard as the inventors of writing. As markers in this new field, I have selected from among those discoverers Palamedes and Orpheus, thinking that, given that those two were attracted to opposite poles, they might afford us a comprehensive glimpse of what the Greeks themselves thought of writing as a physical production—that is to say, letters, books, and writing tablets. With what types of invention was writing associated or contrasted? In what categories of more or less novel objects was it classified, and according to what conscious criteria? Finally, from what type of activity does writing stem? What type of intelligence is it thought to mobilize or use? To what powers is it linked, delegated, or provisionally allotted?

I should like to begin the present inquiry into the cognitive potentialities of writing and its heroes in the Este region of Venetia, two thousand years before Isabella became the marchesa of Mantua and took such an interest in the Invenzione, a collection of pictures and paintings assembled in the Studiolo. In the 1960s a rather strange discovery was made in the territory of the Venetii: a sanctuary dating from 500 B.C. The offerings found in its precinct consisted of a collection of writing materials: alphabetical tablets, bronze engraving chisels, and styluses. Linguists expert in the Venetian language tell us that the deity of this literary temple was called Reitia, the One Who Writes, who engraves (the root **rei* has the same meaning as the root of *graphein*). Reitia, the goddess of the activity of writing, reigned over a large scriptorium, the archives of which have come down to us in the form of metal tablets that were covered with wax, on which letters could be written, writing exercises engraved as dedications to Reitia, whose name is in each case inscribed at the top. The goddess of writing received, as homage, complete spelling primers, lists of letters, lists of vowel groups, and the fifteen consonants repeated sixteen times over. Thanks to this collection of offerings, historians of Italic writing have been able to produce a detailed history of the diffusion of Venetian, starting with the model alphabet of the Etruscans and concluding with the alphabet of consonants diffused, together with syllabic punctuation, by a literate clergy. It was in a similar sanctuary that, under the patronage of Reitia, priests familiar with Etruscan, Greek, and Latin invented a writing and a language that was diffused by scholarly teaching, which operated by using letters rather than sounds, appealing to the concept of words, and concentrating on reproducing these in isolation from any particular context.

At about the same time, around 500 B.C., in the region of Aphrati or Lyttos, in Crete, a small Greek city drew up a contract on the basis of which it engaged a scribe called Spensithios, an expert in Phoenician or "purple" letters. His job, clearly specified, was to write, to record in writing all public business, both religious and civic, both the affairs of the gods and the affairs of men, as the Greek text puts it, so that these should be remembered. The scribe Spensithios was engaged for life, with responsibilities that were to be hereditary and a rank that was equal to that of the *cosme*, the chief magistrate of the city. This master of writing, this writer who suddenly made his appearance in the mountains of Crete, seems a less strange figure once he is associated with a series of others who emerged between 520 and 480. Archaic statues of scribes stood on the Acropolis. The figures were seated stiffly, in a hieratic, Egyptian-looking pose, with their writing tablets on their knees. In the Eleatic territory, at Olympia, there were "clerks" who headed the colleges of magistrates. Similarly, in Teos, a new master of Phoenician letters appeared, a *phoinikographeus*, who was required to read out curses against those who attempted to undermine the political constitution, curses that he himself had engraved in the name of the city.

It seems that at the end of the sixth century some Greeks were tempted to set up scribes as masters of writing, but they avoided that temptation. For, however great his privileges, the scribe was first and foremost a magistrate, unlike the priests of Venetia, assembled around the sanctuary of writing. In Crete and in Teos, the man who wrote in Phoenician or purple letters did so for the citizens as a whole; he did it for the city, which had decided to set out its laws and decisions in writing. In contrast, the Etruscan setting of the Venetian priests is reminiscent of the civilization of the banks of the Euphrates and the oriental tradition of Mesopotamian scribes. It is a matter of a difference of inspiration, for it was from Etruria that the Romans, and we ourselves, too, derived the idea of book deities, gods who dictated or wrote, "opening a new furrow":

the Etruscan religion was founded upon great books. It was just such books of divine origin or inspiration that in Rome encouraged the idea that a civilized people should rely on prestigious written texts. Sumer was subject to Enki, the sovereign god who carried on his chest the tablet of destinies; in Babylon, the gods were constantly recording reality; in Egypt, the god Thoth reigned. In contrast, the Greek gods were positive illiterates, and remained so until the Hellenistic age. In Greece, it was men who kept written records of both their own affairs and the affairs of the gods, or at least of those who were integrated into the politico-religious system. The temples, the sanctuaries of the gods, belonged to the public domain in which the decisions of the assembly were made public and the decrees of the city were posted up in the agora, the public square, for all to read.

It was in this context that writing acquired a first and crucial measure of autonomy: between the figure of the scribe employed in the service of the city and the confirmed public space, the idea of *isonomia* took shape—equality before the law, a law that was written down for the rich and the poor alike. Concurrently, in Samos, in about 350, one of the first geometric formulations of the civic space was produced by a scribe, a "grammatist" employed by Polycrates. Meanwhile, in Miletus, the philosopher Anaximander was bold enough to draw (write) the first map of the inhabited earth, and with the introduction of spherical astronomy, written geometry took off, discovering the ideal properties of subjects such as right angles and circles.

Sandwiched between gods indifferent to writing tablets and men busy with their scriptural practices, writing found itself a hero. His name, Palamedes, conveys an idea of his skill. *Palamē* was the word for the palm, the hand that seizes hold and makes things and is capable of sleight of hand and the dexterity shown by a potter with his wheel or a helmsman guiding his boat: an inventive and instrumental hand that has mastered many techniques and skills. Palamedes was anything but cackhanded: he was a winner, whatever the game. He figures in the *Cypria*, the seventh-century B.C. epic by Stasinus of Cyprus, which traces the origin of the Trojan War down to the point where the *Iliad* begins. In this poem comprising eleven books, Palamedes is represented as a rival of the *polutropos* Odysseus, the man of a thousand tricks and the hero of cunning intelligence. Their rivalry begins when Palamedes foils the subterfuge employed by Telemachus' father, who feigns madness to avoid having to go off to make war on Troy. On several occasions when the Greeks find themselves in a quandary, it is Palamedes who finds the way out. He is skilled at getting them out of tight corners.

He arouses the jealousy and hatred of Odysseus, who kills him during a fishing expedition, in the course of which Palamedes no doubt tried to show off his nets and traps to him and Diomedes, who helped to perpetrate this murder at sea. The story, quite often used by Aeschylus, Sophocles, and Euripides, shows now one, now the other of these heroes of inventive intelligence in alternating episodes in which Palamedes seems all the more dazzlingly noble when set in contrast to his rival in cleverness, who is led to plot his ruin in the most dastardly way. Palamedes' fate was thus to die young, midway between the earth and the sea, and between great expectations and false starts. But his short life was filled with ceaseless intellectual activity, a whole series of discoveries and inventions of the most diverse nature. He was the first to plan the positions of the army beneath the walls of Troy and to organize the night watch. But in addition this tactician-cum-logistics expert (he also masterminded the army supplies) invented the games of draughts and knucklebones, trictrac (an early form of backgammon) and the first dice. He invented the spelling book, the alphabet, and ingenious numbering, "that most eminent of discoveries," and, in parallel, the science of weights and measures. He seems an alternative to Aeschylus' Prometheus, one who, as he listed his inventions, could, like Prometheus, claim: "For the whole of Greece I have imposed order upon an existence hitherto confused and similar to the condition of animals."

His many and diverse inventions were prompted neither by necessity nor by want. Palamedes is not noted for discoveries, such as fire, clothing, or forms of sustenance, that would mark out the separation between men and beasts. Rather, his inventiveness and heuristic fecundity flourished in tight situations, times of crisis and apparent *aporia*, when there appeared to be no way out: a famine, for example. The Greek army was pinned down at Aulis, supplies were insufficient, and the available food was unfairly divided. Discontent was rife, rebellion simmering. Palamedes took the matter in hand, introducing the troops to Phoenician letters and using them, in this situation in particular, to organize the distribution of rations. So effective was his method that the unrest died down once the men could see that the allotment of food was not only just but irreproachable: each received an identical portion of the same weight. In such circumstances, letters could be used as numbers. At the same time, during this phony war in Aulis, when boredom was demoralizing the troops, Palamedes produced dice from his pockets and handed out *psēphoi*, pebbles or counters, through which the Greek army discovered the pleasure of guessing weights and measures.

The common factor behind an alphabet, counters, games of chance, and series of numbers lay not only in Palamedes' active intelligence but also in certain deep affinities that, for the Greeks, linked objects that we might tend to classify in different categories. Before the appearance of what is known as the acrophonic system, the letters of the alphabet also served to designate numbers. Numerical notation used the signs of the alphabet, so that to know one's letters was also to know one's numbers. And, like all Greeks, Plato considered that there was no radical difference between counting and games such as knucklebones, dice, or trictrac. Among the inventions of Thoth, the *Phaedrus* places numbers and letters on the same level as geometry and trictrac, or dice and astronomy. In Greece, calculations were usually made using counters called *psēphoi*, a word also used for accounting units, voting tokens, counters for board games, and the knucklebones used in divinatory practices, in oracular consultations. The difference between a gaming table and a calculating table is so slight that, when archaeologists chance to come upon such objects in the course of excavations, it is impossible to tell which they were. An abacus or a calculating table would take the form of a stone or wooden surface marked by *diagrammata*, tables made up of lines sometimes parallel, sometimes divided by a transversal, perpendicular line. Similarly, a whole tradition shows that the *psēphoi* counters represented units that constituted a "set" endowed with particular properties. The old man in Plato's *Laws* remarks that there is not much difference between playing trictrac with dice and counters, and busying oneself with studies relating to commensurable and incommensurable quantities. As Socrates says in the *Gorgias*, both are affairs of *logos*.

This speculative aspect of writing veering toward numbers and geometry is balanced, amid the activities of Palamedes, by a more literate dimension that leads one to reflect upon the potentialities of writing in general. First came a practical discovery made by an expert in communications: it involved signaling by means of bonfires, a code, and a message relayed through the darkness from one signal point to the next. When the time would come for Palamedes' father Nauplius to avenge his son, he would light misleading signals to lure the ships of the Greeks and wreck them on the reefs. Even before that, Nauplius was to learn of Palamedes' unjust death from another message: a letter engraved on the oars of a ship. The epistolary genre figured at the heart of the speech in praise of writing that Palamedes made before a court where he appeared, charged with high treason. "Anyone who is away and has crossed the expanse of the seas can know exactly what is happening far away, in his own house and his own country." He was referring to the missive-letter, a mute thing that could make its voice heard as far away as was desired and that, mysteriously, made the rest of those present seem deaf when the eyes of its recipient read it in silence (silent reading came to be practiced in Greece at a very early date, whatever Augustine may claim). Another product of letter writing was the will, known as a disposition, which was indeed initially a "disposition" or arrangement of letters and words. "A dying man can let his sons know, in writing, how he is dividing up his fortune, and each heir knows what he is receiving." What Euripides' Palamedes has in mind is a sealed, written text, as was commonly used in the fifth century, a unilateral will that could in this way remain secret until it took effect after the writer's death. Palamedes foretold the omnipotence of writing: "The misfortunes provoked by quarrels and disputes can be ended by a tablet, a tablet that rules out lies." But the man who thus professed his absolute faith in the truth of letters and writing was to die the victim of false writing: a forgery devised by Odysseus to destroy Palamedes, his rival. A false letter, purporting to be from Priam, was dictated under cover of night to a Phrygian prisoner and, together with Trojan gold to pay for services rendered, was dropped treacherously on the pathway running through the Greek camp. This written forgery, constituting convicting evidence against Palamedes, condemned to death the hero of letters, who had proclaimed that an invisible voice could make itself heard through mute signs; it was matched, in tragic fashion, by the message Palamedes' brother engraved on a ship's oar. But in its intention to punish the betrayers, this aroused all the violence that accompanies deception in any form, including writing that lies. This aspect of Palamedean writing within the private sphere of secrecy and death, away from the openness of the civic and political space, conjures up the as yet indistinct figure of the reader, an individual reading to himself mute signs that are invisible to others, a reader who is already a private man and would soon become his own scribe, a possible alternative to the geometrician who inscribed his ideas upon the sky.

Palamedes seems quite at home in the land of inventors. But as a discoverer of writing, Orpheus, for his part, seems to be wearing a mask or even to have completely lost his way there, though only for a very short time, the duration of a scene that was the talk of the town in fourth-century B.C. Athens, when the question of authors and their function in libraries began to be debated. In reality, Orpheus' beginnings involved both the voice and writing, and even established a partnership between the two. In the first place there seems to have been Orpheus' singing, a forerunner of speech that attracted to it the most mute of living creatures, "the animals of silence." But writing was already there, too, inhabited by that same voice, and it is clear that a whole tumultuous rush of books and discourses was written around the songs of Orpheus.

Possibly the co-presence of the voice and the book at the center of Orphism is best revealed by the strange question raised about Orpheus' competence in material writing. This drew from the shadows the Orpheus of books, Orpheus the writer, and placed him in the full glare of light focused upon a debate conducted in the mid-fourth century B.C. The debate was sparked by an accusation made by an Athenian intellectual by the name of Androtion, one of the Atthidographers and a former pupil of Isocrates, who was active in the political and literary world between 380 and 330. Androtion claimed that the books said to be by Orpheus were wrongly attributed to him, as was shown by a clinching ethnographic reason. The reason was, quite simply, that the inhabitants of Thrace, Orpheus' birthplace, were uneducated or even illiterate people who scoffed at the very idea of using writing. The books that circulated under Orpheus' name must therefore be "myths," mere fictions that had to be recognized as the work of some forger. This accusation was all the more grave because at this time the Thracians were reputed to be the most savage and bloodthirsty of all barbarians. Up there, along the coasts of the Black Sea, they would fight to the death over the spoils from Greek shipwrecks, yet would abandon on the shore chests full of written scrolls of papyrus, as if these were objects of no value at all. Similarly, in the course of an episode in the Peloponnesian War—one of the most horrific, according to Thucydides—the Thracians, wielding their short swords (which the Greeks did not consider to be proper weapons of war), massacred all the children of Mykalessos in their school. It seemed as if the destiny of these Thracians who were so scornful of writing was to attack everything that belonged to the intellectual domain—books, instruments, and human beings alike. How could a Thracian possibly be a man of letters, a member of the group of writers who, like Androtion and the Atthidographers, wrote books about books? How could there possibly have been an Orpheus who was a writer?

The question raised by Androtion presupposed the existence of the book as an object. It targeted Orpheus' proprietary rights over the books and papyrus scrolls circulating under his name. Up until the fifth century B.C. the Greekness of Orpheus had gone unchallenged. Pindar had suggested that he was fathered either by Apollo or by Oeagrus, himself a Thracian, as his name indicates. And Orpheus was usually represented clothed in the Greek manner, surrounded by Thracian warriors tamed by the singing of the lyre player. In the fourth century, however, his Thracian connections caused his purely bookish skills to be questioned. The book was now regarded as a product of literate scholarship, and how could Orpheus, a native of Thrace, possibly prove that he had been an expert master of writing? What was at stake was certainly his ability to read and write, for two fourth-century defenders of Orpheus, studied by I. M. Linforth, responded to Androtion's attacks by asserting that Orpheus certainly had presented human beings with writing, which he had learned from the Muses, and so, on those grounds, he was the founder of culture in general, the founder of *enkuklios mathesis*, the encyclopedic kind of knowledge that in the fourth century B.C. was defined by Plato and Isocrates. This Orpheus skilled in writing and recognized by the fourth century also penetrated the figurative tradition. On a hydria in Palermo (Fondazione I. Mormino No. 385), Orpheus is to be seen dressed in the Thracian fashion, holding his lyre and accompanied by two women, both Muses, one of whom is presenting him with an open book, a papyrus scroll, beneath which the painter has depicted a half-open chest of books. This is Orpheus in his library, every bit as much an intellectual as the Apollo who is sometimes represented on contemporary vases, playing his lyre while perusing an unrolled scroll book.

Whether to be discredited or rehabilitated, Orpheus was now judged from the point of view of books, as would be any author in relation to the writing of his works. This was writing as seen and conceived by the intellectuals of the fourth century. There were two sides to the debate surrounding Orpheus the writer. The first emphasized and explained the written nature of the Orphic discourse. Meanwhile, the second argued that the disagreement or misunderstanding over writing was not unfounded and that the interplay between the voice and the book probably was important, for this might well be precisely where the essence of Orphism lay.

Fourth-century Orpheus is a voice unlike any other. While other bards and lyre players celebrate the high deeds of men and the gods, but always for the benefit of human beings as a group, Orpheus' voice begins beyond a singing that recites and recounts. His is a voice that sang before articulated speech and one whose exceptional status is marked by two characteristics. The one assigns Orpheus to the world of music before poetry, music without words, a domain in which he imitates nobody, for he himself is the beginning and the origin. The other, which is noted in Timotheus' *Perses*, has to do with creativity: Orpheus' lyre is not a technical object, an object constructed and fashioned, like Hermes' lyre, designed for the socialized space of music (festivals and banquets), or for an architectonic activity, like the instrument that the god gave to Amphion, the architect, who with his lyre playing charmed the stones into moving into position so as to construct a wall for Thebes. On the contrary, Orpheus is himself the creator of the lyre or cithara. His activity is that of a *teknoun*, not that of a *tektainesthai*.

When Orpheus' song sounds forth, it has never been sung before. Its importance lies in its effects rather than its content, and first and foremost in its centripetal power, which attracts around the voice all living beings, both animate and inanimate, whether they be on the earth, in the sky, or in the sea. It is a voice unknown to the closely packed circle of listeners, but one around which trees, stones, birds, and fish all gather, full of joy. When men come upon the scene, their appearance is warlike and wild, but their aggression and wildness is soon pacified and turned aside. These barbarian warriors clad in the Thracian fashion or in animal skins have left their forests, just as the birds have left the sky and the fish have abandoned the sea. Before this primeval voice becomes a cosmogony, a theogony, then an anthropogony, it harbors an extreme liberty that can encompass everything without ever foundering in confusion and chaos, yet fully accepting every single animated living creature and every single thing, together with all their excessive and necessarily unrestrained aspects. Above all, it is willing to give up the idea of a world that is ordered, separate, and characterized by fragmentation and division—that is to say, the world of others, as represented in the accounts of the six divine generations. As soon as Orpheus' voice reaches the wider human world, beyond that first circle of Thracian warriors, it is written down and turns into books, many books full of writing.

The writing sets out rules, prescribes certain patterns of conduct, authorizes certain ways of behavior, first and foremost a dietary regime. Euripides' Hippolytus, who is presented as a follower of Orpheus, ascribes equal importance to, on the one hand, a vegetarian diet and, on the other, the cult of "the many writings"—in other words, the books of Orpheus. At this point, Euripides introduces an image of rising smoke that evokes both the coils of incense emitted by the pure sacrifices made by the Orphics and also, from the point of view of those who hold such things in scorn, the vanity and futility of such arcane texts. In Plato's *Republic*, those same books are said to recommend sacrifices that produce fragrant smoke. But as well as dietary regimes and bloodless sacrifices, they prescribe ceremonies called initiations *(teletai):* ceremonies born from a book, written down and disseminated by the Orphic literature. These initiations that are set out in writing. in books, testify to the fifth-century opposition, strongly emphasized by Pausanias, between, on the one hand, initiation at Eleusis, a visual ceremony and spectacle, and, on the other, the Orphic mysteries, which for their part were written down and designed to be read.

Orpheus' incantations live on as his books are read aloud; and painted vases and mirrors testify to the co-presence of voice and books. On a fourth-century Etruscan mirror, now in Boston, Orpheus is to be seen singing amid a throng of animals, at his feet a round box overflowing with papyrus scrolls: Orpheus the writer surrounded by spellbound animals. But on an Apulian vase, published in 1975, Orpheus, this time in the underworld and dressed in Thracian fashion, stands, lyre in hand, before one of the dead, who is seated in a kind of niche or *heroon*. In his left hand the inhabitant of the underworld, an initiate and probably a disciple of Orpheus, clasps a scroll, a portable book, like the one found at Derveni in a tomb dating from the first half of the fourth century. An incantation from a book has the same power as singing; it triumphs over the harmful forces of oblivion: anyone who has mastered writing and becomes a reader of Orpheus does not die as others do. However, the relation between book and voice becomes even more immediate and explicit when Orpheus, purged of his body through the violence of women, becomes simply a head, a severed head washed up on a beach in Lesbos, a head that begins to sing and dictate. Again, there are vases and mirrors that represent this head, its lips parted and its eyes fixed upon a scribe working on his wax tablet, with his stylus in his hand. Such technical means are surely superfluous, though, for the voice on its own sets the written signs on the tablets. The song of Orpheus produces writing; it becomes a book; it is written down in hymns and incantations, and in cosmogonies and theogonies, vast compositions that take in all six generations of the divine powers. The discovery of the Derveni Papyrus, an Orphic book of Plato's day, indicates clearly enough that the writing of Orpheus is an open-ended text. His speech continues through exegesis—that is, through the commentaries that it prompts educated initiates to write. The papyrus found at Derveni is a text of philosophical hermeneutics, which refers to the system of Anaxagoras and its ideas of separation and differentiation. Its spirited exegesis sets out to show that what Orpheus says and thinks is always correct and that the meaning of the words that Orpheus deliberately uses to express the world has existed ever since the time when things separated out, giving birth to the world and all its parts. The song of Orpheus generates interpretations, gives rise to exegetic constructions that become or are an integral part of the Orphic discourse. This is polyphonic writing, a book with several voices.

Orphism thus involves a choice of writing, and an impulse to produce a plural book, an impulse that runs as deep as others' renunciation of the world and of the political and religious values of the city. For the kind of salvation that is cultivated amid circles of the purified and intellectuals can also be achieved through literature. It can be won through writing that coincides absolutely with the Orphic way of life, writing that tells of Orpheus' triumph over death and oblivion. The literate initiates of Orphism became the champions of books but at the same time rejected the world, setting up for themselves a secret library that revolved around Orpheus' unique voice.

The Orphic path thus runs in the opposite direction to that of the cognitive possibilities discovered by a hero such as Palamedes, a Promethean figure who depends on a practical intelligence, as adept with the concrete as with the conceptual. In contrast, in the space of Orpheus and the writing of his disciples, the sole purpose of the eschatological vocation that prompts them to write is knowledge, real knowledge of the genesis of the gods and of the world, knowledge that extends to the extreme isolation of the individual.

CHAPTER FOURTEEN

The Double Writing of Mythology (between the *Timaeus* and the *Critias*)

"Mythology," right from the start, seems not to have been a simple idea. At least, not in Greece, where it was indigenous, and in the Homeric world, where it surfaces as the verb *mythologeuein*.[1] Here, surely, Odysseus does not lie, and he is certainly nothing like a noble savage. Besides, who, even today, could detect a primitive state of nature in the stories of the *Odyssey*? On the Phaeacian stage, the epic enacts a representation of itself.[2] We arrive at the point where the bard and the Muses inspiring him make room for Odysseus to tell his own adventures and stories: the impossible return journey from Troy, his ship passing between Scylla and Charybdis, the Land of the Dead, the Cattle of the Sun, the pleasuring of Calypso, and, as the end of the year approached, the melancholy that overtook him. He tells his story point by point, and it is his own story, told with no Muses present, a story that he calls a *muthos*, not to draw attention to the marvels that it contains but to indicate the personal (rather than collective) nature of what is told. When he reaches the episode with which he started, Odysseus brings his performance to a close, saying, "Why repeat myself? Why *mythologize* what I was saying *[emutheomēn]* yesterday evening? I hate to repeat *[muthologeuein]* a story already told." My reason for rendering the Greek form *muthologeuein* as the verb "mythologize" is to note that repetition, which is so common in the oral tradition, is here rejected, and to show how, in this avant-garde company of bards, each one a virtuoso in the reuse of formulas as soon as they are coined, the cunning behind the narrative capitalizes on its ability to think about storytelling and all the possible representations of the tale. To refer to the option of mythologizing is, at the very least, to distance oneself from the constraints that might seem to weigh upon a society in thrall to its stories as much as to its mores and customs.

Others, to be sure—other Greeks—do tell each other the stories of the tribe, and to good purpose. But, as we have seen, at a very early date, say around 800 B.C., we find this influential use of the expression "to mythologize" introduced with a view to guarding against endless reiteration, rambling, and drivel,[3] and avoiding precisely the kind of stories that, we are told in hushed tones in Plato's *Politicus*, recorded "portents, . . . many [of which] did happen and will happen again."[4] We should note that the expression "to mythologize" made its appearance at approximately the same time as the theologian Hesiod was preparing to write his genealogy of the gods and his account of the origin of kingship.

So, in Greece at any rate, "mythology" got off to a good start, with a phrase expressing rejection and even a touch of demythologizing, as Hesiod's Protestant colleague, Rudolf Bultmann, would say.[5] And it would certainly be disappointing to find that, once set out on Plato's writing tablets, this mythology turned into a simple idea without a shadow of polyvalence. Before we venture into the Platonic studio, here is as useful a warning as any. Behind Plato the philosopher, who experimented with the dialogue form, there lurks another, a very alchemist in the transformations that he achieved. We should remember that Plato was something of an adept at such an art. On more than one occasion he sought to fabricate myths, some would say with a certain success. In Plato's studio that seems so like an alchemical laboratory, our best policy is quickly to select a corner that affords us a good angle or vantage point. Let us position ourselves at the intersection of the *Critias* and the *Timaeus*, concentrating on their prologues,[6] in order to appreciate their interplay. The two prologues are highly cinematographic: first a close-up of Critias, followed by a flashback to Solon the ethnographer arriving in Egypt, then a panning back to Critias questioning Socrates, and so on. The *Timaeus*, to take this first, presents an account of the creation of the world and of man, the creation of the world in its general structure and the creation of the beings that live in it. After the World Soul, the demiurge creates Time and the numbers of Time, according to the principle of choosing what is best. Then comes blind Necessity, which is opposed to that activity. But the demiurge manages to win Necessity over. Then comes the creation of the elements out of the basic figures of geometry: the world is written not in words, *grammata*, but in triangles that constitute its prime elements, its true "letters" or *stoicheia*.

The link between the *Timaeus* and the *Critias* does not operate as might be expected—that is to say, moving on from the general to the particular—for the story of creation seems to be simply an episode in one particular history, that of Athens, the history of a city or rather *the* city.[7] In the opening words of the *Timaeus*, Socrates refers to the intellectual feast or banquet that his interlocutors, Timaeus, Hermocrates, and Critias, attended the previous evening.[8] To refresh the memories of the guests, Socrates summarizes their conversation: it consisted of an outline of the ideal city, the political project of the *Republic*. For the benefit of his hosts, he then sketches in the theme of the discussion that he hopes will now develop. Socrates would like them to give him a private view of what the ideal city would be like in action, in full working order. "Suppose, for instance, that on seeing beautiful creatures, whether works of art or actually alive but in repose, a man should be moved with desire to behold them in motion."[9] To put this more precisely, what might the exploits or *athloi* of the ideal city be? What would become of the *kallipolis* once it was cast into the rapids of History?

Critias is eager to speak, for he is widely experienced in the politics of the time (he may have been one of the Thirty Tyrants).[10] Socrates' talk of the ideal city has put Critias in mind of the story of Solon in Egypt, as recounted to him by his grandfather, a story that tells of the Egyptian origins of Athens. Solon was at a loose end, so set sail for Sais and decided forthwith to question the Egyptian priests about their most ancient traditions, *ta arkhaia*, *archaiotata*. Anxious not to be misunderstood, "he attempted to tell them the most ancient of our traditions, concerning Phoroneus, who was said to be the first man, and Niobe; and he went on to tell the legend *(muthologein)* about Deucalion and Pyrrha after the Flood, and how they survived it, and to give the genealogy of their descendants *(genealogein)*; and by recounting the number of years occupied by the events mentioned he tried to calculate the periods of time."[11]

As is well known, Solon was soon brought down to earth with a bump. The Greeks in general and he in particular have not the slightest idea of what is truly ancient. The Greeks are perpetual survivors, lucky to escape repeatedly from a series of cataclysms. Egypt, in contrast, thanks to its favored geographical position, which affords it protection from catastrophes, has always remained the same. The priests of Sais know for sure that even before the greatest cataclysm of all, Athens—that is, the original Athens—already existed. This was an Athens founded by Erichthonius, the offspring of Gaia and a drop of semen let fall by Hephaestus. This primitive Athens had a set of perfect laws. Its classes were strictly separate (priests, warriors, artisans, and producers); its educational system was based on the sciences. Its heroism and its greatness made it superior to all other cities. Its greatest exploit was its victory over Atlantis, an arrogant power bent on conquering the whole earth. But then, one terrible night, both the Athenian army and the entire island of Atlantis were swallowed up by the waters of the sea. That ancient Athens of nine thousand years ago was imitated by the Egyptians, who modeled their own institutions on those of Athens and also preserved in their archives an exact account and description of that distant past.

Socrates expresses his delight. Critias' story of Atlantis, which is summarized in the *Timaeus*,[12] provides historical verification for his own ideal city, bringing it to life, with all its struggles and clashes with other states. There can be no doubt about it: the Athens unearthed in Egypt by Solon in the course of his ethnographic travels is identical to the ideal city *(kallipolis)* imagined by Socrates. It is rediscovered intact in the central archives of the Egyptian state. The rest of Critias' story is promptly deferred, as befits its importance: the birth of Athens, which now acquires the status of a "true account" *(alēthinōs logos)*[13] deserves to crown the other two accounts that are expected, the one of the birth of the world, the other of the genesis of the human race. Ancient history will complement and round off natural science.[14] The *Timaeus* itself is presented not as a "true account" but rather as probable discourse, *eikōs logos* (but also *eikōs muthos*), a discourse-account that sets out to say how things should be rather than how they are.[15] Probable discourse, *eikōs logos,* designates a genre, an *idea*, a literary form: most likely the kind of philosophical rhetoric that is mentioned in the *Phaedrus,* the subject of which is the soul itself and the function of which is to direct the behavior of human beings.[16] It is a psychagogic genre.

We now begin to glimpse the complexity of these two interwoven prologues. Socrates sparks the recovery of memories: a grandfather's story is resuscitated; behind Critias we discover a family chronicle featuring several gaps and children playing at being rhapsodes recounting how Solon visited the Pyramids once he had finished writing his *Laws* and singing his poems. Furthermore, between the *Timaeus*, on the one hand, and the *Critias*, on the other, Critias' story is duplicated, with variations that affect both the material and the bases of the story.[17]

What information about "mythologizing" and the transmission of what are said to be the most ancient of traditions are we to expect from Plato the philosopher, who sets on stage Socrates, who himself introduces Critias, who, in his turn, has Solon speak and, through Solon, the Egyptian priests? What is this literary genre from which stem prologues that have much to say about "mythology" and inquiry into the earliest beginnings, while at the same time claiming, through the intermediary of the Egyptian priests, to tell the truth about the origins of the Athenian city? Can it be that we have chanced upon the exceptional informant whom every anthropologist of ancient societies dreams of meeting? The native informer who little by little reveals all that is most deeply implicit in his culture and unveils its deepest secrets, in short, the informer inside, who acts as the eyes and ears of the ethnologist outside? Were any researcher to come upon a Hellene who could tell what a myth is, how it is fabricated, how it is transmitted, to whom it is addressed, what effects it produces, what kind of things become part of the collective memory, and how myth differs from history, one can well imagine how delighted he or she would be.

It is with just such a piece of good fortune that Luc Brisson's *Platon, les mots et les mythes* (published in 1982) opens. It claims that in the prologues of the *Timaeus* and the *Critias* Plato provides us with an "ethnological"[18] description of myth "in the primary sense of the term." He there sets out for us the theory that underlies traditional stories, and he fully illuminates "the fundamental elements that are in effect present in all myths."[19] This is surely a sensational discovery, which should, once and for all, resolve all our debates on mythology and its essence. However, upon reflection, and once the surprise has worn off, one may perhaps suspect that, somewhat presuming upon his intimacy with Plato, Brisson may have whispered in his ear one or two of our own ready-made ideas on myth in general, such as the notion that "a myth never reports an actual or recent experience," with which Brisson begins his chapter entitled "Information"[20] (information for whom?). It may indeed be reasonable to remind his readers that myths have to do with collective memories, that they are transmitted orally, and that they die when they come into contact with writing. However, what is more surprising is to find him using expressions such as "a myth *never* reports . . ." or "it *always* evokes. . . ."[21] Such statements seem to stem more from some superficial modern definition of myth than from remarks made by our informant Plato. Can we really be certain that the unforgettable stager of the last days of Atlantis is a communication theorist[22] providing irreproachable testimony of the "primary sense" of this thing called "myth"? I am, I must confess, bothered by two observations. The first, which is extremely down-to-earth, is that this discourse, the subject of which is supposed to be the nature of myth, is mainly a matter of *logos*. Hermocrates refers to the account that Critias is about to deliver as a *logos* that "is derived from ancient tradition" (20d1); and Critias takes over from him, declaring it to be a "strange," *atopos*, *logos* but nevertheless one that is "wholly true," *alēthēs* (20d8–9). *Logos* is again the term used when Critias the Elder sets about relating the account-discourse, or *logos*, brought back from Egypt by Solon (21a8, c5, d3, d7, etc.). And Critias, whether in his Elder or his Younger incarnation, remains faithful to the word *logos* right to the end of his contribution to the discussion. That fidelity of his in truth seems logical enough given that, at 26c–d, the narrator congratulates himself upon producing "true discourse," the *logos alēthēs* about what Socrates thought he had himself already presented as a *muthos*, a fiction, or to be more precise (26c5–8) a *plastheīs muthos*, thereby confirming that the story of Atlantis truly is an *alēthinos logos*. Can our informant Plato really be a theorist of "myth" even though the word that constantly rises to his lips is not *muthos* but *logos*?

Second, the prologue to the *Timaeus* does not hide the purpose of the *logos* delivered by Critias: the account promised *truly* is the most ancient story of Athens. So the discourse rediscovered in the archives of the poets of Sais may properly be used "as a tribute of praise, chanted duly and truly in honor of the Goddess."[23] Critias has expressed that very hope, and Socrates has not the slightest doubt about it: "What story should we adopt, Critias, in preference to this? For this story will be admirably suited to the festival of the Goddess which is now being held, because of its connection with her."[24] The explicit intention of the prologue is thus to show that the Egyptian *logos* contains the most suitable of all hymns to be sung in praise of Athena and her city. Yet it turns out that the true story of the earliest Athens is not marked by orality and the workings of memory, as one would expect in a "traditional tale." Instead, it is traced back solely to writing. The true account of the true ancestors, the authentic "offspring of the gods"[25] is based upon the writings of the Egyptian priests, a graphic activity that is doubly remarkable: first, because it is commonly held to be harmful, if not "deadly,"[26] to the spoken substance of a story fashioned by tradition; and second, because, according to Plato, the invention of writing in the land of Theuth is set in contrast to the outright condemnation of the written word expressed by the king Thamous who is set on stage in the *Phaedrus*.[27] On the basis of that condemnation it has been assumed, possibly over-hastily, that in Greece or even in the West generally, writing was deemed to be of secondary importance.

In the ancient Egypt evoked in the *Timaeus*, writing seems to have appeared just as the state was being organized. It is presented as a universal model that is valid for all peoples, ancient Athens included.[28] There was no need for any inventor of writing—Theuth, Sechat, or Palamedes—for writing was already there. The priests and scribes were already at work, recording in archives "any event . . . that [was] noble or great or in any way conspicuous" throughout the inhabited world. As the priests of Sais declared, "All such events are recorded from of old and preserved here in our temples."[29] Writing proceeds according to the criteria of all that is noble, great, and conspicuous. Within those limits, it is faultless. Complete and uncontaminated, the writing of the priests composes a past in the present of an unchanging Egypt that knows nothing of catastrophes, cataclysms, or breaks in temporality. This is perfect history, ultra-history, to be read just as it is written, in the unbroken continuity of an endless sequence of names, words, sentences, and episodes. Two concepts specified in the prologue to the *Timaeus* pinpoint the written nature of this Egyptian history of the earliest Athens: exactness *(akribeia)* and the exhaustiveness of an unbroken narrative *(panta . . . heksēs dielthein / ephеksēs diienai)*.[30] Those are the very same terms, *epheksēs autā diienai*,[31] as are used to describe the continuous recitation of the Homeric poems, the epic fixed in an official written text that is sometimes attributed to one of the Pisistratids, sometimes placed under the patronage of Solon.[32] The entire text was read by relay, "with each reader taking over where the last one left off" *(eks hupolēpseōs, eks hupobolēs)*.[33] The recitation would be performed by rhapsodes on the occasion of the Panathenaea which (according to Proclus, at any rate)[34] took place on the very festival days when, fulfilling Socrates' wish, Critias hymned the praises of Athena in the most appropriate fashion, digging out the aforementioned account of the authentic origins of the city.[35]

The revelation of the history of the true ancestors of Athens was thus brought by Solon from Egypt, where it had been consigned to the archives of the priests. This authentic "mythology" was told in sacred written texts; its truthful discourse was inalterable and told of an ideal city now recaptured in a genealogical memoir. The land of Greece, in all its sterility, presented the most negative of contrasts. As a result of its geographical position, it repeatedly suffered from floods, cataclysms, and catastrophes. Unlike the unchanging Egyptians, the Greeks were swept along by their broken history, repeatedly making new starts that were soon forgotten, and forgetting all that had gone before. A long sequence of bewildered survivors, brutish mountain people, illiterate shepherds from the high pastures where they tended their flocks, one after another all passed away. They were not scribes or priests, but ignorant, illiterate folk, knowing no more than a handful of proper names, *onomata* without context, without traditions, without stories.[36] This was the degree zero of orality, in a society that was destitute: "Since . . . they and their children for many generations were themselves in want of the necessities of life, their attention was given to their own needs and all their talk *[logoi]* was about them."[37] Words were in short supply, so it comes as no surprise to learn that these virtually mute living creatures for a long time lived and died "inarticulate," with no letters *(grammata)*.[38] In other words, they were illiterate, unable to pronounce written signs and so incapable of leaving written records behind them. It was a traditonless society in which people died, as they had lived, in silence. Just as there had been nothing before them, so there was nothing after them. Not one of them was concerned about "the thing before" *(tā en tois prosthen)* or about "what happened in the past" *(tā palai pote gegonota)*.[39]

Critias' story postulates a necessary link between the absence of writing and ignorance of any tradition. The prologue to the *Critias* endorses this by proclaiming a kind of cultural law: "For legendary lore [i.e., mythology] and the investigation of antiquity are visitants that come to cities in company with leisure, when they see that men are already furnished with the necessities of life, and not before."[40] The leisure to which Critias refers is first and foremost leisure in which "people are equipped . . . with letters and all such arts as civilized states require," as the *Timaeus* puts it.[41] Mythology begins when illiteracy ends, when the illiterate with no interest in "before" or the past are succeeded by people who set about researching into ancient times, *anazētēsis tōn palaiōn*. Such research is inseparable from what Critias calls *muthologia*.[42] But this is a different kind of mythological writing: not the ideal and perfect writing of the priests in Egypt, but writing marked by a series of new starts, without memories. This kind of mythology is committed to inquiry, research into what it imagines to be "the most ancient of traditions," the content of which, ironically enough, is presented in those naive, laughable stories that Solon one day ventured to tell, like a child,[43] there in the Nile delta, in the presence of the priests of Sais.

In the two accounts, Critias presents two different facets of mythology: the one in a society only just delivered from its illiteracy, which still confuses origins with the immediate past; the other in the holy land of Egyptian priests who continue to preserve in their books the authentic version of the beginnings of the city. Those two facets of mythology correspond to two different forms of mythography, two different ways of writing mythology, between which Solon mediates to the best of his ability. The various elements of his career qualify him perfectly to do so. As a retired legislator, a respected writer of laws—and the writing of laws is very much a part of the Platonic project—Solon can be regarded as a potential poet of the origins of Athens: he could have been a poet even greater than Homer or Hesiod,[44] if only he had completed the story that he brought back from Egypt, instead of first treating poetry as a secondary string to his bow and eventually abandoning it altogether. As a mediator, he thus falls between two stools. He might have presented the Athenians with a grand poem on the origins, in the form of a hymn addressed to the goddess, but in the event he turned out to be just a mediocre framer of laws. It is true that in a land of illiterates, he is respected for testifying to the sacred writings of the priests of Egypt. But there, in the temples of Sais, Solon produced the infantile babble of illiterates and recited the puerile *muthoi* of little children.

There can be no doubt about it: the true ancestors are those of the written Egyptian archives. But those Athenians of yesteryear are invisible, and all that reaches our ears from the sacred texts that speak of them is a muffled "rumor," a *phēmē*.[45] The prologue to the *Timaeus* does not conceal the extent to which conjuring up memories of the origins of Athens is risky, perilous, in short, unreliable. In the first place, the Egyptian story is now generally forgotten: the grown man has forgotten the child that he was in the presence of his grandfather.[46] Then there is the matter of the little "drama"[47] enacted in the festival of the Apatouria.[48] This was a ritual, a festival, but not yet one in honor of the goddess. It involved a sacrifice and competitions, in which children played at being rhapsodes—as it were, a preliminary for the Panathenaea, the great festival in which all citizens took part under the sign of Athena and autochthony.[49] The Apatouria was the festival of all the "brothers," held when the boys who had reached the legal age of puberty—that is to say, sixteen—were introduced into those cities in miniature, the phratries. Their names were entered in the phratry registers *(phratorikā grammateia)* on the day of the *koureōtis*, when a victim known as the *koureion* was sacrificed to mark the occasion of the shearing of the locks of the youths presented to the assembly.[50] When the little Critias was six years their junior, he played at declaiming and chanting the poems of Solon, as an "entertainment."[51] Surrounded by their families, the future "brothers," those not yet old enough to join the phratry, mimed the rivalry of poets competing as rhapsodes, as if in counterpoint to the festival and competitions that seem to have coincided with Critias' discovery of the Egyptian story and its recitation as a hymn at last worthy of Athena. Proclus tells us that this was the time of the Little Panathenaea. In the course of this celebration, the goddess was offered a *peplos*, an embroidered robe displaying an image of the Giants being vanquished by the Olympians, the victory won by Athena and the other gods over the chaotic powers of warfare. And that victory of the goddess was not only represented on the woven robe, but was also celebrated in song throughout one whole night, during a *pannuchis* when the *hieros logos* of Athens was recited, telling of the birth of Athena, the story of Erichthonius, and the triumph over the Giants.[52] The real "archaeology" of Athens could be heard through the trifling rhapsodies of children who loved Solon's poems and the *muthoi* about Deucalion, Phoroneus, and Niobe. The Egyptian story was threatened on every side by time, forgetfulness, and death, and was soon to be submitted to a night-long trial in which Critias, looking back over his life, came around to thinking that he could remember his grandfather's story perfectly well.[53] It was not long before he declared himself ready to recount it point by point and even boasted that he had retained this story in his mind "as though it was incised there in wax in indelible letters."[54] Truly, the paths of transmission are sinuous and impenetrable, and certainly not linear.[55]

At the crossroads where these prologues intersect, we thus find two paradigms of mythology: two contrasting written versions that both find their place within the conceptual framework of Plato's text, which we certainly do not expect to inform us about the Egyptian ways of writing the history of the Greeks. This is discourse on mythography, but it is designed for the experimental theater of a philosopher who suggests how it should be used: namely, as a simulator, a textual apparatus that makes it possible, with the aid of an artifice, to represent what is really going on. To test the efficiency of this simulator, let us investigate what it suggests about mythology itself and about what we might call "the beginnings of mythography."

First, let us consider the mythological writing that was the less incongruous of the two kinds. "To mythologize" in Solon's way was to research into ancient times, to tell the story of the first man of Argos or of Sicyon, to recite genealogies and count generations, beginning with the Flood or with Deucalion and Pyrrha, or to set about reciting stories about the gods, what Plato, in the *Republic*, calls *theologia:*[56] the representation of the gods is one species of the mythological genus or genre. This was a sample of the kind of learning produced by a category of citizens who enjoyed plenty of leisure and most of the commodities on offer in organized, literate cities. The description more or less fits a fifth-century *logographer*,[57] Hellanicus of Lesbos (480–400), for example.[58] He must certainly have been a man of leisure, for he produced no fewer than four "monographs," in which he collected all the known stories circulating among his contemporaries. These focused principally upon four names or figures: Phoroneus, Deucalion, Atlas, and Asopus. At the same time, Hellanicus, who was pursuing his own researches in the field, published a list of the priestesses of Hera in Argos. He also listed the names of the victors in the Carnean Games of Sparta, thereby providing exremely useful information for all those who, like Critias' Solon, "by recounting the number of years occupied by the events mentioned, . . . tried to calculate the periods of time."[59] The third field of inquiry in which he was active produced foundational stories *(ktiseis)* and works that we should describe as ethnographic (stories about Persians, Scythians, and barbarian customs generally). This set of "foundational" stories included the first "archaeology" or "history" of Attica. Hellanicus, a native of Lesbos, was the earliest of the Atthidographers,[60] the first in a whole line of prose writers of *logopoioi* who belonged to the well-to-do circles of Greek society and who, over a century and a half—notwithstanding the philosopher of the *Timaeus*—persisted in setting down in writing "everything fine, great, or conspicuous that [had] happened" in Attica. Traditions on Athena and Poseidon, the most ancient royal genealogies, the organization of the Panathenaea, the institution of courts of law: these were the typical subjects for research *(anadzētēsis)*, verification *(eksetadzeia)*, and minute criticism *(akribeia)*, all three terms being keywords for this kind of writing, which even had a role to play in the political discourse of Hellanicus' day. In 411, when the Assembly was setting up the Constitution of the Thirty, it was suggested by Clitophon "that the commissioners elected should also investigate *[prosanadzētēsai]* the ancestral laws laid down by Cleisthenes when he was establishing the democracy."[61]

These accounts of the origins of the city, which in the fifth century took the form of a history-memoir, incorporated a high proportion of *muthologia*.[62] Hellanicus' works thus corroborate what Critias claims. The works of these researchers, leisured writers of prose and sophists specializing in "archaeology," constituted the first more or less substantial written records of what Solon called "mythologizing." The beginnings of mythography also had a part to play further afield, in important innovations that were being introduced in the city. The most fundamental of these, at the beginning of the sixth century, had been the establishment of written records of laws, public announcements of community matters, and records of collective decisions.[63] Also very early on—certainly before 500—the Greek cities took to distinguishing between the affairs of the gods *(tā theia)* and the affairs of men *(tā anthrōpina)*. This was not in order to marginalize one side and devote all their attention to the other, but rather so as to manage both better. "Political" writing, that of the city, was devoted to publicizing on stelae the calendars and the sacred laws—all that defined the whole set of practical relations that linked the gods to the civic community. The sacrifices appropriate for Erechtheus, Athena, and Pandora were engraved on stone even before the logographers set about writing down the exploits of Cecrops and the high deeds of Athena.

That kind of history-memoir produced in the fifth century certainly contributed to the recording in writing of large portions of traditional stories and lore. But the effect of objectivization that might reasonably be expected from procedures of inquiry and writing in domains linked with "archaeology" and "mythology" was strongly counteracted by the all-inclusive nature of this discourse of self-identification, which, as it noted the continuity between the present and what came before, fostered a traditional view of that past.[64] It did so to such a degree that, in the patriotic circles where, in the course of the fourth century, a general interpretation of the time of origins and the past was elaborated, a statesman such as Demosthenes declared forthrightly that all those old Athenian exploits stemmed from myth. In other words, they possessed the dignity and force that goes with myth, but it was necessary to distinguish between high deeds already raised to the rank of myths and others, closer in time, that had not yet been transformed into *muthoi*[65]—or, as we used to say, which had not yet entered into history. But that distancing and, consequently, objectivization of the stories about Deucalion or Athena's relations with Hephaestus began in the early years of the fifth century—to be precise, when, even before Herodotus, Hecataeus of Miletus set about "writing down" what he called the accounts *(logoi)* that were circulating in Greece, and showing how "multiple and ridiculous" they were. He gave us the version of Heracles' descent to the underworld in "what appeared to him to be its true form"—in other words, the version that was the least characterized by "marvels" and so possessed the most verisimilitude for him and his contemporaries.[66] Herodotus, the inquirer, was more radical. His unambiguous intention was to reject the affairs of the gods altogether. However, when he writes of the affairs that date "from the time of human beings,"[67] Herodotus retains the word *myth* to convey anything that is unbelievable, improbable, and absurd,[68] or, to be more precise, anything that is "other" than a historical narrative. He thus makes the same exemplary distinction as that made not only by early philosophers, such as Xenophanes of Colophon, but also by the initiators of mathematical demonstration and the men who discovered geometrical reasoning. Not only was the "otherness" of "myth" thus established, but, as a result, it now tended to be excluded as an outdated form of discourse lacking rigor and outclassed by new forms of thought and modern ways of reasoning and arguing.

Condemned as a matter of principle by Herodotus and strictly shunned by Thucydides, who opted for the present rather than the "mythical" and the perils of the past, a whole body of literature in the style of Hellanicus nevertheless now played its part in the mutation of one part of what Plato called "mythology" into something new, which was eventually dubbed "mythography."[69] At the beginning of the third century B.C. several different practices seem to have helped to turn the writing of *muthoi* into a specific genre. Between 290 and 280 the Delians charged a poet from Andros with the task of writing down "the myths of their land," *muthoi epichōroi;*[70] not long after, in Magnesia-on-the-Meander, the Magnesians assembled a whole body of documents relating to their history and origins, which had been put together by various "poets and historiographers."[71] Such self-identifying discourse could be of practical use in the event of frontier conflicts or territorial claims, as is testified by some arbitrational treaties.[72] Local myths could play a decisive role here. It is even reasonable to suppose that such discourse was sometimes used much earlier, in similar debates that appealed to the very nature of the stories, designed as they were to hold their own against the stories of neighboring cities and also to distinguish one city's stories from those of its rivals.

In parallel, meanwhile, the "mythographic" genre was becoming distinctive, thanks to a different debate. This involved a literate public in which, in a poetic context, people were learning to differentiate the magical accounts of the stories about metamorphoses and to distinguish a story about the verifiable past, an "archaeological" account, from *muthoi* that were pure inventions.[73] This involved literary or *poietic* criticism, which got under way with tragedy and Sophocles' reflections on the tragedies of other writers, such as Aeschylus and Thespis, and also on his own.[74] Tragedy, a product of the art of writing, was soon seen as a way of writing a *muthos*, of constructing a plot out of a story that was bound to be "known to everyone" as it was part of the "mythology repertoire."[75] In his *Tragoidoumena*, Asclepiades of Tragilos, a pupil of Isocrates, analyzed the myths recounted by the tragic poets and, it seems, compared them to their traditional versions.[76] At the end of the fourth century, Philochorus, another Atthidographer, wrote five volumes on the *muthoi* of Sophocles.[77] Continuing in the line of such exercises in literary theory, the newly founded Library of Alexandria undertook the huge task of classifying all books and genres. An important part in this adventure was played by Callimachus, a friend and reader of Philochorus, who organized the inscription on tablets[78] of an inventory of "all those who have shone in the various forms of culture and all the texts that they have written." On the basis of the information provided by his library, which was so rich in "mythological memoirs,"[79] he also composed his extremely "mythographic" *Aitia*. Eventually the time came when a purged mythology, reduced to a limited number of items, became a "library," such as the handbook attributed to Apollodorus. In this way, the writing down and correcting of *muthoi* became an established tradition in itself, its purpose being "to classify myths and to make them as readable as possible."[80]

Plato's extremely active involvement in the beginnings of mythography was essentially prompted by a philosophical project that led him to ponder upon the astonishing power to "inspire belief" at work in the mythological "machine." And the reason why, using his kinsman Critias as an intermediary, he embarked upon an analytical critique of the history-memoir of the Athenians who were more or less contemporary with the first written account of their city's origins was that, as a reformist philosopher, he dreamed of replacing frivolous stories about Deucalion or Phoroneus with a "mythologeme" of the ideal city, a paradigm "set high in the luminous heavens."[81] There could be no city of philosophers until such time as the recollection of the Forms became the origin from which the real *Republic* stemmed, even if it took the miniaturized form of a more or less Phoenician history. What Plato wanted was an idealized mythology, a simple form that eluded the complexity of the inventories and the tortuous wandering ways of Critias, Solon, and many other Greeks besides.

But mythology is not something simple. Not in Greece, or elsewhere. The *Odyssey* sets the tone with its air of knowing that it is very boring always to hear the same stories. Furthermore, there is room for a whole spectrum of views on it. Demosthenes, robed to deliver a funeral oration, tells the Athenians that, through their exploits, they win a place in myth, and everyone is very pleased about this. A century earlier Herodotus, in his new guise as an Ionian inquirer, slings out myth yet never spurns any story from the tradition or any genealogy of the divine powers. But there is more to the matter. And this very local model of the twofold writing of mythology points the way. Ever since Claude Lévi-Strauss and Georges Dumézil (whatever one thinks of them), there have been essentially two ways of perceiving myth, and hence two ways of analyzing it: either as a narrative genre, a domain organized by certain modes of narration, or as a system of representation that always goes beyond the narrative genre that is one particular aspect of mythology. In short, Dumézil and Lévi-Strauss make the same choice as Plato. They consider mythology to be fundamentally a structure of thought, a *cosa mentale* over and above its momentary narrative appearance. In all likelihood, the philosopher of the *Timaeus* would have been interested in the (extremely linguistic) theories of A. J. Greimas, for whom mythology is a semantic code capable of "generating" the whole spectrum of mythical stories, whatever their form.[82] But certainly, in Greece, quite independent of Plato's philosophical project, mythology existed both as a framework and as a lore. On the one hand, it was a more or less tightly packed system of thought that covered the entire range of Greek culture. This invites us to resist being overly impressed by strict chronology and its frequently false constraints and, instead, to read the whole of Greek culture in a unitary manner—with all its beliefs, its lore, its practices, and its different types of accounts—regarding all of these as a system of interrelating correspondences with various categories and modes of logical organization. On the other hand—or, to be more precise, *within* mythology considered as a framework for thought—there was mythology that was lore and the various contexts in which that lore was paraded. It encompassed Odysseus, the Atthidographers, certain philosophers, and the "mythographers," those who were true to that name and to whom Diodorus Siculus refers. This mythology as lore was long the place for historical memoirs that took a variety of narrative forms, such as "archaeology," funeral orations, and foundational discourse, and it was eventually taken over by people who claimed to be professionals in the matter of writing down myths. So there was a specifically native way of thinking about mythology. But what is special here is that those natives happen to be our informants. There was, then, a Greek way of doing things that our own analysis of myths must take into account and integrate into our own interpretations.[83]

CHAPTER FIFTEEN

Orpheus Rewrites the City Gods

The death and life of Orpheus, in between Dionysus and Apollo: the crossroads embodied by Orpheus might afford the reader the best possible vantage point from which to gain a new perspective on Greek polytheism and a new way of conceiving of the divine powers as they relate both to one another and also to the human race.[1]

The new way of seeing is essential to the vision of Orpheus and those who identified so wholly with his way of life—namely, the renouncers who suddenly appeared in Greece in the sixth century B.C., intent on refashioning polytheism and rethinking the system of thought and action so closely pegged to the set of social and political relations known as a city. Their rethinking proceeded as a rewriting, but it did retain in its pantheon and throng of gods two actors of particular importance by reason of not only their high standing but also, clearly, their complicity, their interaction, and the remarkable interchanges in which they delighted to engage more or less everywhere, including Delphi, the major site of panhellenism ever since the eighth century B.C.

By using this chiasmic structure we might hope to eliminate the plot that is spontaneously suggested by the figure of Orpheus and his destiny, placed, as he is, in between these two gods who confront each other just as they do in the representations of painters and illustrators echoing the narrative of Ovid's *Metamorphoses.* The plot in question is an essentially biographical one in which Dionysus, identified with all that is nocturnal, cedes to Apollo all the advantages that stem from his striking resemblance to Orpheus, the cithara player. Yet the death and violent dismemberment that confines Orpheus' singing voice to the head that is severed from his trunk seems to belong by right to the fanatical cult of the non-Greek-speaking Thracian god, namely the Dionysus of Pangaeus who, as Erwin Rohde puts it, has not yet been purified by the light of Greek humanity. The dichotomy thus suggested (between the Apollonian and the Dionysiac Orpheus) seems to be supported by details in certain vase paintings: one, for example, shows an Orpheus, holding his Thracian audience spellbound, who is crowned with a laurel wreath, dressed as a Greek, and seems so Apollonian that only the multicolored clothing of his warrior entourage prevents us from taking Apollo for his father.[2] In parallel, vases bearing depictions of his death are sometimes painted on the reverse side with a scene showing Dionysus cavorting amid his maenads in a manner horribly reminiscent of the undisguised frenzy of the murderous women who closed in upon an Orpheus as handsome as Apollo.[3] In truth, how can one possibly not credit Apollo with all the aspects of the behavior of Orpheus and his followers that seem naturally traceable to him: the music and the singing, the extreme pursuit of purity, and even the fervent vegetarianism? That was certainly the view that was both shared and ratified by many modern scholars right down to the 1940s. Some suggested that a chronological gap separated Apollonian Orphism from the Orpheus confronted by or involved with Dionysus. Others from the start favored an Apollonized Orpheus preaching a reformed Dionysiac religion.[4]

It is true that there was plenty of scope for varied interpretation between the appearance of the first musician, Orpheus, and the last neo-Platonic spate of writing produced in Orphic circles. There was material enough for hermeneutics to work on in between the end of the sixth cenury A.D., the time of Olympiodorus' Alexandria, and the earliest beginnings in about 570 B.C., when Orpheus first appeared striding firmly on his way, apparently flanked by two Sirens, large aggressive birds with women's heads. A black-figure lecythus, now in Heidelberg,[5] affords us our first glimpse of this master of song, armed with his lyre, making his way between those powers with their death-dealing voices, hybrids whose sexuality veers from virginal, through androgyny, to bearded masculinity. Over the past twenty years, some important discoveries have made it possible to focus more precisely upon certain aspects of Orpheus and Orphism, considered at once as a system of representations, a body of theological discourse, and a set of practices and modes of behavior.[6] For there are three relatively autonomous levels to Orphism as it is generally understood. First there is a tradition about Orpheus, which tells of his birth, his life, his descent to the underworld, his spellbinding singing among the Thracians, and his tragic end, torn to pieces by a pack of murderous women. In this domain, the abundant iconography of the fifth and fourth centuries has revealed previously unnoticed details. For example, one Apulian amphora, published in 1976, displays Orpheus in the underworld playing his lyre before a dead hero seated in a small chamber; and this dead man, whose face is painted to resemble a mask, is grasping in his left hand a papyrus scroll, an Orphic book just like the real one discovered in 1962, close to a tomb at Derveni, not far from Thessalonika.

Then there is the level of the writings and the voice of Orpheus, which produced what an exasperated Plato called "a tumult of books." A singing voice caused written signs to be set down on Thracian tablets. These texts constitute an Orphic library that tells of the birth of the world and the genesis of the gods. They are known as the *Theogonies*.[7] Meanwhile, other books prescribe a dietary regime or recommend pure sacrifices of fragrant fumes. The latter are itemized in a work entitled *Thuepolikon*, which Plato mentions in a passage in the *Republic*.[8] An Etruscan mirror, now in Boston, depicts a box of books lying at the feet of an Orpheus surrounded by animals drawn out from their world of silence. The box contains a piece of writing entitled *The Initiation* and also a *Teletē* designed to be recited or chanted, which recounts how the child Dionysus is lured by the Titans and then put to death in the course of a most horrible sacrifice. One item that forms part of this literature made up of fragments and citations frequently interlaced with neo-Platonic exegeses is the Derveni Papyrus. It is a long philosophico-religious text dating from the early fourth century, and it constitutes the earliest Greek book in our possession. It consists of discourse on words and things, and is based on a cosmotheogony by Orpheus, in which the principle of all things is Night. The philosophical commentary, stemming directly from the philosophy of Anaxagoras and the operations of separation and differentiation, aims to show that what Orpheus thinks and says is always correct and that the meaning of words consciously adopted by the founder has existed ever since the time when things were separated out so as to form the world and all its parts. The words sung by Orpheus are charged with cosmic truths.[9]

The third level of Orphism is that of the practices followed by those who live in the Orphic manner, people faithful to the *bios orphikos,* in accordance with the strict rules that are noted in Plato's *Laws:* abstain from meat, never eat beef, offer the gods only cakes and fruits dipped in honey, remembering that it is impious and impure to eat meat and to let blood defile the altars dedicated to the gods. We are now in possession of documentation on these devotees of Orpheus, self-styled as Orphics: three bone tablets written in the early fifth century and discovered in 1978 on the shores of the Black Sea, at Olbia, in a space adjacent to the agora and surrounded by altars, which is close, dangerously close, to the sanctuary of the Delphinian Apollo.[10] That is no mirage of strange exoticism on the part of the Soviet archaeologists who deciphered the graffiti left by those ancient believers in Orpheus in a Greek town of the Propontis. For upon the underside of each of these tablets, these Orphics—restored to the light of day along with Delphinian Apollo—had scratched the name of Dionysus. And on the upper side of the second tablet, one of them had even drawn a rectangle divided into seven by straight lines, no doubt to persuade the more imaginative of their readers to believe that the Dionysus named truly had been divided into that Apollonian number of parts. The Kern fragment 210a reads as follows: "The Titans divided the child's limbs into seven parts."

But is it a matter of Apollo *or* Dionysus or of Dionysus *and* Apollo? The Black Sea Orphics seem to favor the conjunction of an Apollonian Orpheus with the powers of Dionysus. And that remains the case where the co-presence of the two gods takes the form that Herodotus gives it when he describes the prohibition, in Egypt, against burying the dead in a woolen shroud as "Orphic and Bacchic,"[11] and likewise where the association is expressed by the mask of the Orphic Hippolytus set on stage by Euripides:[12] the young man observes a vegetarian diet and quivers with purity but "plays the Bacchant," brandishing the writings of Orpheus, no doubt the same Orpheus who, according to one well-established tradition, instituted the mysteries of Dionysus.

But now it is time to tackle another question. Who are these people who arrange to be buried grasping a scroll of papyrus and who hold blood in such horror, produce cosmogonies, dream up strange stories about the birth of the gods, and even invent an anthropogony on the basis of the tortured bodies of Dionysus and his murderers? And what is it that they seek, as they cling to their Orpheus and his mute incantations? In truth, they seek just one essential thing: salvation. They want to save themselves in the only way possible: by fleeing the world. The Orphics are renouncers. They practice sanctity and cultivate purification techniques in order to distance themselves from others, from those who are tainted by murder and defilement. By returning to the Golden Age, the time of beginnings, the Orphic way of life seeks utterly to reject bloodshed on the altars of the gods and stands equally for a radical rejection of meat eating and—indissolubly—the values of the city, with its religious system of distinct divine powers, differentiated gods, and a necessary separation of the gods from the human race. Their uncompromising rejection of all this is expressed roundly by their condemnation of the communal consumption of meat and the social links instituted in the city by the sacrifice of an animal victim on an altar, followed by commensality that involves feasting upon meat.

Unlike a similar form of mysticism, such as the way of life and thought of the disciples of Pythagoras, Orphism was at no time in its history tempted to reform politics or to imagine the city and ceremonial in a different form. For the faithful followers of Orpheus who opted for writing and books to signal their otherness effectively, renouncing the wordliness of the city meant more than simply discovering in vegetarianism a foretaste of life with the gods, the gods who existed before this world and the bloodstained altars now devoted to them. The mysticism of these intellectuals and theologians also involved investing much effort in the reinvention of the genesis of the world and the rewriting of the entire history of the gods. For their attitude to the gods chimed with their attitude to sacrifice: it was part of a system in which the political, social, and religious aspects of life were perfectly harmonious. Just as to abstain from meat eating was to put oneself beyond the city, since the practice of blood sacrifice was part and parcel of political life, to renounce the gods worshiped by all the others amounted to calling into question the whole edifice of city life. Greek polytheism was such that it infiltrated social life and became a part of politics. In short, in the organization of the public space, the relations between the divine powers defined a symbolic dimension that had been foundational but still played an active and unerringly effective role through the network of gestures, practices, and ceremonies that activated the divine powers, playing upon the antagonisms that existed between them—gods who were differentiated according to the places, sanctuaries, and spaces that were respectively associated with them.

Orphism was not content to be wary of the polytheism of the others. But it could not reject it entirely without cutting itself off from a common language, the very language that made it possible for the sect to state its own view of the criminal blindness of those others and the misguided piety that trapped them in a repetitious cycle of murder. The Orphics were therefore obliged to rethink the ineluctable gods and to reinvent the order of the divine powers, producing a new genealogical theory for them. More radically still, the Orphics were forced to rethink the multiplicity of the deities. And this, it would seem, is the background against which the question of Apollo and/or Dionysus was raised in Orphism and in connection with the figure of Orpheus himself.

Pursuing our line of inquiry, we must first formulate the question at the cosmo-theogonic level at which the coming-to-be of the gods is recounted in a series of poems, the style of which becomes increasingly refined as more new palimpsests are deciphered. The Orphic gods are very strange,[13] starting with the First Born, the First Genitor, at once masculine and feminine, known as Phanes-Metis or Protogonos in the Derveni Papyrus, and also as Erikepaios. This being constitutes a repeated affront to the human form, with two pairs of eyes, golden wings, the voices of a lion and a bull, and two sets of genitals, one of which adorns the upper side of the thighs. But there is also a Zeus, in the fifth reign, who passes his power over to his son and, instead of being the sovereign assured of reigning in perpetuity over the gods, on the advice of Night replaces the First Born back within his body, thus turning himself into the matrix, the shell of an egg as large as the All. As if this were not enough, the same god then becomes the husband of his mother and impregnates his married daughter who is once again his mother—thereby committing double incest. The Church Fathers, who persisted in a stubborn, voyeuristic interest in all these couplings, at this point found their crimson blushes paling to a greenish hue. This cosmo-theogony consists, in effect, of a debauchery of baroque deities and polymorphic monsters. However, the luxuriance of these multiform gods is neither gratuitous nor meaningless. It makes sense of the coming-to-be. Originally, in the beginning, there is a totality, the unity of All. Phanes-Metis is complete within the perfect orb of primordial Night. In the course of the five reigns that follow, this fine unity undergoes the trial of separation and fragmentation through the processes of differentiation. The five reigns begin with Phanes and end with Zeus, passing by way of Night, who is so close to Phanes, then Ouranos and Gaia, then Cronos and Rhea. Zeus, the last in line, is born from Rhea-Demeter, then marries Demeter "II," before becoming the spouse of Demeter "III," the Demeter-Core who produces the child Dionysus. This Dionysus was already present in the First Born, and it is he who inaugurates the sixth and last generation of the gods.

Differentiation, which is the motor of this coming-to-be, proceeds first through sexual activity, then through marriage, which effects the separation of the various divine powers. It is worth pointing out that the first conjugal union in the world of the gods takes place during the third reign. There is no *gamos* before that of Ouranos and Gaia. However, Phanes does beget upon Night (actually, the second Night, who is called his daughter) the flower of his own body, in all its youth. This is the first figure with sexuality, but at this stage there is still no marriage. As Proclus, who produced an excellent exegesis on Orpheus, comments, "For those who are the most in unity, there is no conjugal union." Sexuality introduces difference, but it is the conjugal relationship that institutes it and founds it, by consummating the separation that it effects down to the fifth reign, that of Zeus. There are two sides to conjugal union, however: the one is degenerate, since it involves the doubly incestuous marriage of the son to his mother and the father to his daughter; the other is regenerative, for, heeding the advice of Night, Zeus inaugurates the second creation of the world by absorbing the First Born into his own body. He becomes a pregnant god who realizes within himself both the unity of all things and the distinction of each one. The Orphic book of Derveni, for its part, confirms this process of differentiation by a genesis of words and things: multiple names are given to one and the same god. The vocabulary used in this papyrus is philosophical. It is the vocabulary of Anaxagoras and separation, *diakrisis*. In particular, in column 17, it states that all things already existed in advance but received their names only when they became separate: in the order of words, naming duplicated the sexual activity that separated and made things distinct. In this particular instance it is Aphrodite and her father Zeus who become distinct. In the Derveni Papyrus, in which the exegesis strives to show the veracity of the words of Orpheus, the linguistic discourse seems to be an extra means of conceiving of unity through the interplay of figures of separation, made possible by the rightness of the names given by Orpheus.

In the light of all this discourse, with its abundant multiplicity of gods, what of Dionysus and Apollo? Let us first consider Dionysus. For he is as much the last sovereign as he is the first. The last is the child to whom Zeus passes his royalty, a child described as greedy, *eilapinastēs*, one who is fond of banquets.[14] It is an unusual epithet for a god, but is used in Cyprus, where it is applied to Apollo, also a god who enjoys fine fare, but one who has a stronger vocation for the art of butchery and as a sacrificer. The child Dionysus thus seems to have, as it were, a predisposition toward feasting and thus toward the sacrifice that is to come. Then there are the toys with which the Titans lure the little god into their clutches: the spinning top, a rhombus that is really a devil, the apples, and the mirror. And finally, there are the brutish Titans themselves, who tear him to pieces, slaughter him, then boil and roast his flesh. It is deliberate, cruel behavior that, with a few scholarly distortions, mimes the act of murder that is implicit in all blood sacrifices. The human race, plunged in forgetfulness and ignorance, does not yet realize that it was born then and there, on the scene of the crime committed by the Titans, who proceeded to taste the flesh of the child before being blasted by the thunderbolt of Zeus. The seed of the human behavior associated with altars and cities began to germinate somewhere there, amid the remains left by those criminal sacrificers.

That is one Dionysus, in a most extreme state of dispersion, an emblem of human dereliction and of the prisonlike regime imposed upon the fragment of divinity that is buried deep within each individual. The child god bears the marks of that dispersion in his flesh, for he has been cut into seven pieces, while his heart, abandoned and rejected, is saved from destruction, affording the promise of another, new life of which he is both the last and the first anatomical receptacle. That is how the last king of the gods is also the first. Even if some details in this story remain obscure, Dionysus, as the First Born changed by metamorphosis into a greedy infant, carries within himself the plenitude of all origins, the very plenitude that is soon ripening within Zeus who, by absorbing his heart, an organ totally composed of condensed blood, incorporates Dionysus within himself. The reign of the Golden Age begins inside a masculine body, a matrix alien to femininity, in accordance with the same logic that, conversely, foisted upon marriage and sexuality all the problems of differentiation.

In this great drama in which Dionysus is, without question, the protagonist, Apollo may seem to have no more than a walk-on part, so discreet and limited are his appearances. In all, he appears only three times, although admittedly twice at strategic points that are reenacted in Delphi, in the panhellenic sanctuary that, of all sanctuaries, is the one most strongly marked by the double sovereignty of Apollo and Dionysus. Apollo's first appearance is that of a distant yet fundamental presence. Plutarch, always more Apollonian than even the Delphians, is scandalized by it. He puts it down to a mistake on the part of Orpheus, suggesting that the Thracian enchanter who descended into the underworld was misinformed when he was told that the Delphic oracle was a means of prophecy used by both Apollo and Night.[15] That is a tradition that Plutarch the theologian is quick to refute, yet it is a by no means unprecedented one. Ancient

Delphic traditions refer to the sovereignty of Night in the earliest days of the oracle, before Themis, Dionysus, and eventually Apollo ever appeared on the scene.[16] Furthermore, in Orphic thought, the greatest oracular power ever, including whatever gods were yet to appear, was Night, the daughter of Phanes-Metis, who at her birth not only received her scepter and her legislatory authority but also was endowed with the most sublime powers of prophecy. By presenting himself as the co-adjutant of Night in the Delphic scene retouched by Orpheus, Apollo secures for his most dazzling sanctuary the backing of the primordial deity who, in the eyes of the Orphics, was the very embodiment of true oracular knowledge.

In view of this, Apollo's second intervention makes perfect sense. He now becomes implicated in the tragedy of Dionysus. He makes his entrance immediately after Dionysus has been done to death. There are two versions of this story. In that of Callimachus,[17] it is Apollo who, as the victim's brother, receives the members of Dionysus' body from the hands of his murderers. It therefore falls to him to gather up the remnants of the murdered child and to place them in a cauldron, in accordance with an ancient mode of burial for heroes. Apollo installs this vessel alongside the prophetic tripod positioned at the center of his sanctuary. However, in the version recorded by Clement of Alexandria,[18] it is Zeus who charges Apollo with the task of burying the remains of Dionysus: Apollo, "without disobeying him," carries off the pieces of the dismembered body and deposits them at the foot of Mount Parnassus, in the very sanctuary where a very firmly established tradition locates a tomb of Dionysus. In a more philosophical vein, the neo-Platonic glosses were later to draw attention to the figure of an Apollo who recomposes the broken body of Dionysus, puts it back together, and even discovers the magical quality of the number seven as he counts the pieces into which the Titans have torn it.[19] This exegesis on the death of Dionysus, on which the emergence of the human race is founded, suggests an interest in the question of the one and the many, but at the same time it certainly does not do away with the solidarity between the two brother gods, here brought together at the same moment at the foot of Mount Parnassus.

The third appearance of Apollo emphasizes his role as a deity who watches over a cosmogony that is totally oriented toward Dionysus and his resuscitation. As he begins his hymn on the creation of the world, Orpheus invokes the son of Leto, the powerful Phoebus or Apollo, the god who sees everything. He addresses Apollo as the sun god, Helios, saying, "Now, for the twelfth time, I hear your prophetic voice; it is you who have spoken; I call upon your testimony."[20] Does this not show that Orpheus places the whole of his theology under the sign of one single god who occupies the first position, in the same way that Night is primordial—a god to whom Orpheus, by his birth, is himself so close. The alternative polytheism that is here put together in discourse on the gods woven around Dionysus and Apollo is innovative even within a religious space in which already, in one panhellenic tradition, the essential element in the pantheon tended to be expressed by a single fascinating couple: Dionysus and Apollo. These two closely related powers are so much in harmony in the theogonic architecture that their conjunction really does, at this point, seem unquestionably to triumph—except, precisely, that the logic of mysticism raises the question of a single-minded kind of priority, involving an exclusive relationship with one god in particular, one who, as it were, holds himself apart from the other gods. That is the situation in cases of possession or in *thiasoi* in which the maenads or Dionysiac initiates are defined by a status that they share with their god. For whoever sees Dionysus face to face, the god is quite different from the Dionysus of civic liturgies. The initiate becomes *bacchos*, as does Dionysus himself in his Mysteries, where he is called *bacchos*, *baccheios*, or even *baccheus*. In parallel fashion, but in a slightly different mode, Orpheus, the man seeking absolute purity, conceives of salvation as a similar all-encompassing and possessive relationship with a single god. The choice of that god immediately distances him, in very visible fashion, from the differentiated pantheon of the polis.

In his own life, Orpheus himself makes just such a radical choice. In the first tetralogy based on stories about Dionysus that Aeschylus composed, he set on stage an Orpheus seized by pious love for a god greater than the rest.[21] His excessive piety leads him to his doom. Such is the plot of the *Bassarai*. Every day at dawn, Orpheus climbs the rocky Mount Pangaeus, the highest mountain in Thrace, for he wishes to salute the Sun as it rises, to be the first to see it and to honor it. For Orpheus, the Sun is "the greatest of the gods," and he bestows upon it the name Apollo. It was said that Dionysus resented this and sent women with a name as barbaric as their manners to attack him: the Bassarai. They tracked Orpheus down, seized hold of him, tore him to pieces, and dismembered him. The body of Orpheus was thus reduced to fragments, dispersed, and lay scattered around until such time as the grieving Muses came to Mount Pangaeus, collected up the scraps of the tortured body and took them to a place called Leibethra, to bury them. The most immediately striking point indicated by the title that Orpheus gives to the god of his choice is that his piety is of a type associated with the Mysteries, for "the greatest of the gods" is not an expression used in city cults and rituals. It seems to have been reserved for powers honored in ancient Mysteries, such as those of the great gods of Andania or the great goddesses of Arcadia.[22] Furthermore, in Greece, the Sun, Helios, is a god who does not fit into the general framework. He is not only extremely ancient but also noticeably absent from the usual altars set up in the public space. To make him more his own, Orpheus gives him another name: he calls the Sun Apollo. That is exactly the reverse of the practice of the Pythagorean tradition, a practice from which the Orphics liked to distinguish themselves, even as devotees of Apollo.

Orpheus' choice certainly has an exclusive air about it. That, at least, is what Dionysus seems to think. For, without a doubt, there is an element of resentment here, as there always is when a god feels neglected or deprived of the honor that is his due. It is not a psychological reaction, rather a structural one, which is natural in polytheism since this sets up a collection of powers that are carefully balanced and adjusted to working together. The pantheon apparatus is directly threatened by any decision to turn one particular power into "the greatest of the gods." One reason for Dionysus taking offense in this case is that this is his particular terrain, given that Mount Pangaeus lies in his domain. This is the mountain where Lycurgus, the king of the Edonians, the man with an axe, Dionysus' enemy and Thracian tormenter, underwent the punishment that he deserved for his foolish refusal to recognize the god: he was torn to pieces by the teeth of wild horses. But now, in the particular instance that we are considering, Dionysus is more than just a vague poliad deity whose territory happens to be called Mount Pangaeus. For the man praying on the mountaintop is the theologian in whose thinking Dionysus holds such a preeminent position. Small wonder that the polarity usually cultivated in theological discourse is eclipsed by such overt antagonism, even if it is true that Apollo is only an extra name given to the Sun, and even if the Bassarai are Thracian women let loose by the god of Mount Pangaeus and not maenads possessed by the god with the power to drive humans mad. Yet the death inflicted upon this devotee of the Sun and Apollo makes him strangely reminiscent of the child in the Orphic theogony: there is the same mutilated body, torn into the same number of scattered pieces, and they are collected and buried in similar fashion, although by the Muses rather than Apollo. Furthermore, just as in the one case the heart is saved, in the other it is the head that escapes the violence. Thanks to this, a new kind of life is conferred upon Orpheus. The live head rolls down to the sea, and the waves bear it away to another shore, where it continues to sing. Orpheus is transfigured but still himself, now a bodiless, shadowless voice that continues to sing and prophesy. Several vase paintings show Apollo, laurel wreath in hand, overseeing the transcription of the words of Orpheus by a disciple who is seated facing the open-mouthed head and is equipped with a tablet and a stylus.

In certain versions, at this point Dionysus reappears, now as a divine protector of Orpheus who welcomes the head to the island of Lesbos and has it buried in his Baccheion.[23] Dionysus is as solicitous toward this Orpheus as the Apollo of Delphi was toward Dionysus his brother. That Apollo, moreover, presides over an open sanctuary alongside the sanctuary of Dionysus and shares what remains of Orpheus with his brother god: this Lesbian Apollo is allotted the lyre of the musician who sang his praises. Yet another version relates that in Thrace itself, at the summit of Mount Haemon, a sanctuary of Dionysus shelters the tablets of Orpheus and in this way preserves the writing dictated by his voice.[24] This is a Dionysus who bears a definite resemblance to the oracular god who, in Thrace, took care of the burial of Orpheus, warning the people of Leibethra that their town would be destroyed if the bared bones of the murdered victim continued to offend the eyes of the Sun.[25] Even in Thrace, Dionysus is not the sworn enemy of Orpheus. Nor is he an unambiguous adversary. In Ovid's *Metamorphoses*[26] he laments the death of his devotee and mourns for the man who invented his Mysteries. The Bassarai are first and foremost simply wild Thracian women, as fierce as their masculine partners whom Porphyry evokes in his *On Abstinence*.[27] Carried away in the madness of their human sacrifices, these men stuff their mouths with their victims, and their frenzy reaches such a pitch that they even fall upon their fellows and tear each other apart. But in truth the only real enemies of Orpheus are women or, to be more precise, the Thracian women. As the tradition recorded in the *Symposium*[28] recalls, death comes to Orpheus from the race of women. That is why he hastens to choose the destiny of a swan when it comes to his reincarnation in the drama staged by Plato. Orpheus refuses to be born from a female womb because of his hatred of the women who so cruelly tore him apart. In several depictions, the imagery of the fifth century presents the same version of what happened as that recorded by Ovid and Pausanias: the violence of the Thracian women should not be confused with that of the Bacchae. The murderesses of Orpheus are certainly frenzied women, but ones who elude the control of Dionysus, just as overflowing Bacchic passions sometimes do in the course of Dionysiac festivals. It is even said that the excessive audacity of the Thracian women stemmed from wine and that from that day forward their menfolk never went into battle sober.[29] The Orphic tradition, which is consistently misogynous, suggests that Orpheus' singing could triumph over anything, attracting to it even stones and forest animals, subjugating Satyrs and Sirens, and winning over the frenzied Thracian warriors. It could triumph over anything except the female species, before which it was powerless. The voice of Orpheus failed when he faced the race of women, and they treated him with the same fundamental cruelty as that of the murderers of the infant Dionysus. However, the god of Mount Pangaeus does not identify himself with the women of Thrace. Besides, on that mountain of his, Dionysus is a god remarkably different from what he is elsewhere. Herodotus encountered him and discovered him to be an oracular god.[30] His sanctuary towered above the forest-clad, snowy mountain peaks, and there he dwelt among the Satres tribe, Thracians who extracted gold and silver from the mines of Mount Pangaeus. This oracular Dionysus of the mountain lived surrounded by his prophets and was served by a woman who delivered his oracles exactly as she did in Delphi, in the temple of his brother Apollo, who thus seems to be duplicated in the land of Thrace. So up on Mount Pangaeus there lived a Dionysus who resembled his brother, the Apollo of Delphi. Was this a lure, a mirage in a mirror? In the only extant verse fragment of his tragedy about Orpheus and the Bassarai, Aeschylus dismisses that notion. The fragment features an Apollo masked as Dionysus or, vice versa, a Dionysus masked as Apollo: "Apollo, you who are wreathed in ivy *[kisseus]*, you who are a diviner inspired by Bacchus *[baccheiomantis]*."[31] It is impossible to say where this invocation came in the tragedy, but interpreters of Aeschylus consider it to refer to an Apollo who is identical to Dionysus, one and the same god, but with two different names, as Macrobius, writing in late antiquity, put it.[32] After all, Orpheus, to be sure, knew the silent names of the deities better than anyone else.

In his devotion to the Thracian Sun, the theologian of an alternative polytheism picked out the holy mountain where the god of the return to the One, Dionysus in his various metamorphoses, appeared most closely to resemble the Apollo of prophecy who, in the company of Night, was promoted to the rank of a primordial power. Orpheus' rewriting of the theogony exploited and enriched the complementarities at work between Dionysus and Apollo, and his account was all the more incisive because it left its mark upon the body and flesh of the writer who had that alternative vision of the gods and men.

Notes

The abbreviations of the titles of periodicals, collections, and editions are taken from *L'Année philologique.*

Preface to the English-Language Edition

1. In parallel to these analyses, I have been working on the problems of polytheism, especially in a programmatic essay, "Experimenting in the Field of Polytheisms," *Arion* 7, no. 2 (1999): 127–149, and in a preliminary volume, *Apollon le couteau à la main* (Paris, 1998).

2. See Marcel Detienne, *The Creation of Mythology*, trans. Margaret Cook (Chicago, 1986), pp. 85–86.

3. Or mythology is "transcribed." Transcription is a procedure that I and others have tried to clarify in an expressly comparativist work: Marcel Detienne, ed., *Transcrire les mythologies. Tradition, écriture, historicité* (Paris, 1994).

4. See the survey and discussions in "Return to the Mouth of Truth," preface to the American edition of Marcel Detienne, *The Masters of Truth in Archaic Greece*, trans. Janet Lloyd (New York, 1999), pp. 15–33. Also useful on certain points is Richard Buxton, ed., *From Myth to Reason? Studies in the Development of Greek Thought* (Oxford, 1999).

5. See Geoffrey Lloyd, *Adversaries and Authorities* (Cambridge, 1996).

6. This is the perfectly respectable view of Claude Calame, *Poétique des mythes dans la Grèce antique* (Paris, 2000).

7. See Jean Bollack, *La Grèce de personne. Les mots sous le mythe* (Paris, 1997), especially pp. 131–180. The hypothesis of a "coherent and interconnected body of stories" into which "poets, in their guilds, were initiated" is an interesting one, but all the same, it does not confine "mythology" to completely literary relations from Homer down to the writers of tragedy. That is a philologist's view, which "historians," trained in the cult of a handful of great texts, tend to prolong in interpretations vaguely described as ritualistic, such as those produced by Richard Seaford, *Reciprocity and Ritual: Homer and Tragedy in the Developing City-State* (Oxford, 1994).

8. See Marcel Detienne, afterword, "Revisiting the Gardens of Adonis" (1989, trans. Froma Zeitlin), in *The Gardens of Adonis*, trans. Janet Lloyd (Princeton, 1994), pp. 133–145; postface, "Retour sur la transgression d'un meurtre sacrificiel," in *Dionysos mis à mort* (1977; 2nd ed., Paris, 1998), pp. 219–230.

FIVE: The Danaids among Themselves

1. An investigation into the powers of Hera in the Greek pantheon led me back to the stories of Argos and the network of traditions on the Danaids, which I had previously attempted to analyze in a series of seminars that are briefly summarized in *L'Annuaire de l'École Pratique des Hautes Études (Section V, Sciences Religieuses)* 84 (1975–1976): 279–283. In 1982 I returned to the mythology of Argolis, and although my work centered on Hera the sovereign was not yet ready, I took part in a workshop organized for Nicole Loraux and in a project entitled "Masculin/Féminin." Eventually the present essay appeared in *Arethusa* 21, no. 2 (1988).

2. L. Curtius, "Die Töchter des Danaos," in *Jahreshefte des Österreichischen Archäologischen Instituts* 39 (1952): 17–21 (crater from Tarantum, fifth century B.C.).

3. Aristotle, *Politics*, I.3.2.1253b9–10; and the remarks of J.-P. Vernant, *Myth and Society in Ancient Greece*, trans. Janet Lloyd (New York, 1988), pp. 59–60.

4. Plato, *Laws*, IV.719c1.

5. Here are two useful references selected from a wide-ranging and closely packed bibliography: C. Bonner, "A Study of the Danaid Myth," *Harvard Studies* 13 (1902): 129–173; *Aeschylus' "Supplices": Play and Trilogy*, ed. A. F. Garvie (Cambridge, 1969).

6. Callimachus, F. 65 and 66, ed. R. Pfeiffer; Aeschylus, F. 355, 16–28, ed. H. J. Mette.

7. Herodotus, II.171. See also an essay not unrelated to the present one: "The Violence of Wellborn Ladies: Women in the 'Thesmophoria,'" in *The Cuisine of Sacrifice among the Greeks*, ed. M. Detienne and J.-P. Vernant, trans. Paula Wissing (Chicago, 1989), pp. 129–147.

8. Aeschylus, *Supplices*, 817–840.

9. The question of incest does not arise for, contrary to the claims of E. Benveniste, "La Légende des Danaïdes," *Revue de l'histoire des religions* 136 (1949): 129–138, there was no prohibition against unions between first cousins. Furthermore, an appeal to the epiclerate does not really seem viable, at least to judge from the summary of an analysis by L. Gernet, "Observations sur les 'Suppliantes,'" *Revue des études grecques* (1950): xiv. The evocation of the bird that is impure if it feeds on the flesh of other birds is indissociable from this marriage, "which cannot be pure *(hagnos)* when the woman is taken *against her will and the will of her father*" (*Supplices*, 226–228).

10. Iamblichus, *Life of Pythagoras*, 48, ed. Deubner, 27, 1–3, and 84, 49, 4–6; also Pseudo-Aristotle, *Economica*, I.4.1.1344a10–13.

11. J. Toutain, "Le Rite nuptial de l'*anakaluptērion*," *Revue des études anciennes* (1940): 345–353. See now Anne-Marie Vérilhac and Claude Vial, "Le Mariage grec du VIe avant notre ère à l'époque d'Auguste," *BCH*, suppl. 32, École Française d'Athènes (1998).

12. Pausanias, II.4.6–7.

13. Vernant has emphasized this point in *Myth and Society in Ancient Greece*, p. 94.

14. *Danaïs*, F. 1, ed. Kinkel.

15. Aeschylus, *Supplices*, 287–289.

16. Melanippus, F. 757 *PMG*, ed. Page, together with the comments of G. Giangrande, "Interpretationen griechischer Meliker," *Rheinisches Museum* 114 (1971): 118–124; and the essay by A. Moreau, "Les Danaïdes de Mélanippide: La Femme virile," *Pallas* 32 (1985): 59–60; also Moreau's analyses in *Eschyle, la violence et le chaos* (Paris, 1985), pp. 58–59, 195–202, 297–301.

17. The data can be found in Plutarch, *De mulierum virtutibus*, 245E; see the com-

parison drawn between the Danaids and the courageous women of Argos in Clement of Alexandria, *Stromateis*, IV.120.3.

18. Plutarch, *De mulierum virtutibus*, 245E.

19. Pausanias, II.38.4.

20. Pausanias, II.15.5; Akousilaos, *F Gr Hist*, 2.F.1 and 23A Jacoby; *Iliad*, 21.195–197, 14.200–201.

21. Hesiod, F. 126 West-Merkelbach.

22. [Pseudo-Apollodorus], *Library*, II.1.1; *Schol. ad Lycophron*, 177, ed. Scheer, 86, 22–23.

23. *Phoronis*, F. 1 Kinkel; Akousilaos, 2.F.23A Jacoby; Plato, *Timaeus*, 22A.

24. Pausanias, II.20.3.

25. Hesiod, F. 123 West-Merkelbach.

26. Pausanias, II.19.5–6.

27. *Schol. Sophocles*, *Electra*, 4, ed. Papageorgias.

28. Fire discovered by chance, in a tree struck by lightning: Diodorus, I.13.3; Vitruvius, 33.16–23. See T. Cole, *Democritus and the Sources of Greek Anthropology* (Atlanta, 1967).

29. Hesiod, *Theogony*, 563, ed. West (1966, 323), together with the *Scholia vetera*, ed. L. Di Gregorio (Milan, 1975), 85, 17–20.

30. Musaeus, F. 4 Diels-Kranz; Hesychius, *s.v. Melias karpos.* In Thebes, Melia was an *autochthonous* nymph; following her union with Apollo, she engendered Ismenius (Callimachus, *Hymn to Delos*, 79–80).

31. Hesiod, *Works*, 145. See *Iliad*, 16.143.

32. Hyginus, *Fab.*, 274.8 Rose.

33. Hyginus, *Fab.*, 143. See Clement, *Protreptica*, III.44.1.

34. Hyginus, *Fab.*, 274.8.

35. Pausanias, II.15.5; Tatian, *Speech to the Greeks*, 39.148–149.

36. *Oxyrrh. Pap.*, X.1241.c.IV.3–4.

37. Pausanias, VIII.15.5.

38. Pausanias, VIII.15.9.

39. Pausanias, II.25.4.

40. Hyginus, *Fab.*, 169e, ed. H. J. Rose; [Pseudo-Apollodorus], *Library*, II.4.4.

41. Theophrastus, *Peri Eusebeias*, F. 18, ed. Pötscher. On the relation between water and seeds in the ceremonial of sacrifice, see J.-L. Durand, *Sacrifice et labour en Grèce ancienne* (Paris, 1986), pp. 123–133.

42. Callimachus, F. 75.10–11, ed. Pfeiffer.

43. An account is given in Pindar's version, *Pythian* 9.112–116, which recounts the collective marriage of the Danaids, after the night of bloodshed.

44. [Pseudo-Apollodorus], *Library*, II.1.4.

45. Aeschylus, F. 131, ed. H. J. Mette.

46. Pausanias, II.37.4; Strabo, VIII.6.8.c.371. See R. Baladié, *Le Péloponnèse de Strabon* (Paris, 1980), pp. 87–88.

47. Callimachus, F. 66, ed. R. Pfeiffer: Amymone with three of her sisters. There were in Argos, probably within the city, four wells, said to have been sunk by the Danaids: Strabo, VIII.6.7–8.c.370–371.

48. Aeschylus, F. 355, 16–17.

49. Aeschylus, *Prometheus*, 865; Pindar, *Nemean* 10.6.

50. Pausanias, II.19.6.

51. *Orphicorum fragmenta*, F. 163, ed. O. Kern.

52. Aeschylus, *Eumenides*, 213.

53. J. Modrzejewski, "La Structure juridique du mariage grec," *Annuaire scientifique de la faculté autonome des sciences politiques d'Athènes "Panteios"* (1981): 53–60.

54. Pausanias, II.17.3–4.

55. Hesiod, F. 129.3, ed. West-Merkelbach; Pausanias, X.10.3–5.

56. See J. Pouilloux and G. Roux, "L'Hémicycle des rois d'Argos," in *Énigmes à Delphes* (Paris, 1963), pp. 46–51.

57. [Pseudo-Apollodorus], *Library*, II.1.5.

58. For an interpretation of the punishment of the Danaids, standing for "female bodies," see the perceptive and convincing essay by Giulia Sissa, "Neither Virgins nor Mothers," in *Greek Virginity*, trans. Arthur Goldhammer (Cambridge, Mass., 1990). Since then, several rewarding studies have appeared, of which the following are particularly worth mentioning: Froma Zeitlin, "The Politics of Eros in the Danaid Trilogy of Aeschylus," in *Playing the Other: Gender and Society in Classical Greek Literature* (Chicago, 1996), pp. 123–171; and Marcel Piérart, "Omissions et malentendus dans la 'Périégèse': Danaos et ses filles," *Kernos*, suppl. 8, *Les Panthéons des cités* (1998): 165–193.

SIX: A Kitchen Garden for Women, or How to Engender on One's Own

1. Ovid, *Fasti*, V.195–260.

2. Zeus Heraïos: *IG* I², 840.20–21 (Sokolowski, *LSC* [Paris, 1969], 1, 19–20). See F. Salviat, "Les Théogamies attiques, Zeus Tēleios et l''Agamemnon' d'Eschyle," *BCH* (1964): 647–654. The "keys of marriage" belong in Hera's hands. They should not be allowed to stray into those of Zeus.

3. *Iliad*, 14.200–210.

4. Ovid, *Fasti*, V.243–244.

5. Ovid, *Fasti*, V.195.

6. Ovid, *Fasti*, V.196–229.

7. See "La Panthère parfumée," in *Dionysos mis à mort* (1977; 2nd ed., Paris, 1998), pp. 114–116 (=*Dionysus Slain*, trans. Mireille Muellner and Leonard Muellner [Baltimore, 1979]). The anenome, evoked at 228 by "the son of Cinyras"; also Ovid, *Metamorphoses*, X.519–520.

8. Ovid, *Fasti*, V.251–258. In Argos, Chloris is close to Hera "in bloom": D. Porte, "La Fleur d'Olène et la naissance du dieu Mars," *Latomus* 42 (1983): 877–884.

9. Ovid, *Fasti*, I.204.

10. Ovid, *Fasti*, I.927–930.

11. "Who sleeps alongside," *parakoitēs* (928).

12. *Homeric Hymn to Apollo*, 305–352.

13. *Schol. B Veter. Il.*, II.783a, ed. Erbse.

14. Lucian, *Dialogue on Sacrifices*, 6.

15. Aristotle, *The Generation of Animals*, II.3.737a 27–34.

16. Aristophanes, *Birds*, 694–696.

17. On Ares, the wish to drink blood, mortality, and the god of war wounded and lying among the dead in the blood and the dust, see N. Loraux, "Le Corps vulnérable d'Arès,"

in *Le Corps des dieux*, ed. C. Malamoud and J.-P. Vernant, Le Temps de la réflexion 7 (Paris, 1986), pp. 335–354.

18. Aristotle, *History of Animals*, I.13.493b3; VII.1.581a12–15.

19. Pausanias, II.13.3.

20. Ovid, *Fasti*, V.228; Ovid, *Metamorphoses*, X.519–520, cf. n. 7.

21. *On the Generation of Animals*, IV.8.777a5–9.

22. *On the Generation of Animals*, IV.8.777a14–15.

23. *On the Generation of Animals*, I.19.726b7–10.

24. A more complex model is to be found in G. Sissa, "Il Corpo della donna," in S. Campese, P. Manuli, and G. Sissa, *Madre materia: Sociologia e biologia della donna greca* (Turin, 1983), pp. 83–145. On the humors of the body and the principles of the mechanism of the vital fluids, which in symbolic thought are invariants, see the program of research directed by F. Héritier-Augé between 1977 and 1988 ("La Mauvaise odeur l'a saisi," in *La Fièvre, Le Genre humain* 15 [1987]: 7–17). See Helen King, *Hippocrates' Woman: Reading the Female Body in Ancient Greece* (London, 1998).

25. Aristotle, *On the Generation of Animals*, I.21.730a32; III.1.749b1.

26. *On the Generation of Animals*, III.1.749b–751a.

27. *On the Generation of Animals*, IV.5.774a1–3.

28. *On the Generation of Animals*, I.19.728a1–3; II.3.737a27.

29. See E. Lesky, *Die Zeugungs- und Vererbungslehren der Antike und ihr Nachwirken*, Akad. Wiss. Lit. Mainz, Abh. d. geist- und socialwiss. Kl, 1950, 19 (Wiesbaden, 1951); and G. E. R. Lloyd, *Science, Folklore and Ideology* (Cambridge, 1983), pp. 86–111.

30. Plutarch, *Table Talk*, IV.10.672c. Following skirmishes at Urbino in May 1973, a vigorous counter-attack came from G. S. Kirk in the London *Times Literary Supplement*, 18 August 1978 ("The Spicy Side of Structuralism"), triumphantly flourishing a Sumerian lettuce in between a nipple and a woman's head of hair. Jean Bottéro had already provided me with copious information in June 1975, when I was investigating the further reaches of Flora's garden. A richer symbolism has in this way emerged in both the Oriental and the Greek worlds, and as a result, greater attention has been paid to multiple versions and to the differences between the Adonia of Byblos and those of Alexandria and Athens. (I myself tackled this subject in the *Dictionnaire des mythologies*, ed. Y. Bonnefoy [Paris, 1981], pp. 1–4). At the same time, even more scholarly analyses have appeared on the ethnographic context, symbolic configurations, and intellectual operations at work in the relations between plants and animals. They have, of course, been influenced by the methods of Lévi-Strauss, the analytical strength of which I again praised in "Retour sur la transgression d'un meurtre sacrificiel," the postface to Marcel Detienne, *Dionysos mis à mort* (1977; 2nd ed., Paris, 1998), pp. 219–230.

SEVEN: Misogynous Hestia, or the City in Its Autonomy

1. I am thinking of G. Nagy, *The Best of the Achaeans: Concepts of the Hero in Archaic Greek Poetry* (Baltimore, 1979), especially pp. 118–141. I have drawn attention to the audacities of a violent Apollo in a provisional essay entitled "L'Apollon meurtrier et les crimes de sang," *QUCC* (1986): 7–17. See now my *Apollon le couteau à la main* (Paris, 1998).

2. In the interests of brevity and perhaps because the essential point here is still valid,

see my *Masters of Truth in Archaic Greece*, trans. Janet Lloyd (New York, 1996), pp. 89–104.

3. As Louis Gernet showed in a legal analysis of the Games in Book XXII of the *Iliad*, which first appeared in 1948 and was reprinted in *Droit et Société dans la Grèce ancienne* (Paris, 1955), pp. 9–18.

4. On the model of the *dais eisē* in Homeric society, see S. Said, "Les Crimes des prétendants, la maison d'Ulysse et les festins de l'*Odyssée*," in *Etudes de littérature ancienne* (Paris, 1979), pp. 14–23.

5. [Pseudo-Apollodorus], *Library*, III.11.2.

6. G. Berthiaume, *Les Rôles du Mageiros. Étude sur la boucherie, la cuisine et le sacrifice dans la Grèce ancienne* (Leiden, 1982), pp. 62–64; and the data provided by J. Svenbro, "À Mégara Hyblaea: Le corps géomètre," *Annales ESC* (1982): 954–955.

7. A formula used in the past by P. Levêque and P. Vidal-Naquet, *Cleisthenes the Athenian*, trans. David Ames (Atlantic Highlands, N.J., 1996).

8. On the testimony of Plutarch, *Lycurgus*, 12.3, and Dicearchus, F. 72 Wehrli², see the study by L. Piccirilli in *Le Vite di Licurgo e di Numa* (Rome, 1980), pp. 253–254.

9. Louis Gernet's essay "Sur le symbolisme politique en Grèce ancienne: Le Foyer Commun" (1951), reprinted in *Anthropologie de la Grèce antique* (Paris, 1968), pp. 382–402, opened up the way for other studies. More recent works have revealed the richness of the information and the diversity of the aspects of Hestia: G. Tosi, "Contributo allo studio dei pritanei," *Arte antica e moderna* 33 (1966): 10–21, 151–172; Stephen G. Miller, "Hestia and Symmachos," *Opuscula romana* 9 (1973): 167–172; Miller, *The Prytaneion: Its Function and Architectural Form* (Berkeley, 1978); R. Merkelbach, "Der Kult der Hestia im Prytaneion der griechischen Städte," *Zeitschrift für Epigraphie und Papyrologie* 37 (1980): 77–92; L. Giangiulio, "Edifici pubblici e culti nelle nuove iscrizioni da Entella," *Annali della Scuola Normale Superiore, Classe di Lett. e Filosofia* 12, no. 3 (1982): 945–963. Following the discovery of the decrees of Entella, which draw attention to the publicizing of "political" texts in the sanctuary of Hestia, another document from Paros has produced more information about the function of the archives of the sanctuary of Hestia: W. Lambrinoudakis and M. Wörrle, "Ein hellenistisches Reformgesetz über das öffentliche Urkundenwesen von Paros," *Chiron* 13 (1983): 283–368. This new material suggests that it would be worthwhile further developing the line of inquiry opened up by J.-P. Vernant in "Hestia-Hermes: The Religious Expression of Space and Movement in Ancient Greece," in *Myth and Thought among the Greeks* (London, 1983), pp. 127–175. On the paradigm of Hestia in Aristotle, see M. Vegetti, "Akropolis/Hestia. Sul senso di una metafora aristotelica," in *Poikilia. Mélanges J.-P. Vernant* (Paris, 1987), pp. 357–368.

10. *Homeric Hymn to Hestia (I)*, 5–6; *Homeric Hymn to Aphrodite (I)*, 21–23.

11. *Homeric Hymn to Aphrodite (I)*, 24.

12. J. and L. Robert, *Bull.*, 1968, 465 (R.E.G., 1968, 514), suggest that a dedication to the Prytaneion of Ephesus (published by D. Knibbe, "Epigraphische Nachlese im Bereiche der ephesischen Agora," *Jahreshefte Wien* 47 [1967], Beiblatt 42), in honor of Hestia and the *themelioi*, the deities of the earth's stability, refers to two figures. One is Apollo the architect, the other Apollo the founder of cities, who is skilled in "weaving" foundation stones (Callimachus, *Hymn to Apollo*, 57–58, ed. F. Williams [Oxford, 1978], 56–57). The walls of Troy, among others, were built by Apollo and Poseidon (*Iliad*, VII.452–453). Hestia is a founder who invented the way to build houses (Diodorus, V.68).

13. *Hymn to Aphrodite (I)*, 30–32. See Pindar, *Nemean* 11.6–77; Sophocles, F. 726 Radt; Plato, *Cratylus*, 401a; Pausanias, V.14.5.

14. *Homeric Hymn to Hestia (I)*, 5–6. The Hestia of beginnings is here described as *prōtē* and *pumatē*.

15. Artemidorus, *Onirocritica*, II.37, ed. R. A. Pack, 173, 9–12.

16. In other words, even if not all cities necessarily have a Prytaneion, they do "at least" have an altar or sanctuary consecrated to Hestia, Hestia Koinē.

17. An allusion to the essay by J. Labarbe, "Les Premières démocraties de la Grèce antique," *Bulletin de l'Académie Royale de Belgique, Literature, and Moral and Political Sciences* (1972): 223–254.

18. R. Meiggs and D. Lewis, *A Selection of Greek Historical Inscriptions*, 4th ed. (Oxford, 1980), n. 8 (A.I.1–2), pp. 14–17. Contrary to the commentary (p. 17) by these two historians, here Hestia is not "the goddess" (why?), but the power of the Common Hearth. I am following the interpretation of C. Ampolo, "La *Boulē dēmosiē* di Chio: Un consiglio 'popolare'?" *La Parola del passato* (1983): 401–416. Nothing seems certain. One suggestion is that this is the constitution of Erythrae (O. Hansen, *L'Antiquité classique* 54 [1985]: 274–276).

19. Pausanias, I.18.3, edited with commentary by L. Beschi and D. Musti (Milan, 1982), p. 324.

20. Apart from works on the Prytaneion, see also the study by P. Schmitt-Pantel, "Les Repas au prytanée et à la tholos dans l'Athènes classique. *Sitesis, trophē, misthos:* Réflexions sur le mode de nourriture démocratique," *Archeologia e storia antica* 2 (1980): 55–68.

21. F. Sokolowski, *Lois sacrées d'Asie Mineure* (Paris, 1955), n. 50, ll.12–13. On the Delphinion of the Singers of Miletus, see F. Graf, "Apollon Delphinios," *Museum Helveticum* (1979): 7–9.

22. For example, in the Thasos dedication published by F. Salviat, "Dédicaces de magistrats à Thasos," *BCH* (1958): 319–328.

23. The first collection of documentation was put together by F. Croissant and F. Salviat, "Aphrodite et les magistrats," *BCH* (1966): 460–471.

24. Pindar, *Nemean* 11.1–10: here Hestia is "prytanic."

25. Demosthenes, XIX.189–190. For a history of "political food" and modes of commensality in Athens between the sixth and the fourth centuries, see Schmitt-Pantel, "Les Repas au prytanée et à la tholos dans l'Athènes classique."

26. But there were also some people who were fed "for life" in the Prytaneion: priests of Eleusis, figures chosen by Apollo, victors in the Olympic Games. Schmitt-Pantel, "Les Repas au prytanée et à la tholos dans l'Athènes classique," pp. 56–57, remarks that "there is one image of Athens' past" that stands in contrast to the communal eating of the fifty *prytaneis*, the permanent representatives of the democratic city, who were installed in the *tholos*, "the place of political abstraction *par excellence*" (pp. 64–67).

27. Plutarch, *Solon*, 24.5=F. 89 Ruschenbusch and T. 493 Martina.

28. See L. Ziehen, "*Parasitoi*," in *Realencyclopädie der klassischen Altertumswissenschaft* (Stuttgart, 1949), pp. 1377–1381. There is a great variety of terms: *sunestai, sunsitoi, sumbiotai, sunthoinoi, sitothètai*(?) as well as *paredroi* and *hierophagoi*.

29. Aristotle, *Politics*, III.6.1322b26.

30. Probably the citizens of the first class, those who are "well-born" *(eugeneis)*, who have enjoyed the rights of citizenship for three generations (one of the conditions for be-

coming a *timoûchos* in Massalia: Strabo, IV.1.5) and can, on that account, "accede to any magistracy or priesthood," as is the case for the *demiourgoi* who act as public authorities in the city of Delphi (G. Roux, *L'Amphictionie de Delphes et le temple d'Apollon au IVe siècle* [Paris, 1979], pp. 62–65). See Claude Mossé, who considers the matter more generally in "Citoyens actifs et citoyens 'passifs' dans les cités grecques: Une approche théorique du problème," *Revue des études anciennes* 81 (1979): 241–249.

31. Diogenianus, IV.68 (=*Par. gr.*, I.242.5–7, ed. Leutsch and Schneidewinn), II.40 (=*Par. gr.*, I.201.16–17); Zenobius, IV.44 (=*Par. gr.*, I.97.1–4).

32. Plutarch, I.46 (=*Par. gr.*, I.328.8–10); Diogenianus, II.95 (=*Par. gr.*, II.35.3).

33. Callimachus, *Hymn to Demeter*, 108.

34. *Hymn to Hestia (I)*, 5–6.

35. F. Sokolowski, *Les Lois sacrées des cités grecques* (Paris, 1969), n.151A.252–257. Apart from the commentaries by R. Herzog, "Heilige Gesetze von Kos," *Abhandlungen der preussischen Akademie der Wissenschaften* 6 (1928): 5–10, 42–56; D. Wichtel Kaestner, "The Coan Festival of Zeus Polieus," *Classical Journal* 71, no. 4 (1976): 344–348; and S. M. Sherwin-White, *Ancient Cos* (Göttingen, 1978), pp. 158–165, 322–323, I am endebted to Jesper Svenbro for precious information collected in the course of research for an as yet unpublished work on "the political body," based on the ritual of the Polieus of Cos. A foretaste is provided by his article "Le Partage sacrificiel selon une loi sacrée de Côs (IVe siècle av. J.-C.)," in *Anthropozoologica. La découpe et le partage du corps à travers le temps et l'espace* (Paris, 1987), pp. 71–76.

36. L. 28: here Hestia is called Hetaireia. This has been emended to Tamia, an epithet admittedly attested in Isthmos, a deme of Cos (see Sok., *L.S.C.*, n.169A9), but also to Prytaneia and Damia by Sokolowski (*Les Lois sacrées*, p. 256), who claims that Hetaireia is unusual, even unprecedented. In Crete, Zeus is called *hetaireios* (Hesychius, *s.v. hetaireios*, l.6483, ed. K. Latte; Diphile, F. 20 Kock), in relation to the division of society into *hetaireiai* and its organization into *syssitia* (H. van Effenterre, *La Crète et le monde grec de Platon à Polybe*, 2nd ed. [Paris, 1968], pp. 86–87).

37. Herzog, "Heilige Gesetze von Kos," p. 43: 3 *phulai* of 3,000 and 9 *chiliastues* of 1,000.

38. 151A.i.38: *oikēma* to *damosion*. This probably relates to Hestia.

39. The procedure consisted of each of the three tribes in turn bringing nine oxen, which began by mingling (*summisgontai*, 1.7–8) in the agora; then the three finest were paraded before the priest "to see if one of them would be chosen" (J. Svenbro's interpretation). The same procedure was repeated for the other two tribes. After this (1.16–17), if not one of the oxen had been selected, an ox was chosen from each *chiliastus*, and these too were encouraged to intermingle (*summisgontai*, 1.17). This time one would be chosen as a victim for Zeus, a prayer said, and an *apokērutteinu* organized (l.18), which Svenbro correctly interprets as meaning "being put up for sale" (*apokēruttein*, "put up for auction").

40. "What is emphasized here is the idea of the unity of the civic group, all the elements of which had momentarily to be fused as a whole" (Gernet, "Sur le symbolisme politique en Grèce ancienne," p. 393).

41. By receiving the monetary "value" of the ox, in the name of all the citizens, Hestia did not forfeit the unificatory role implied by her title of Hetaireia.

42. 151A.35–43.

43. 151A.19–22: the prime portion—that is to say, the skin and a thigh—went to the *gereaphonos* of the kings *(basileis)*, while the rest of the meat went to the city. In the case of Zeus Polieus, the sacrifice took place on the day following the ceremony of choosing a victim: 151A.38–44.

44. 151A.19: *hypokuptein.*

45. J. Svenbro's pertinent interpretation.

46. Sherwin-White, *Ancient Cos*, pp. 158–165.

47. Even if she is Hetaireia, not Tamia as at Isthmos.

48. Artemidorus, II.37, ed. R. A. Pack, 173, 10: *enthēkē tōn prosodōn.*

49. K. Latte, *Kollektivbesitz und Staatschatz in Griechenland* (1946–1947), reprinted in *Kleine Schriften* (Munich, 1968), pp. 294–312. The importance of this inquiry was pointed out by L. Gernet: "Dans la cité antique, il y a État à partir du moment où il y a Trésor d'État," *Anthropologie* (1968): 397.

50. K. Latte, *Kollektivbesitz und Staatschatz in Griechenland.*

51. Herodotus, III.57.

52. See J. Labarbe, *La Loi navale de Thémistocle* (Paris, 1957).

53. Thucydides, I.80.4. See I.142.1. Sparta was characterized by the poor state of its "public finances," Aristotle, *Politics*, II.9.36.1271b10–15.

54. This absence is noted by Miller, *The Prytaneion*, 14n.21. But all the same there was a Hestia, probably a "communal" one, alongside Moira.

55. Pausanias, III.11.11: Moira and Hestia "for the Spartans." In the *megaron* of Delphi, the Moirai stood close to the altars of Hestia and Poseidon: G. Roux, *Delphes, son oracle et ses dieux* (Paris, 1976), pp. 98–99.

56. Aristotle, *Politics*, III.14.22.1285b9–11. The twofold royalty blocked the development of Hestia and the Communal Hearth. Just as there were no *syssitia* under the sign of Hestia, there was no Hestia under a regime of *syssitia.*

57. M. M. Austin, *Greece and Egypt in the Archaic Age* (Cambridge, 1970), pp. 22–23, 58–69; J. Boardman, *The Greeks Overseas*, 2nd ed. (London, 1980), pp. 118–133.

58. As Herodotus, II.178, most explicitly formulates it. See Austin, *Greece and Egypt in the Archaic Age*, p. 30.

59. Boardman, *Greeks Overseas*, p. 120. The sanctuary was identified by a dedication "to the gods of the Greeks."

60. Hermeias, *The Apollo of Gryneion*, in Athenaeus, IV.149d = F. 112 Tresp.

61. As was decisively shown in a work by L. Robert begun in 1934 and reprinted in 1962: *Opera minora selecta*, vol. 2 (Amsterdam, 1969), pp. 972–976, 983–987. A drinking cup from the same period bore a dedication to Kōmaios (Apollo): E. Simon, "Neuerwerbungen des Martin von Wagner Museums Würzburg," *Archäologischer Anzeiger* 83 (1968): 135–136.

62. The problem of females in the service of Hestia Boulaia arises in Ephesus, at any rate, where the dedications of female *prytaneis* were found. They were published by D. Knibbe, *Forschungen in Ephesos*, IX, 1, 1, Österreichische Akademie der Wissenschaften (Vienna, 1981), F. 1 (62–63) and F. 4 (64), and mentioned by Merkelbach, "Der Kult der Hestia im Prytaneion der griechischen Städte," pp. 84–87. One of them, a girl named Tullia, asks Hestia, the most ancient of the goddesses and the guardian of the eternal fire given by Zeus to the city, to give her children—even "children who in every respect resemble their mother." It is true that another dedication refers to a masculine Hestiouchos

and his companion Kalathēphoros. As for the title Hestia of the city, bestowed upon certain priestesses in Sparta (*I.G.* V[1].583, 584, 586), this seems to have been introduced under the Roman empire. However, it would be interesting to investigate all this further.

63. This seems to have been the case at Hermione, Pausanias, II.35.1: no *agalma*, but instead a statue, an altar (*bōmos*), where sacrifices were made to Hestia, who seems to have enjoyed the same privileges as Vesta, if we are to believe Ovid, *Fasti*, VI.299: fire is her image, the flames of the altar embody her. See G. Dumézil, *La Religion romaine archaïque*, 2nd ed. (Paris, 1974), p. 330.

64. The Virgin-Hestia, positioned close to the hearth (Porphyry, in Eusebius, *Prepar. Evangel.*, III.11), and the old woman of Artemidorus, II.44, ed. R. A. Pack, 179, 3–4. But there is also room for a matronly figure of Hestia in the Prytaneion: the one sculpted by Scopas for the city of Paros (Pliny, *Natural History*, 36.25) and, now, the relief by Pharsalus, studied by S. G. Miller, "Hestia and Symmachos," *Opuscula romana* 9 (1973): 167–172.

65. A first version of this chapter may be found in *Quaderni di storia* 22 (1985): 59–78. But since then Hestia has not found her historian! On questions concerning Hestia, see Pauline Schmitt-Pantel, *La cité au banquet. Histoire des repas publics dans les cités grecs*, Collection de l'École Française de Rome157 (Farnese Palace, Rome, 1992).

EIGHT: Even Talk Is in Some Ways Divine

1. E. Bernheim, *Einleitung in die Geschichstwissenschaft* (Leipzig, 1889).

2. See the meticulous Africanist J. Vansina, *De la tradition orale. Essai de méthode historique* (Tervuren, 1961), pp. 69–100. To know "how to detect false rumors," see pp. 98–100.

3. Plutarch, *Nicias*, 30.1; *On Gossip*, 13.508a–c.

4. Hesiod, *Works*, 764.

5. *Iliad*, 3.150–160.

6. Aeschylus, *Agamemnon*, 687. See N. Loraux, "Le Fantôme de la sexualité," *Nouvelle revue de psychanalyse* 29 (1984): 11–31, especially 27–28.

7. Aeschylus, *Helen*, 2.

8. F. 2 Allen.

9. *Iliad*, 20.203–204. On *kleos*, the hero, the memory of his high deeds: for the *Iliad*, see G. Nagy, *The Best of the Achaeans* (Baltimore, 1979); for the *Iliad* and the *Odyssey*, see P. Pucci, *Odysseus Polutropos: Intertextual Readings in the "Odyssey" and the "Iliad"* (Ithaca, N.Y., 1987), pp. 216–221. For a suitably "deconstructed" book, see M. Detienne and P. Pucci, "Autour du Polytrope," *L'Infini* 23 (1988): 57–71.

10. *Odyssey*, 24.196–203.

11. J. Svenbro, *La Parole et le marbre* (Lund, 1976), pp. 36, 65.

12. *Odyssey*, 20.100–121.

13. Herodotus, 9.90–92.

14. Pausanias, 9.11.7.

15. Pausanias, 7.22.1.

16. Philichorus, F. 192 Jacoby.

17. *Iliad*, 2.250: *panomphaios*, glossed *klēdonios*. Zeus Phemios at Erythraea (Dittenberger, *Sylloge*^{3}, 1014, 25).

18. *Iliad*, 2.86–94.

19. *Odyssey*, 24.413–414.
20. *Aeneid*, 4.174–190.
21. *Scholia to Aeschines*, I.128.
22. See M. Detienne, *L'Invention de la mythologie*, 2nd ed. (Paris, 1987), 154–189.
23. *Laws*, 8.838a–839d.
24. *Laws*, 1.625a–b.
25. *Laws*, 12.966c.
26. *Laws*, 2.664a–d.
27. *Laws*, 2.664d.
28. *Laws*, 2.663e–664a.
29. Such a figure is suggested by Maurice Olender in *Le Genre humain* 5 (1982): 71–80.

NINE: An Ephebe and an Olive Tree

1. [Pseudo-Apollodorus], *Library*, III.14.1, ed. J. G. Frazer (commentary and notes, vol. 2, pp. 78–79). See L. Preller and C. Robert, *Griechische Mythologie*, vol. 1, part 5 (1894; rpt., Berlin, 1964), pp. 202–204. In his report entitled "La Grèce archaïque," published in the proceedings of the *Deuxième Conférence Internationale d'Histoire Économique: Aix-en-Provence, 1962*, vol. 1 (Paris, 1965), pp. 70–71, Édouard Will tried to show that olive cultivation was developed at the cost of the cultivation of other foodstuffs and that oil was used as a commodity to barter in exchange for the wheat that Attica needed. Several of the laws and measures introduced by Solon seem to indicate the promotion of olive cultivation. In the first place, the planting of olive groves was subject to certain regulations: the trees had to be planted in rows, at regular intervals of at least 9 feet (Pollux, V.36; Plutarch, *Solon*, 23.7=F. 60b Ruschenbusch). Second, it was forbidden to uproot olive trees anywhere in the territory of Athens, unless it was to the advantage of one of the city sanctuaries, or a deme, or for the use of a citizen, in which case a maximum of two trees per year could be taken ([Demosthenes], *C. Macartatos*, 71). See L. Gernet, in his edition of *Plaidoyers civils* (Paris, 1960), vol. 2, p. 120n.1. Finally, of all the products of Athens, Solon allowed only oil to be sold abroad. The exportation of everything else was forbidden (Plutarch, *Solon*, 24.1=F. 65 Ruschenbusch).

2. Sophocles, *Oedipus at Colonus*, 694–705. See the notes in the editions of C. E. Palmer (Cambridge, 1869) and R. C. Jebb (Cambridge, 1885).

3. Artemidorus, *Oneirocr.*, IV.57 Pack.

4. Euripides, *Ion*, 1435–1436; Aeschylus, *Persians*, 616–617; Porphyry, *De antro nympharum*, 33. On the funerary uses of olive trees, see F. Cumont, *La Stèle du danseur d'Antibes* (Paris, 1942), pp. 13–14.

5. Plutarch, *Quaest. conviv.*, 723F.

6. Pliny, *Natural History*, 16.234; Theophrastus, *H. Pl.*, 13.2 and 5. In his commentary on Pliny, *Natural History*, 16.234 (Collection des Universités de France [Paris, 1962], p. 180), J. André writes: "The olive tree lives for between 1,000 and 2,000 years."

7. Pliny, *Natural History*, 17.129, ed. J. André.

8. R. Billiard, *L'Agriculture dans l'Antiquité* (Paris, 1928), 259–269.

9. Herodotus, VIII.55.

10. See G. Kruse, *s. v. Morios*, *RE* (1933), c. 307. Some interpretations are content to draw attention to the purely linguistic connection between Zeus Morios and the *moriai*, without taking into consideration the religious significance and the mythical represen-

tations of the olive tree in Athens and in other parts of the Greek world. The present analysis, on the contrary, suggests an interpretation that underlines the affinities of the Attic olive tree with a whole mythical tradition in which the olive is not only a fateful tree but also the soul of a man, as is confirmed by the latter's representation as a human sprig. Comments to this effect are to be found in J. E. Harrison, "Some Points in Dr. Furwängler's Theories on the Parthenon and Its Marbles," *CR* 9 (1895): 89; O. Gruppe, *Griechische Mythologie*, vol.2 (Munich, 1906), pp. 879–880 and 1197–1198; A. B. Cook, *Zeus*, vol. 3, part 1 (Cambridge, 1940), p. 762; F. Vian, *La Guerre des Géants* (Paris, 1952), p. 256.

11. The *glaukōpis* Athena corresponds to the *glaukōpis* olive tree (Euphorion, F. 140 Meineke): *The Homeric Hymn to Demeter*, 23, evokes the olive trees laden with shining fruit (*aglaokarpos elaiai*) that were deaf to the cries of Persephone when she was abducted by Hades.

12. Istros, 334 F. 30 Jacoby (*Comm.*, 644–645); Philochorus, 328 F. 125; Androtion, 324 F. 39. See Latte, *s.v. Moria*, *RE* (1933), c. 302–303.

13. Aristotle, *Athen. Polit.*, IX.2; Lysias, VII, ed. L. Gernet (see the observations of vol. 1, pp. 107–110). See U. Wilamowitz, *Aristoteles und Athen*, vol. 1 (Berlin, 1893), pp. 240–242.

14. J. Fink, "Lieferanten der Athena," *Gymnasium* 70 (1963): 133–136 (together with pl. XIII). See P. E. Corbett, "Attic Pottery of the Later Fifth Century from the Athenian Agora," *Hesperia* 18 (1949): 306–307 (together with pls. 73 and 74). It should also be remembered that several traditions state that olive picking should be carried out by young boys and girls who are virgins (Palladios, *De agric.*, I.16.14) or else by men who can "swear that they have just left the beds of their legitimate wives, not those of any other women" (*Geoponica*, IX.2.5–6). See A. Delatte, *Herbarius*, 3rd ed. (Brussels, 1961), p. 76.

15. See Aristotle, *Athen. Polit.*, 60.3; *IG*, II^2, 2311, 52–53; and the remarks of L. Deubner, *Attische Feste* (Berlin, 1932), p. 34.

16. Vian, *La Guerre des Géants*, pp. 247–248.

17. Aristides, II, *Athena*, ed. Dindorf, vol. 1, p. 16; Vian, *La Guerre des Géants*, p. 255n.20, who notes this testimony, points out that *hugieia* carried the strong meaning of *valetudo*, along with all the implications of *valeo*.

18. *Schol. in Plat. Parm.*, 127a, ed. Greene, 48.

19. Philochorus, 328 F. 9 Jacoby (with the *Commentary*, III, B. *Suppl.* I [Leiden, 1954], 276). In opposition to Pfuhl and Deubner, Jacoby is correct in his belief that *thallos* means "olive branch."

20. *Lex rhet.* in *Anecdota graeca*, I.242. 3-4 Bekker. The *Promachia* of Sparta (Nilsson, *Griechische Feste* [1906; rpt., 1957], p. 470, and nn. 2 and 3), draw a distinction of the same type between, on the one hand, the citizens of Sparta and the *perioikoi* and, on the other, the citizens and the young boys still being trained and taking part in the *agogē*: the citizens wear a crown of reeds *(kalamos)*, while the others are not crowned (Athenaeus, 674A).

21. Hesychius, *s.v. stephanon ekpherein*. The masculine olive tree corresponds to the tuft of wool reserved for newborns of the female sex, which constitutes an allusion to the wool work and weaving *(talasia)* for which girls are responsible. J. Harrison, *CR* 9 (1895): 89–90, noted the relation between this Athenian custom and the place of the *moriai* in Attic religious representations.

22. Pollux, IX.17; Hesychius, *s.v. astē elaia;* Eust., 1388.7–8. See Cook, *Zeus,* vol. 3, part 1, pp. 760–761.

23. See V. Chapot, *REA* (1929), pp. 7–12. As J. Bingen reminds me, in the calendar of Erchia, the expression *en astei* means "in Athens" (see G. Daux, *BCH* [1963]: 623).

24. See Van der Kolf, *s.v. Meleagros, RE* (1931), c. 446–478. For a fuller interpretation of the firebrand of Meleager, see "La part du feu" in P. Ellinger, "La Légende nationale phocidienne," *BCH,* suppl. 27, École Française d'Athènes (1993): 246–268.

25. Phrynichos *ap.* Paus., X.31.4 (*TGF*², 721, F. 6); Bacchylides, V.141–142; [Apollodorus], I.8.2. See the studies of J. T. Kakridis, *Homeric Researches* (Lund, 1949), pp. 14–15 (which refers to his other works).

26. On the customs of the seventh and tenth days, see L. Deubner, "Die Gebraüche der Griechen nach der Geburt," *RhM* 95 (1952): 374–377.

27. Tzetzes, *Schol. in Lycoph.,* 492, ed. Scheer, vol.2, p. 178, 11–18; Malalas, *Chronographia,* VI, ed. Dindorf, 165, 8–9. The importance of this version was recognized by G. Knaack, "Zur Meleagersage," *RhM* 49 (1894): 310–313.

28. [Plutarch], *Parall. gr. et rom.,* 26, p. 312A: Doru, which is here associated with Ares, Meleager's father, as in the tragedy by Euripides (*TGF*², 515–539), can only mean the shaft of a spear or hunting spear.

29. Sophocles, *Electra,* 419–423. See J.-P. Vernant, *Mythe et pensée chez les grecs,* 3rd ed. (Paris, 1985), pp. 166–167 (=*Myth and Thought among the Greeks* (London, 1983).

30. See *Iliad,* I.234–235: the scepter by which Achilles swears a solemn oath is a staff "which will never again put out leaves and branches from the moment it parted from its stump in the mountains, and it will sprout no more."

31. *Homeric Hymn to Demeter,* 239–241. See C. M. Edsman, *Ignis divinus* (Lund, 1949), pp. 224–229.

32. Herodotus, I.108.

33. Herodotus, VII.19.

34. See L. Séchan, *Etudes sur la tragédie grecque dans ses rapports avec la céramique* (Paris, 1926; rpt., 1967), p. 357.

35. See A. Severyns, *Le Cycle épique dans l'École d'Aristarque* (Paris, 1928), pp. 342–345.

36. Malalas, *Chronogr.,* V, ed. Dindorf, 138–139. The value of such objects as talismans probably also explains their presence in sanctuary treasuries. Cf. the golden olive tree in the temple of Amphairaus (*IG,* VII.3498).

37. *Odyssey,* XIX.109–114.

38. Thetis, speaking of her son, says, "He shot up like a young [sprig]. I tended him like a [sprig alongside a vine . . .] and sent him out to fight the Trojans" (*Iliad,* XVIII.56–59).

39. Simonides, F. 564, in *PMG,* ed. Page.

40. Pausanias, II.7.7–9. On the complex ritual of Sicyon, see A. Brelich, *Paides e Parthenoi* (Rome, 1969), pp. 377–387.

41. Hesiod, *Works,* 144–146; *Theogony,* 185–187. See J.-P. Vernant, *Mythe et pensée chez les grecs,* pp. 31–35. Also called to mind are the Phrygian Corybantes whom the Sun saw rising out of the ground and growing like great trees (*PMG* F. 985b5–7, ed. Page).

42. Tzetzes, *Schol. in Lycophron,* 480, ed. Scheer, vol. 2, 172–173; see Weizsäcker *s.v. Dryops, Roschers Lexikon,* c. 1204–1205; also the factual data provided by P. Ramat, "Su alcune tracce del totemismo nell'onomastica greca: Gli etnici in *opes,*" *RFIC* 40 (1962): 170–171.

43. See Heckenbach, *s.v. Kaineus, RE* (1919), c. 1504–1505; M. Delcourt, "La Légende de Kaineus," *RHR* (1953): 129–150.

44. Aeschylus, *Seven*, 529–530. See Fiehn, *s.v. Parthenopaios, RE* (1949), c. 1932–1934.

45. An upright spear is not only an image of war but also "a qualitative representation of a man standing up, and of his power as an agent" (E. Cassin, "Symboles de cession immobilière dans l'ancien droit mésopotamien," *L'Année sociologique*, 3rd series [1952] [Paris, 1955]: 131[=*Le Semblable et le différent. Symboles du pouvoir dans le Proche-Orient ancien* [Paris, 1987], p. 305).

46. R. Hanslik, *s.v. Orestheus, RE* (1939), c. 1016, is careful to distinguish between Orestheus, the son of Deucalion and the king of Aetolia, and Orestheus, the son of Lycaon, who lived in the part of Arcadia known as Oresthasion (see E. Meyer, *s.v. Oresthasion, RE* [1939], c. 1014–1016).

47. Hecataeus of Miletus, *FGrHist*, 1.F.15.

48. Phytius is associated with Leto Pythia, Poseidon Phytalmios, and Phytalos, Demeter's host who receives the gift of a fig tree by way of thanks for his hospitality. See J. Schmidt, *s.v. Phtalmios, Phytia*, and *Phytios*, and also K. Ziegler, *s.v. Phytalos, RE* (1941), c. 1175–1178.

49. *Iliad*, IX.533–534.

50. See J. Herbillon, *Les Cultes de Patras, avec une prosopographie patréenne* (Baltimore, 1929), pp. 55–74; Wilamowitz, *Der Glaube der Hellenen*, vol. 1, part 3 (Berlin, 1959), pp. 374–380.

51. *Iliad*, IX.534: *thalusia*. See M. P. Nilsson, *Griechische Feste*, pp. 330–332.

52. *Iliad*, IX.536–537.

53. See, for example, the myth of Artemis *Chitonē*, recounted in the *schol. in Callim. Hymm.*, I.77b, ed. Pfeiffer, vol. 2, 45.

54. See Nilsson, *Griechische Feste*, pp. 183–184.

55. For a whole tradition, a child is a branch, *thalos* (*Iliad*, XXII.87; *Homeric Hymn to Demeter*, 66, 187, etc.; see L. Broccia, "*Phallos* in Asclepiades," *La Parola del passato* 6 [1951]: 54–61); a young sprig, *ernos* (Aeschylus, *Eum.*, 660–661; Pindar, *Nem.* 6.37; etc.); a young bush, *phuton* (Plato, *Euthyd.*, 2d; Theocritus, XXIV.103–104), that his father has planted on his land and that he tends as would a careful gardener (Aeschylus, *Suppl.*, 592–593). In similar fashion, in the city men are like plants in the field or trees in the orchard of those who govern them (Plutarch, *Moralia*, 329B). An old man, meanwhile, is a dry stump with withered leaves (Aeschylus, *Ag.*, 79–80). A crater with slender columns, now in Bologna, shows two contrasting herms, one of which, sporting a black beard and black hair, is being honored by a young woman, while the other, with a white beard and white hair, is receiving homage from an old man, standing next to a leafless tree: J. Marcadé, "Hermès doubles," *BCH* (1952): 617–618 and fig. 22.

56. *Iliad*, IX.539–542.

57. In epic, the wild boar is an animal as fearsome as a lion (*Iliad*, XI.293). Like the lion it symbolizes aggressive fury and power (*Iliad*, V.782–783; XVII.20–21, 281–283). Achilles shows how strong and courageous he is by hunting lions and killing wild boars (Pindar, *Nem.* 3.46–47). See now Alain Schnapp, *Le chasseur et la cité. Chasse et érotique dans la Grèce ancienne* (Paris, 1997). Elsewhere, before the fight that sets two teams of young Spartans against each other, in the Plataniste (Pausanias, III.14.8–10), two wild boars are loosed in a fight, the result of which prefigures the outcome of the trial that takes place there. Finally, Tydeus, another of Oeneus' sons and a violent warrior, is linked

with the wild boar in the Theban tradition: he either displays a painted boar on his shield ([Apollodorus], *Library*, III.6.1, ed. J. G. Frazer), or, when he visits Adrastus, wears the skin of a boar (Hyginus, *Fab.*, 69; Statius, *Theb.*, I.488–489).

58. The relations between Odysseus and his maternal grandfather Autolycus are summed up in the hospitality that the latter offers Odysseus when he comes of age. In the company of his maternal uncles, Autolycus' sons, Odysseus kills a huge boar against which he stands alone without flinching (*Od.*, XIX.395; cf. the Macedonian custom of not allowing a youth to take part in meals with the adult men until he has killed a boar without resorting to the use of a net: Athenaeus, 18A).

59. *Schol. in Eur. Hippol.*, 35.

60. *Iliad*, IX.547–548.

61. The version of Malalas, cited in note 27, above.

62. *Iliad*, XVII.20–60.

63. See P. Vidal-Naquet, *The Black Hunter*, trans. Andrew Szegedy-Maszak (Baltimore, 1986), pp. 106–128.

64. See L. Robert, *Études épigraphiques et philologiques* (Paris, 1938), pp. 296–307; C. Pélékidis, *Histoire de l'éphébie attique* (Paris, 1962), pp. 110–113.

65. See N. C. Conomis, "On the Oath of the Athenian Ephebes," *Athena* 63 (1959): 119–131.

66. See my early observations in "La Phalange: Problèmes et controverses," in *Problèmes de la guerre en Grèce ancienne*, ed. J.-P. Vernant (Paris, 1968), pp. 119–142, especially 126–127.

67. *Syll.*^{3}, 527, 140–160; *Inscr. Cret.*, I (1935), 84–85. On the political problems posed by the Dreros oath, see, for example, E. Kirsten, *s.v. Dreros*, *RE*, *Suppl. B.* VII (1940), c. 141–144; and R. F. Willetts, *Aristocratic Society in Ancient Crete* (London, 1955), pp. 182–185.

68. On the expression and its reference to autochthony, see L. Robert, *Études anatoliennes* (Paris, 1937), p. 320.

69. This type of combat belongs in the file of information collected by A. Brelich, *Guerre, agoni e culti nella arcaica* (Bonn, 1961); *Paides e Parthenoi*, vol. 1 (Rome, 1969), especially pp. 200–204.

70. See R. F. Willetts, *Aristocratic Society in Ancient Crete*, pp. 11–14; Willetts, *Cretan Cults and Festivals* (London, 1962), pp. 201–202.

71. R. F. Willetts, "A Neotas at Dreros?" *Hermes* (1957): 381–384.

72. See the remarks and information provided by R. F. Willetts himself in his *Aristocratic Society*, pp. 120–121; and also in *Cretan Cults*, pp. 176–177.

73. Unsurprisingly, the half-Athenian, half-Cretan politico-religious myth of the olive tree had a part to play some decades ago in a comparative study entitled *Problèmes de la terre en Grèce ancienne*, ed. M. I. Finley (The Hague, 1973), pp. 293–306.

TEN: The Crane and the Labyrinth

1. The visual encyclopedia edited by H. Kern, *Labirinti*, vol. 2 (Milan, 1981), which is a compendium of references, lists works on labyrinths, especially those in Greece.

2. Hesiod, F. 140 West-Merkelbach (=[Apollodorus], III.1.2; *Schol. AB Il.*, 12.292.

3. Bacchylides, XVII.53–57, ed. B. Snell; Hyginus, *Astronom.*, II.5.

4. [Apollodorus], III.1.3; Euripides, *The Cretans*, F. 4.23–24, ed. Cantarella.

5. For example, the magical cow belonging to the king's herd, the riddle about which has to be solved by diviners, for this is the only way to find Glaucus, whom his father Minos is seeking ([Apollodorus], III.3; Aeschylus, *The Cretans*, F. 164, ed. H. J. Mette).

6. *Od.*, XI.568–571; Plato, *Gorgias*, 523f; *Apologia*, 41a. See Helbig, *s.v. Minos*, in *Roschers Lexikon*, II, 2 (1894–1897), c. 2995–97; and E. Bethe, "Minos," *Rheinisches Museum* 65 (1910): 200–232.

7. [Apollodorus], III.15.1; Antoninus Liberalis, *Metamorphoses*, 41.

8. [Apollodorus], III.1.4: *exagriein.*

9. [Apollodorus], III.1.4.

10. Euripides, *The Cretans*, F. 4, ed. Cantarella: *aiskhistēnosos* (l. 12). On Pasiphae, the pathological nature of her desire, and the fascination that boundlessness holds for Euripides, see A. Rivier, *Études de littérature grecque* (Geneva, 1975), pp. 43–60, who suggests that Euripides' text is based on the "intact structure" of the mythological account.

11. Euripides, F. 2a.12, ed. Cantarella: *[tau]rou memiktai kai broto[u diplei phusei].*

12. Theseus is a political hero, often the subject of ideologies both in fifth-century Athens and, even more, in modern hermeneutics. See Claude Calame, *Thésée et l'imaginaire athénien*, 2nd ed. (Lausanne, 1996).

13. *Poetics*, 8.1451a16–22, edited with commentary by R. Dupont-Roc and J. Lallot.

14. *Poetics*, 8.1451a1–2, 36–38.

15. K. Friis Johansen, *Thésée et la danse à Délos. Etude herméneutique* (Copenhagen, 1945).

16. In C. Robert's interpretation, *Die griechischen Heldensagen*, vol. 2, part 2 (Berlin, 1966–1967), pp. 677–678, the Minotaur duplicates the bull of Marathon, a local monster, which has nothing to do with Crete.

17. [Apollodorus], II.5.7; Diodorus, IV.13.4. In Pausanias' version, I.27.9–10, the Cretan bull is a monster sent by Poseidon, who is angered at not having received the highest honors from Minos. On Heracles and the bull, see Robert, *Die griechischen Heldensagen*, vol. 2, part 2, pp. 456–458. Once he has overcome the bull with his bare hands, Heracles lets it go: *anetos.*

18. In particular, one of Minos' sons, Androgeus: Pausanias, I.27.10.

19. *Elaunein* and *thuein:* Pausanias, I.27.10 (Athena on the Acropolis); *elaunein* and *katathuein:* Plutarch, *Theseus*, 14.1 (Delphinian Apollo).

20. Johansen, *Thésée et la danse à Délos*, pp. 26–44.

21. The labyrinth, circular, polygonal, or square, drawn and painted on vases, tablets, and coins, always follows an uninterrupted course on its winding way: a single, continuous path leads to the central point. P. Borgeaud, "The Open Entrance to the Palace of the King: The Greek Labyrinth in Context," *History of Religions* 14, no. 1 (1974): 22; W. A. Daszewski, *La Mosaïque de Thésée* (Warsaw, 1977), p. 53n.4. So the figurative model is contrary to the mental model presented here. This may be a deliberate way of demonstrating the autonomy of the iconography.

22. They appear together on the Rayet vase in the Louvre: Johansen, *Thésée et la danse à Délos*, p. 39, figs. 20–21.

23. Callimachus, *Hymn to Delos*, 310–313: *Mukema, hagrion . . . huia, gnampton hedos skoliou laburinthou.*

24. The face, like that of the Gorgon, is yelling and monstrous, a full-face, terrifyingly shrieking mask: J.-P. Vernant, seminar on the mask of Gorgo, in *Annuaire du*

Collège de France, 1978–1979 (Paris, 1980), pp. 374–393; Vernant, "L'Autre de l'homme: La face de Gorgô," in *Le Racisme. Mythes et sciences*, ed. M. Olender (Brussels, 1981), pp. 141–156; Vernant, *La Mort dans les yeux* (Paris, 1985).

25. All the data can be found in P. Bruneau, *Recherches sur les cultes de Délos* (Paris, 1972), pp. 29–32.

26. Pollux, IV.101: *hekastos huph' hekastoi kata stoichon.* K. Friis Johansen provides an interpretation of the François vase.

27. Pollux, IV.101; [Apollodorus], *Epitome*, I.8.9.

28. Eustathius, 1166.17.

29. Dicearchus, in Plutarch, *Theseus*, 21: *Mimema tōn en toi laburinthoi periodōn kai dieksodōn.*

30. Pollux, IV.101: *ta akra hekaterothen tōn hēgemonōn ekhontōn.*

31. See the remarks of G. Roux, "Le Vrai temple d'Apollon à Délos," *BCH* 103 (1979): 118–119.

32. According to G. Roux, "Le Vrai temple d'Apollon à Délos," p. 119, the dance around the altar is just an ordinary lustral rite, a back-to-front version of an ancient spring agricultural rite, under the sign of the crane.

33. For proof that they invented the alphabet, or at least the letter delta, see Philostratus, *Heroicus*, 11.4.

34. Bruneau, *Recherches sur les cultes de Délos*, p. 31, is fascinated by the gait of the crane.

35. A file of data on the crane has been put together by D'Arcy Thompson, *A Glossary of Greek Birds* (1936; rpt., Hildesheim, 1966), pp. 68–75.

36. 263d. Dionysus, *De Aucupio*, II.18, ed. Garzya: *sopha . . . bouleumata.*

37. Aristotle, *History of Animals*, 8.12.597a 4–32; Aelian, *Nature of Animals*, III.13.

38. Aristotle, *History of Animals*, 8.12.597a31–32: *ektopidzousin eis eschata ek tōn eschatōn.*

39. *Paroemiographi graeci*, I.389–390, ed. Leutsch-Schneidewinn; Suda, *s.v. Geranoi lithous pherousin; Schol. Arist. Birds*, 1137; Aelian, *Nature of Animals*, III.13.

40. Aelian, *Nature of Animals*, III.13.

41. On the Cypselon coffer, Ariadne holds the wreath, standing close to Theseus: Pausanias, V.19.1.

42. This model was used by M. Detienne and J.-P. Vernant in *Cunning Intelligence in Greek Culture and Society* (1974), trans. Janet Lloyd (Chicago, 1991). Its application to Daedalus' labyrinth is noted by F. Frontisi-Ducroux, *Dédale. Mythologie de l'artisan en Grèce ancienne* (Paris, 1975), pp. 135–150.

43. *Schol. V. Il.*, 18.590.

44. [Apollodorus], *Epitome*, I.8.9.

45. [Apollodorus], *Epitome*, I.14. See Sophocles, F. 324 Radt.

46. *Dia ton kochlion linon dieirein:* [Apollodorus], *Epitome*, I.14.

47. This was noticed many years ago by J.-P. Rossignol, professor at the Collège de France, in an essay entitled "Dédale montré pour la première fois sous son vrai jour," in *Les Artistes homériques*, vol. 2 (Paris, 1885).

48. Sophocles, F. 324 Radt.

49. Examples are listed in H. Kern, *Lăbirinti*, vol. 2 (Milan, 1981), pp. 39–42.

50. This thesis is reaffirmed by G. Pugliese Carratelli, "Labranda e Labyrinthos," *RAAN* (1939): 285–300; followed by F. Cordano, "Il Labirinto come simbolo grafico della città," *MEFRA* 92 (1980): 1, 7–15.

51. Hippolytus, *Réfutation de toutes les hérésies*, IX.9.4, ed. Wendland, p. 243. A commentary on the text can be found in J. Bollack and H. Wismann, *Héraclite* (Paris, 1972), F. 59, p. 202.

52. E. Pontremoli and B. Haussoullier, *Didymes* (Paris, 1904), p. 93; B. Haussoullier, "Inscriptions de Didymes. Comptes de la construction du temple d'Apollon Didyméen," *Revue de philologie* 29 (1905): 264–268.

53. Diodorus, V.37.2–3.

54. Hypotheses formulated by E. Pontremoli and B. Haussoullier, *Didymes*, p. 93.

55. Sophocles, F. 1030 Radt: *achanes. To mē ekhon stegēn ē orophon epi tou laburinthou.*

56. P. Tannery, *Pour l'histoire des lignes et surfaces courbes dans l'antiquité* (1883–1884), reprinted in *Mémoires scientifiques*, vol. 2 (Paris, 1912), pp. 14–40.

57. Plato, *Euthydemus*, 291b. This is an example of circular reasoning; and the metaphor is surely sophistic, in the strict sense of the term. In Empedocles' poem, it is the inner ear that is shaped like a whorled shell: J. Bollack, *Empédocle*, vol. 3, part 2 (Paris, 1969), pp. 370–371.

58. In agreement with P. Rosensthiel, "Les Mots du labyrinthe," in *Cartes et figures de la terre* (Paris, 1980), pp. 94–103.

59. *Epigram. Rome*, Kaibel 920, together with the interpretations of L. Robert, *Hellenica* 11–12 (1960): 12–13.

60. Kern, *Labirinti*, p. 20, suggests that the path of the labyrinth may be danced along, but that is not to say that this constituted the "original form" of the dance steps.

61. I was encouraged to make this journey to the labyrinth by Roland Barthes in his last seminar, devoted to the metaphorical power of the labyrinth (1978–1979, Collège de France). An account of this "journey" was included by P. Mauriès in *Le Promeneur* 11 (1982): 1–6; 12 (1982): 2–4, and was later published in *MEFRA* 95 (1983): 2, 541–553.

ELEVEN: The Finger of Orestes

1. R. Parker, *Miasma, Pollution and Purification in early Greek Religion* (Oxford, 1983).

2. *Iliad*, 24.477–483.

3. L. Moulinier, *Le Pur et l'impur dans la pensée des grecs* (Paris, 1952); and J.-L. Durand, "Formules attiques du fonder," in *Tracés de fondation*, ed. M. Detienne (Louvain, 1990), pp. 271–287.

4. H. Van Effenterre and F. Ruzé, *Nomima. Recueil d'inscriptions politiques et juridiques de l'archaïsme grec*, vol. 1 (Rome, 1994), pp. 16–23.

5. L. Gernet, "Delphes et la pensée religieuse en Grèce," *Annales ESC* (1955): 526–542; and Gernet, "Le Droit pénal de la Grèce ancienne," in *Du châtiment dans la cité. Supplices corporels et peine de mort dans le monde antique* (Rome, 1984), pp. 9–35.

6. M. Detienne, "Return to the Mouth of Truth," in *The Masters of Truth in Archaic Greece*, trans. Janet Lloyd (New York, 1996), pp. 7–14.

7. M. Delcourt, *Oreste et Alcméon. Études sur la projection légendaire du matricide en Grèce* (Paris, 1959).

8. Durand, "Formules attiques du fonder," p. 276.

9. Plato, *Laws*, IX.865d.

10. *Odyssey*, I.30.298–300, III.309.

11. Stesichorus' version: PMG, F. 215–219. See also A. Neschke, "L'Otestie de Stési-

chore et la tradition littéraire du mythe des Atrides avant Eschyle," *L'Antiquité classique* (1986): 283–301.

12. Pausanias, II.7.7–9.

13. Pindar, *Pythian* 9.36–37.

14. Pausanias, VII.25.7.

15. Pausanias, VIII.34.1–3.

16. Aeschylus, *The Libation Bearers*, 278–284; Delcourt, *Oreste et Alcméon*, pp. 28–29.

17. Pausanias, II.31.4 and 8–9.

18. Heraclitus, F. 5 Bollack-Wissman.

19. "On the Sacred Disease," 4.

20. Aeschylus, *Eumenides*, 280–285.

21. Delcourt, *Oreste et Alcméon*, fig. 7, pp. 94–95.

22. Delcourt, *Oreste et Alcméon*, pp. 95–102.

23. E. Rohde, *Psyché* (Paris, 1893; rpt., 1952), pp. 599–603 (=*Psyche: The Cult of Souls and Belief in Immortality among the Greeks* [London, 1925]); A. Gotsmich, "Der Maschalismos und seine Wiedergabe in der griechischen Kunst," in *Festgabe für B. Kraff* (Tübingen, 1955), pp. 349–366; F. Vian, "Commentaires à Apollonios de Rhodes," in *Argonautiques* IV, vol. 3 (Paris, 1981).

24. E. Vanderpool, "A Lex Sacra of the Attic Deme Phrearrhioi," *Hesperia* (1970): 47–53.

25. See Marcel Detienne, *Apollon le couteau à la main* (Paris, 1998), pp. 175–234 ("L'Architecte du pur et de l'impur").

26. This inquiry into defilement and its various representations was conducted by a comparatavist group. Some of its results have been assessed by Michel Cartry and myself in *Destins de meurtriers. Systèmes de pensée en Afrique noire*, Cahier 141 (Paris, 1996).

TWELVE: At Lycaon's Table

1. The wolf has already been the subject of an investigation: see M. Detienne and J. Svenbro, "The Feast of the Wolves, or the Impossible City," in M. Detienne, J.-P. Vernant et al., *The Cuisine of Sacrifice among the Greeks*, trans. Paula Wissing (Chicago, 1989), pp. 148–163, 249–253. The richest collection of data is to be found in Giulia Piccaluga, *Lykaon. Un tema mitico* (Rome, 1968).

2. Two essential works on Arcadia are Philippe Borgeaud, *Recherches sur le dieu Pan*, Bibliotheca Helvetica Romana 15 (Rome, 1979); Madeleine Jost, *Sanctuaires et cultes d'Arcadie*, École Française d'Athènes, Études péloponnésiennes 9 (Paris, 1985).

3. Herodotus, VI.105–6. See Borgeaud, *Recherches*, pp. 195–202.

4. See Michael Jameson, "Apollo Lykeios in Athens," *Archaiognosia* 1, no. 2 (1980): 213–35; also Stephen F. Schröder, "Der Apollon Lykeios und die attische Ephebie des 4 Jhs.," *Athenische Mitteilungen* 101 (1986): 167–184. The wolf crosses Apollo's path in Argos, Cyrene, and Tarsis in Cilicia. See Carla Mainoldi, *L'Image du loup et du chien dans la Grèce ancienne, d'Homère à Platon* (Paris, 1984), pp. 22–28; Louis Robert, "Deux inscriptions de Tarse et d'Argos," *BCH* (1977): 88–132.

5. *Asios*, F. 8 Kinkel, in Pausanias, VIII.1.44.2. See P. Borgeaud, *Recherches*, pp. 41–45. Thanks to Pelasgus, the Arcadians are thus "proselenes," according to Hippys of Rheghium, a fifth-century B.C. historian who was extremely interested in foundations: *F Gr Hist*, 554.F.6 Jacoby.

6. Pausanias, VIII.1.5–6.
7. Pausanias, VIII.4.1.
8. Pausanias, VIII.2.1–7.
9. See Borgeaud, *Recherches*, pp. 73–192.
10. Epimenides, cited by Apollodorus, *F Gr Hist*, 244.F.134a Jacoby. See Borgeaud, *Recherches*, pp. 66–67.
11. Hesiod, F. 163 Merkelbach-West; and W. Sale, "The Story of Callisto in Hesiod," *Rh. Mus.* 105 (1962): 122–141.
12. Pausanias, VIII.42.1–7. See Louise Bruit, "Pausanias à Phigalie," *Mètis* 1, no. 1 (1986): 71–96; Jost, *Sanctuaires et cultes d'Arcadie*, pp. 312–317.
13. Pausanias, VIII.42.5–7.
14. Plato, *Republic*, VIII.565d.
15. Jost, *Sanctuaires et cultes d'Arcadie*, pp. 221–222. This was a pan-Arcadian god.
16. See Michel Cartry, ed., *Sous le masque de l'animal. Essais sur le sacrifice en Afrique Noire* (Paris, 1987).
17. See Charles Malamoud, *Cuire le monde. Rite et pensée dans l'Inde ancienne* (Paris, 1989), pp. 253–273.
18. M. Detienne, "Dealings with the Gods," in Giulia Sissa and Marcel Detienne, *The Daily Life of the Greek Gods*, trans. Janet Lloyd (Stanford, Calif., 2000), pp. 166–178. I have suggested a less simple interpretation of the practice of sacrifice, in *Apollon, le couteau à la main* (Paris, 1998).
19. Pausanias, VIII.2.1–3.
20. Pausanias, VIII.2.3.
21. Pausanias, VIII.2.3–4.
22. Jost, *Sanctuaires et cultes d'Arcadie*, pp. 251–254.
23. Hecataeus; *F Gr Hist*, 1.F.6a, ed. Jacoby (*Addenda*, I [1957], 1*–2*).
24. Nicolas of Damascus, *F Gr Hist*, 90.F.38, ed. Jacoby. A closer examination of the sacrificial vocabulary of the various versions might be rewarding. The data are collected in Borgeaud, *Recherches*, pp. 46–51; Mainoldi, *L'Image du loup*, pp. 11–18; Jost, *Sanctuaires et cultes d'Arcadie*, pp. 261–263.
25. Pausanias, VIII.2.6, VIII.38.7.
26. See Detienne and Svenbro, "The Feast of the Wolves, or the Impossible City," pp. 152–160.
27. Detienne and Svenbro, "The Feast of the Wolves, or the Impossible City," pp. 158–163.
28. This is recognized by Jost, *Sanctuaires et cultes d'Arcadie*, pp. 262–263, who is nevertheless inclined, along with W. Sale, to believe that the "pious" versions of Lycaon as a sacrificer are "more authentic." Although I recognize the accuracy of Borgeaud's analyses of the "first Arcadian," I do not believe that Arcas introduced a "definitively humanized culture" (*Recherches*, p. 48).
29. Pausanias, VIII.38.2–8.
30. Pausanias, VIII.38.2–8.
31. In the sanctuary of Zeus Lycaeus reconstructed at Megalopolis, the tables and the altars are still positioned close together (Jost, *Sanctuaires et cultes d'Arcadie*, pp. 221–222).
32. D. Gill, "Trapezomata: A Neglected Aspect of Greek Sacrifice," *Harvard Theological Review* 67 (1974): 117–137.
33. 265e.

THIRTEEN: An Inventive Writing, the Voice of Orpheus, and the Games of Palamedes

This essay was first published in *Critique* 475 (1986): 1225–1234, and is therefore unburdened by the references that will have to be supplied when it appears as two chapters in a volume entitled *Les Dieux de l'écriture*, which is still, I confess, in preparation. A useful compendium that provides a wealth of data is *Les Savoirs de l'écriture. En Grèce ancienne*, ed. M. Detienne (Lille, 1988).

FOURTEEN: The Double Writing of Mythology

1. *Od.*, 12.450–453.
2. Pietro Pucci, *Odysseus Polutropos: Intertextual Readings in the "Odyssey" and the "Iliad"* (Ithaca, N.Y., 1987).
3. Marcel Detienne, *L'Invention de la mythologie* (Paris, 1981), pp. 160–161.
4. Plat., *Polit.*, 268e4–10.
5. See R. Bultmann, "Neues Testament und Mythologie," in *Kerugma und Mythos*, vol. 1, ed. H. W. Bartsch (Hamburg, 1948).
6. Plat., *Tim.*, 17a–26e; *Crit.*, 106a–113b. See Pierre Hadot, "Physique et poésie dans le 'Timée' de Platon," *Revue de théologie et de philosophie* 115 (1983): 113–133: an excellent analysis that I have found very useful.
7. Hadot, "Physique et poésie dans le 'Timée' de Platon," p. 115.
8. Plat. *Tim.*, 17a.
9. Plat., *Tim.*, 19c.
10. See Luc Brisson, *Platon, les mots et les mythes* (Paris, 1982), pp. 34–38.
11. Plat., *Tim.*, 22a6–b3.
12. Plat., *Tim.*, up to 26d.
13. Plat., *Tim.*, 26e6.
14. See Hadot, "Physique et poésie dans le 'Timée' de Platon."
15. Hadot, "Physique et poésie dans le 'Timée' de Platon," pp. 118–119. Thirteen times *e. logos;* three times *e. muthos.*
16. In agreement with Hadot, "Physique et poésie dans le 'Timée' de Platon," p. 127.
17. Analyzed by Patrice Loraux, "L'Art platonicien d'avoir l'air d'écrire," in *Les Savoirs de l'écriture. En Grèce ancienne*, ed. M. Detienne (Paris, 1988), pp. 420–455.
18. Brisson, *Platon, les mots et les mythes*, p. 171.
19. Brisson, *Platon, les mots et les mythes*, p. 22.
20. Brisson, *Platon, les mots et les mythes*, p. 23.
21. Brisson, *Platon, les mots et les mythes*, p. 23.
22. Brisson, *Platon, les mots et les mythes*, p. 21.
23. *Tim.*, 21a1–4.
24. *Tim.*, 26e3–5.
25. *Tim.*, 24d6.
26. Writing "kills myth," according to Brisson, *Platon, les mots et les mythes*, p. 31.
27. See Hadot, "Physique et poésie dans le 'Timée' de Platon."
28. *Tim.*, 23a5–7.
29. *Tim.*, 23a2–6.
30. *Tim.*, 23d3–4, 24a1–2.

31. Ps.-Plat., *Hipp.*, 228b; Diog. Laert., I.2.57.

32. Solon, F. 489 Martina.

33. See Jesper Svenbro, *La parola e il marmo. Alle origini della poetica greca* (Turin, 1984), p. 82.

34. The little Panathenaea, according to Proclus, in *Tim.* I.26.18, 84.25, 85.28 Diehl. But the festival in question is more likely that of the Plynteria, which, in the calendar, follows the Bendidia that are mentioned in the *Republic.* See André-Jean Festugière, *Proclus. Commentaire sur le "Timée"* (Paris, 1966), vol. 1, p. 121n.2, cited by Hadot, "Physique et poésie dans le 'Timée' de Platon," pp. 116–117.

35. *Tim.*, 26e4–5.

36. *Crit.*, 109d–e; *Tim.*, 23c.

37. *Crit.*, 109e3–110a2.

38. *Tim.*, 23c3; *Crit.*, 109d6; *Tim.*, 23a9–b1.

39. *Crit.*, 110a2–3.

40. *Crit.*, 110a3–6.

41. *Tim.*, 23a5–7.

42. *Crit.*, 110a3–6.

43. *Tim.*, 22b5, 23b5.

44. *Tim.*, 21d1–3. See Nicole Loraux, "Solon et la voix de l'écrit," in *Les Savoirs de l'écriture*, ed. Detienne, pp. 95–129.

45. *Tim.*, 27b5.

46. While the elder Critias, who was a contemporary of Solon, did, within his family, make an effort to remember great exploits that "had been forgotten" as time passed and people died, the more or less young Critias seems initially to be very forgetful—at least until Socrates' words jolt his memory. See *Tim.*, 20e4–6, 25e–26a3.

47. See *Crit.*, 108b4 and 108d6, but the word is applied to the performance given before Socrates and his friends.

48. *Tim.*, 21b1–7.

49. From a symbolical point of view, this is more suitable—as Proclus suggests.

50. Jules Labarbe, "L'Âge correspondant au sacrifice du Bouteion et les données historique du sixième discours d'Isée," *Bulletin de l'Académie de Belgique, Classe de Lettres* 39 (1953): 358–394.

51. *Parergon: Tim.*, 21c4. Like the game enjoyed by the younger boys, but on the occasion of one of those festivals in the course of which there were games *played (prospaidzein)* in honor of the gods. There was a serious side to games such as the one that delights Athena at 26e. The double meaning here is analyzed by Hadot, "Physique et poésie dans le 'Timée' de Platon," p. 128.

52. Francis Vian, *La Guerre des géants. Le mythe avant l'époque hellénistique* (Paris, 1952), pp. 250–251. See the interpretations of Proclus in Hadot, "Physique et poésie dans le 'Timée' de Platon," pp. 117, 128–129.

53. *Tim.* 26a–c.

54. See P. Loraux, "L'Art platonicien d'avoir l'air d'écrire," pp. 445–448, who suggests that the *Timaeus* is about one kind of writing, the *Critias* about another kind. The first kind is minimal, the second much more elaborate; the one consists of a pictorial sketch, the other of extremely precise manuscripts.

55. "Plato's fantasy of writing," particularly in his prologues: "to be merely the fab-

ricator of a medium which, in advance but symbolically, creates an archive of discourse in all its versions" (P. Loraux, "L'Art platonicien d'avoir l'air d'écrire," p. 453).

56. Plato, *Rep.*, II.379a5–6.

57. Not "a writer of a legal argument," as understood by the Attic orators, but a writer of prose who produces a historical account or general discourse, as does a *logographos* who models himself on Thucydides (I.21). See Marcel Lavency, *Aspects de la logographie judiciaire attique* (Louvain, 1964), pp. 36–45, a perfect collection of data.

58. Hellan., *F Gr Hist.*, 4 Jacoby.

59. *Tim.*, 22b1–2.

60. Félix Jacoby, *Atthis, the Local Chronicles of Ancient Athens* (Oxford, 1949), pp. 58–59, 68–69, 88–90.

61. Aristot., *Athen. Polit.*, 29.3.

62. In the first place, the *content*, conveyed by the shared lore about the key figures or decisive events of the group. But it is also a matter of what Lévi-Strauss calls "mythism," which confers "a wider symbolic meaning" upon a story.

63. Detienne, *L'Invention de la mythologie*, pp. 29–81.

64. See note 61, above. Where Atthidography is concerned, it is a matter of including the ideal mythology of the city in a funeral oration that is designed to operate as the city's memory: N. Loraux, *The Invention of Athens*, pp. 135–137 and passim.

65. Demosth., *Epit.* See N. Loraux, *The Invention of Athens*, p. 137.

66. Detienne, *L'Invention de la mythologie*, pp. 134–145.

67. See Catherine Darbo-Peschanski, *Le Discours du particulier. Essai sur l'enquête hérodotéenne* (Paris, 1987), pp. 23–83.

68. This was an important stage in the progress of *muthos* and its complex history. See Detienne, *L'Invention de la mythologie*, pp. 99–104.

69. Carl Wendel, "Mythographie," in *Realenc. Alt. Wiss., XVI*, 2, c. 1353.

70. *IG* XI 544 (=*Styll.*[3] 382), 1. 7–8.

71. *I Magnes.* 46, 13 f. (=*FGrHist*, 482.F.1 Jacoby).

72. Gregory Nagy, "The Ainos," in *Métamorphoses du mythe en Grèce antique*, ed. Claude Calame (Geneva, 1988).

73. This area of research has been opened up by Paul Veyne. See Paul Veyne, *Les grecs ont-ils cru à leurs mythes?* (Paris, 1983).

74. See Guiliana Lanata, *Poetica preplatonica. Testimonianze e frammenti* (Florence, 1963), pp. 142–150.

75. See Charles Segal, *La Musique du Sphinx. Poésie et structure dans la tragédie grecque* (Paris, 1987), pp. 13–42.

76. Wendel, "Mythographie," c. 1353–1354.

77. Philoch., *FGrHist*, 328.n.20–23 Jacoby.

78. Rudolf Pfeiffer, *History of Classical Scholarship* (Oxford, 1968), pp. 123–151.

79. *Mnēmē muthologos:* the heading under which Callimachus refers to Xenomedes' work on the founding of Ceos. See Callim., F. 75.54–55 Pfeiffer.

80. Christian Jacob, "Problèmes de lecture du mythe grec," in *Le Conte*, Colloque d'Albi (Toulouse, 1987), p. 408.

81. Detienne, *L'Invention de la mythologie*, pp. 177–189.

82. Algirdas J. Greimas, *Des dieux et des hommes* (Paris, 1985), pp. 11–27.

83. These questions were addressed by a colloquium in Lausanne, the proceedings of

which were published under the title *Métamorphoses du mythe en Grèce antique*, ed. Claude Calame (Geneva, 1988).

FIFTEEN: Orpheus Rewrites the City Gods

1. The notes have been reduced to the minimum. They will appear in a fuller form elsewhere, in a general essay on Apollo and Dionysus, in which Orpheus plays a role. This article was first published in *Archives de sciences sociales des religions* 59, no. 1 (1985): 65–75. See Marcel Detienne, "Oublier Delphes. Entre Apollon et Dionysos," *Gradhiva* 24 (1998): 11–20.

2. For example, the vase of the Painter of Naples, now in Hamburg, published by H. Hoffmann, "Orpheus unter den Thrakern," *Jahrbuch der Hamburger Kunstsammlungen* 14–15 (1970): 31–44, fig. 1.

3. On the iconography, see the catalogue produced by Enrique R. Panyagua in *Helmantica* 70 (1972): 83–135. See Pan. 42 for Dionysus on the reverse side, and Pan. 26 for death and sacrifice with a Dionysiac drinking cup.

4. For more details, see my *Dionysos mis à mort* (1977; 2nd ed., Paris, 1998), pp. 203–204, and n. 139 (=*Dionysus Slain*, trans. Mireille Muellner and Leonard Muellner [Baltimore, 1979]).

5. H. Gropengiesser, *Archäologischer Anzeiger* (1977): 583, fig. 2.

6. See the article by Walter Burkert, "Craft versus Sect: The Problem of Orphics and Pythagoreans," in *Jewish and Christian Self-Definition.*, ed. Ben F. Meyer and E. P. Sanders III (London, 1982), pp. 1–22, 183–189.

7. An extremely detailed genealogy is provided by M. L. West, *The Orphic Poems* (Oxford, 1983), based on an imaginative reconstruction of the Orphic fragments found in the Derveni Papyrus. See L. Brisson's detailed and apposite critique, "Les 'Théogonies' orphiques et le papyrus de Dervéni," *RHR* 202, no. 4 (1985): 389–420. See now *Studies on the Derveni Papyrus*, ed. André Laks and Glenn W. Most (Oxford, 1997).

8. 364e.

9. See Walter Burkert, "La Genèse des choses et des mots," *Études philosophiques* (1970): 443–455.

10. M. L. West, "The Orphics of Olbia," *ZPE* 45 (1982): 17–29; West, *The Orphic Poems* (Oxford, 1983), pp. 15–20.

11. Herodotus, II.81.

12. Euripides, *Hippolytus*, 952–955.

13. On what follows, see "Les Chemins de la déviance: Orphisme, dionysisme et pythagorisme," in *Orfismo in Magna Grecia* (Naples, 1975), pp. 50–79, especially 72–79.

14. *Orphicorum fragmenta*, F. 207, ed. O. Kern.

15. Plutarch, *De sera numinis vindicta*, 22.566c=F. 294, ed. O. Kern.

16. *Scholia in Pindare*, *Pythic*, Argum. 1.

17. F. 643, ed. R. Pfeiffer.

18. F. 35, ed. O. Kern.

19. See the glosses of Olympiodorus, F. 209 and 211, ed. O. Kern. On fragmentation, individuation, see the interpretations of Proclus, and of Nietzsche: G. Sissa, "Dionysos, corps divin, corps divisé," in *Le Corps des dieux*, ed. C. Malamoud and J.-P. Vernant, Le Temps de la réflexion 7 (Paris, 1986), pp. 355–371.

20. F. 62, ed. O. Kern.
21. Aeschylus, F. 83, ed. H. J. Mette.
22. See B. Müller, *Megas Theos* (Halle, 1913), p. 308.
23. *Orphicorum fragmenta*, ed. O. Kern, *Testim.*, 118.
24. *Testim.*, 82.
25. *Testim.*, 129.
26. XI.1–85.
27. II.8.3.
28. 179d.
29. *Testim.*, 116.
30. VII.111.
31. Fr. 86, ed. H. J. Mette.
32. *Saturnales*, I.18.6. Quoting Aeschylus, F. 86, ed. H. J. Mette.

Select Bibliography

Brelich, Angelo. 1958. *Gli Eroi greci. Un problema storico-religioso.* Rome.

———. 1985. *I Greci e gli dei.* Naples.

Brisson, Luc. 1982. *Platon: Les mots et les mythes.* Paris. 2nd ed., 1994.

Bruneau, Philippe. 1970. *Recherches sur les cultes de Délos à l'époque hellénistique et à l'époque impériale.* Paris.

Burkert, Walter. 1972. *Homo Necans: Interpretation altgriechischer Opferriten und Mythen.* Berlin.

———. 1979. *Structure and History in Greek Mythology and Ritual.* Berkeley.

Buxton, Richard, ed. 1999. *From Myth to Reason? Studies in the Development of Thought.* Oxford.

Calame, Claude, ed. 1988. *Métamorphoses du mythe en Grèce antique.* Geneva.

———. 1996. *Mythe et histoire dans l'Antiquité grecque.* Lausanne.

Darbo-Peschanski, Catherine. 1987. *Le Discours du particulier. Essai sur l'enquête hérodotéenne.* Paris.

Detienne, Marcel. 1967. *Les Maîtres de vérité dans la Grèce archaïque.* Paris. New ed., including "Retour sur la bouche de la Vérité." Paris, 1995. Published in English as *The Masters of Truth in Archaic Greece.* Trans. Janet Lloyd. New York, 1996.

———. 1972. *Les Jardins d'Adonis. La mythologie des aromates en Grèce.* Paris. Published in English as *The Gardens of Adonis.* Trans. Janet Lloyd. Hassocks, Middlesex, England, 1972. Revised and expanded ed., Paris, 1989.

———. 1986. *The Creation of Mythology.* Trans. Margaret Cook. Chicago.

———. 1988. *Dionysos mis à mort.* Paris. Published in English as *Dionysus Slain.* Trans. Mireille Muellner and Leonard Muellner. Baltimore, 1979.

———. 1988. "L'Espace de la publicité, ses opérateurs intellectuels." In *Les Savoirs de l'écriture. En Grèce ancienne,* ed. Marcel Detienne. Lille. Pp. 29–81.

———. 2000. *Comparer l'incomparable.* Paris.

Detienne, Marcel, ed. 1994. *Transcrire les mythologies. Tradition, écriture, historicité.* Paris.

Detienne, Marcel, and Jean-Pierre Vernant. 1978. *Cunning Intelligence in Greek Culture and Society.* Trans. Janet Lloyd. Hassocks, Middlesex, England.

Detienne, Marcel, and others. 1989. *The Cuisine of Sacrifice among the Greeks.* Trans. Paula Wissing. Chicago.

Edmunds, L., ed. 1990. *Approaches to Greek Myth.* Baltimore.

Festugière, André-Jean. 1966. *Proclus, commentaire sur le Timée.* Paris.

Finley, Moses I. 1965. *Myth, Memory and History.* The Hague.

Frazer, James George. 1921. *Apollodorus. The Library.* 2 vols. Cambridge, Mass.

Gentili, Bruno, and Giuseppe Paioni, eds. 1977. *Il Mito greco.* Rome.

Goody, Jack. 1977. *The Domestication of the Savage Mind.* Cambridge.
Gordon, R. L., ed. 1982. *Myth, Religion and Society.* Cambridge.
Graf, Fritz. 1993. *Greek Mythology.* Trans. Thomas Marier. Baltimore.
Greimas, Algirdas J. 1985. *Des Dieux et des hommes.* Paris.
Hadot, Pierre. 1983. "Physique et poésie dans le 'Timée' de Platon." *Revue de théologie et de philosophie* 115:113–133.
Jacob, Christian. 1987. "Problèmes de lecture du mythe grec." In *Le Conte.* Toulouse. Pp. 389–408.
Jacoby, Felix. 1949. *A Commentary on the Ancient Historians of Athens.* Vol. 1. Oxford.
Kirk, Geoffrey S. 1974. *The Nature of Greek Myths.* Harmondsworth, Middlesex, England.
Labarbe, Jules. 1952. "L'Âge correspondant au sacrifice du *koureion* et les données historiques du Sixième Discours d'Isée." *Bulletin de l'Académie Royale de Belgique. Classe des Lettres* 39:358–394.
Lanata, Giuliana. 1963. *Poetica pre-platonica. Testimonianze e frammenti.* Florence.
Lavency, M. 1964. *Aspects de la logographie judiciaire attique.* Louvain.
Lévi-Strauss, Claude. 1963. *Structural Anthropology.* Trans. Claire Jacobson and Brooke Grundfest Schoepf. New York.
———. 1964–1971. *Mythologiques.* 4 vols. Paris. Published in English as *Introduction to a Science of Mythology.* Trans. John and Doreen Weightman. London, 1981.
———. 1979. *Textes de et sur Claude Lévi-Strauss, réunis par R. Bellour et C. Clément.* Paris.
———. 1987. "De la fidélité au texte." *L'Homme* 101:117–140.
———. 1987. *Structural Anthropology 2.* Trans. Monique Layton. Harmondsworth, Middlesex, England.
Loraux, Nicole. 1986. *The Invention of Athens.* Trans. Alan Sheridan. Cambridge, Mass.
———. 1988. "Solon et la voix de l'écrit." In *Les Savoirs de l'écriture. En Grèce ancienne,* ed. M. Detienne. Lille. Pp. 95–129.
Loraux, Patrice. 1988. "L'Art platonicien d'avoir l'air d'écrire." In *Les Savoirs de l'écriture. En Grèce ancienne,* ed. M. Detienne. Lille. Pp. 420–455.
Nagy, Gregory. 1979. *The Best of the Achaeans: Concepts of the Hero in Archaic Greek Poetry.* Baltimore.
———. 1988. "Myth and Early Greek Prose: The Ainos."In *Métamorphoses du mythe en Grèce antique,* ed. C. Calame. Geneva.
———. 1990. *Greek Mythology and Poetics.* Ithaca, N.Y.
———. 1990. *Pindar's Homer: The Lyric Possession of an Epic Past.* Baltimore.
Pfeiffer, Rudolf. 1968. *History of Classical Scholarship.* Oxford.
Piccirilli, Luigi. 1975. *Megarika. Testimonianze e frammenti.* Pisa.
Pucci, Piero. 1987. *Odysseus Polutropos: Intertextual Readings in the "Odyssey" and the "Iliad."* Ithaca.
Segal, Charles. 1987. *La Musique du sphinx. Poésie et structure dans la tragédie grecque.* Paris.
Svenbro, Jesper. 1984. *La Parola e il marmo. Alle origini della poetica greca.* Turin.
Vernant, Jean-Pierre. 1965. *Mythe et pensée chez les grecs. Etudes de psychologie historique.* Paris. Published in English as *Myth and Thought among the Greeks.* London, 1983. Revised and expanded ed., Paris, 1985.
———. 1988. *Myth and Society in Ancient Greece.* Trans. Janet Lloyd. New York.
Veyne, Paul. 1983. *Les Grecs ont-ils cru à leurs mythes?* Paris.

Vian, Francis. 1952. *La Guerre des géants. Le mythe avant l'époque hellénistique.* Paris.
Vidal-Naquet, Pierre. 1986. *The Black Hunter. Trans.* Andrew Szegedy-Maszak. Baltimore.
Wendel, Carl. 1935. "Mythographie." In *Realencyclopädie Altertums-Wissenschaft*, vol. 16, 2. Stuttgart. Cols. 1352–1374.

Index